PHILOSOPHY OF THE ARTS

An Introduction to Aesthetics

Gordon Graham

London and New York

First published in 1997
by Routledge
11 New Fetter Lane, London EC4P 4EE

Simultaneously published in the USA and Canada
by Routledge
29 West 35th Street, New York, NY 10001

Typeset in Sabon by RefineCatch Limited, Bungay, Suffolk

Printed and bound in Great Britain by
T. J. International Ltd, Padstow, Cornwall

Brtitish Library Cataloguing in Publication Data
A catalogue record for this book is available from the British
Library

Library of Congress Cataloging in Publication Data
Graham, Gordon
Philosophy of the arts: an introduction to aesthetics / Gordon
Graham.
p. cm.
Includes bibliographical references and index.
1. Aesthetics. I. Title.
BH39.G67 1997
111'.85—dc21 97–1474
ISBN 0–415–16687–X (hbk)
0–415–16688–8 (pbk)

PHILOSOPHY OF THE ARTS

Philosophy of the Arts is designed specifically for readers studying aesthetics for the first time; it is the first comprehensive introduction for students of philosophy, as it will be for those of literature, music, or art. Written in non-technical language, equipped with regular summaries of the argument and suggestions for further reading, this textbook is up-to-date and full of examples from all the arts, from film to poetry, architecture to music.

The chapters consider:

- The value of art: as a form of entertainment, a source of beauty, a means of emotional expression, or something bringing insight and understanding.
- The theories of Hume, Mill, Kant, Habermas and Collingwood.
- Central topics in the philosophy of music: musical expression, music as a language, the uniqueness of music.
- The importance of representation to painting; some central problems of film theory.
- Philosophical issues in the literary arts, for example, 'What does poetry lose in paraphrase?' and a wide-ranging discussion of literary devices.
- The context in the philosophy of architecture for the debates between formalists and functionalists, modernists and traditionalists.
- The Marxist, structuralist and modernist objections to philosophical aesthetics; with the writings of Althusser, Lukács, Lévi-Strauss and Derrida.
- A defence of normative theories of art in Hegel and Schopenhauer.

Ideal for readers who do not necessarily have a background in philosophy and are new to aesthetics, *Philosophy of the Arts* is a clear, accessible introduction to what is often seen to be a difficult but fascinating subject.

Gordon Graham is Regius Professor of Moral Philosophy at King's College, University of Aberdeen. He has published widely on ethics, aesthetics, and social philosophy; his books include *Contemporary Social Philosophy* (1987), *The Idea of Christian Charity* (1990), *Ethics and International Relations* (1996), and *The Shape of the Past* (1997).

For
Christina Marie Kennedy
to whom these questions *matter*

Contents

———◦◯◦———

CONTENTS

CONTENTS

Acknowledgements

—•⊖•—

The content of this book derives in considerable part from lectures given over several years at the University of St Andrews. I owe a great deal to many students for their questions and comments. I am also grateful to my former colleagues there – Berys Gaut for comments on an earlier draft, and Alex Neill for many helpful suggestions and criticisms on the completed typescript. I am specially indebted to William Poole, who made extensive and incisive comments on the whole text and brought to it not only a highly intelligent mind but the invaluable point of view of the interested newcomer to the subject. If there are passages remaining that are obscure and hard to understand, I am the only one left to blame.

Dan Rashid kindly proof-read for me, and Louise Gregory was especially helpful in assembling the list of examples and compiling the bibliography. Earlier versions of some of the themes I discuss were published in papers in the *British Journal of Aesthetics*, the *Journal of Aesthetic Education*, and the *Journal of Aesthetics and Art Criticism*. I gratefully acknowledge their permission to reproduce some of the material here.

I began writing on these issues some years ago, during a visit to The Colorado College, where Mrs Phoebe McReynolds generously shared her office with me, and made me very much at home.

Gordon Graham
King's College, Aberdeen
November 1996

Introduction

————•◦⊙◦•————

The arts are an important part of human life and culture. They attract a large measure of attention and support. But what is art, exactly, and why should we value it? These are very old questions. Philosophers have been concerned with them for over two thousand years. In that time a number of important answers have been developed and explored. The purpose of this book is to introduce newcomers to the field of aesthetics and art theory to the problems encountered by the attempt to answer these questions in a sustained and coherent way, and to familiarize new readers with the thinking of those philosophers who have devoted most attention to them. The purpose of the book is not just to provide information and stimulation for students of philosophy. It also aims to show the relevance of philosophy of art and aesthetics to the interests and concerns of all those, students and others, who are actively concerned with the appreciation and study of works of art of every kind.

Philosophers are not the only people to develop theories of art. Sociologists, musicologists, art critics, and literary theorists have done so as well. But what philosophy has to say on these topics cannot but be relevant to any serious thinking about the arts. At the same time art theory and the philosophy of art soon become lifelessly abstract if they are too far removed from the arts themselves. Therefore a large part of the book is devoted to the examination of specific art forms, not just in order to avoid lifeless abstraction, but in the hope of drawing upon the interests of those whose motivation is primarily a love of music, painting, or literature as an entry to philosophical reflection.

Realizing this hope presents a peculiar difficulty. We can only talk meaningfully about paintings, poems, symphonies, and so on if, quite literally, we know what we are talking about, and a writer on these topics cannot be sure if the examples chosen are known to the audience. So an essential precondition to studying the philosophy of art by means of this book is familiarity with the particular examples that have been chosen by way of illustration. Some aids are provided here for locating the works of art mentioned or discussed (a complete list of these will be found at the back of the book), but

1

it has to be stressed at the outset that readers will need to make an effort to familiarize themselves with the works referred to in the course of the argument.

It is also true that any introduction, however comprehensive it aims to be, can only get the reader started. For this reason, a short list of suggestions for further reading is included at the end of each chapter. *The Philosophy of Art*, edited by Alex Neill and Aaron Ridley, is a particularly useful collection of readings both ancient and modern, and many of the suggestions for further reading will be found in it. Where possible, passages quoted in the text are located in this volume (referred to as *N&R*), while details of their original source can be found in the bibliography.

Additional reading is important. The primary concern of this book is to stimulate the mind and interest of the newcomer who is both open to philosophical argument and interested in the arts. Where it was necessary to make a choice between pursuing interesting lines of thought or merely providing a comprehensive account of the literature, I have chosen the former.

In a book of this length it is not possible to consider every issue in the philosophy of art. The principal concern is to introduce the broad outlines of the commonest theories of art and see how these apply to explicit art forms. Two general conclusions emerge – that it is better for the philosopher of art to explore the question of art's value than to try to arrive at a definition of art, and secondly that the best explanation of its value lies in explaining the ways in which it makes a contribution to human understanding. The course of explaining and exploring these ideas takes us into a more detailed look at music, painting, film, poetry, fiction, and architecture, and leads to the investigation of many interesting and important issues. Even so, there is little direct examination of two interrelated topics that have exercised philosophers of art, namely the objectivity of aesthetic judgment, and the role of the artist's intention in determining the meaning and merits of a work of art. Both topics are touched upon only briefly, but some such omissions are inevitable. Typically philosophy raises more questions than it answers, and the point of an introduction is not to provide a definitive set of solutions to a designated set of problems but to start the mind of the reader on an exploratory journey of its own.

This, then, is an introduction to aesthetics. But what is 'aesthetics'? People write about the arts in many ways. There is art criticism, which aims to explain and interpret individual works of art, and there is history of art, which charts the changes and developments that painting, music, and so on, have undergone over the centuries. Aesthetics is not either of these. It is rather an attempt to *theorize* about art, to explain what it is and why it matters. One striking feature of contemporary theorizing about art, however, is this: there are not merely competing theories, as is to be expected in any subject, but two quite different ideas about how theories should be formulated. Broadly speaking, modern theoretical approaches to art divide into two kinds. First there are those theories which seek to uncover the defining essence of art. The concern of these might be said to be with the *concept* of art as such. Although, as we shall see, there is more to the philosophy of art than this, I shall call these 'philosophical' theories, because their origin is to be found in the works of Socrates and Plato, both of whom tried to understand the things they discussed by formulating definitions of them. Second, and in opposition to theories based upon conceptual abstraction of this kind, is a more recent current of thought which can loosely be called sociological, since it is chiefly concerned with art as a social phenomenon. Its origins are to be found in Marxism, but in this century the Marxist basis has been amended and extended by the ideas and interests of structuralism and poststructuralism. The concern of the sociological approach is with art as an historical phenomenon and a social construction.

Because of the fundamental disagreement between the philosophical and sociological approaches, some exploration of the question, 'How should we theorize about art?' is a necessary preliminary to dealing adequately with the other major topics customarily included in aesthetics. However, though this is a necessary preliminary from the point of view of a logical ordering of the subject, the newcomer to philosophy is likely to find the material with which it must deal rather difficult. From the point of view of the reader, consequently, it is better if the more abstract and theoretical topic of the nature of aesthetics itself is approached after some familiarity with the philosophy of art has been attained. For this reason, it is the last and not the first chapter of the book that deals with theories of art.

To set the stage for the first chapter, it is necessary here to say only that we can combine something of both the philosophical and the sociological approaches if we orientate our discussion around this question, 'What is valuable about the arts?' I shall call answers to this question, 'normative' theories of art, that is to say, theories which aim to explain its value. The next three chapters examine several such theories, both in the form in which they influence our common thinking and in the more precise form in which they are to be found in the writings of famous philosophers. The following four chapters look at their implications for various art forms. Only then do we return to more abstract and more difficult questions about the proper basis of aesthetics and art theory.

1

Art and pleasure

We are going to assume that the most profitable approach to theorizing about art is a normative one. That is to say, for the next three chapters we will treat aesthetics as the attempt to formulate a theory of art that will explain its value, rather than one which, say, seeks to define what art is, or to determine its social function. One way of beginning to formulate a normative theory of art is to ask this question: 'What is it that we expect to get from art?' A spontaneous answer, even to the point of being commonplace, is pleasure or enjoyment. Most people wishing to pass favourable judgment on a book or a film will say that they 'enjoyed it'.

Hume and the standard of taste

Some philosophers have thought that the value of art is *necessarily* connected with pleasure or enjoyment, because, they argue, to say that a work is good is just the same as saying that it is pleasant or agreeable. The best known philosopher to hold this view was the eighteenth-century Scottish philosopher David Hume. In a famous essay entitled 'Of the standard of taste' he argues that the important thing about art is its 'agreeableness', the pleasure we derive from it, and that this is a matter of our sentiments, not its intrinsic nature. 'Judgments' about good and bad in art, according to Hume, are not really judgments at all, 'because sentiment has a reference to nothing beyond itself, and is always real, wherever a man is conscious of it' (Hume 1975: 238). 'To seek the real beauty, or the real deformity, is as fruitless an enquiry, as to seek the real sweet or real bitter' (*ibid.*: 239). That is to say, aesthetic preferences are expressions of the taste of the observer, not statements about the object, and Hume thinks the wide diversity of opinions about art that we find in the world is confirmation of this fact.

At the same time, Hume recognizes, while it is true that opinions differ widely, it is no less widely believed that at least some artistic sentiments can be so wide of the mark as to be discountable. He considers the example of a minor writer being compared with John Milton, the great poetic genius who

4

wrote *Paradise Lost*. Though, says Hume, 'there may be found persons who give the preference to the former . . . no one pays attention to such a taste; and we pronounce without scruple the sentiment of these pretended critics to be absurd and ridiculous'. What this implies is that, even though taste is a matter of feeling things to be agreeable or disagreeable, there is still a *standard* of taste, and the question is how these two ideas can be made consistent.

Hume's answer is that the standard of taste arises from the nature of human beings. Since they share a common nature, broadly speaking they like the same things. When it comes to art, he thinks, 'Some particular forms or qualities, from the original structure of the internal fabric [of the human mind], are calculated to please, and others to displease' (*ibid.*: 271). There are of course aberrant reactions and opinions; people can favour the oddest things. But Hume believes that the test of time will eventually tell, and that only those things which truly are aesthetically pleasing will go on calling forth approbation as the years pass.

On the face of it, Hume's theory does seem to fit attitudes to art. Artistic tastes differ greatly, but at the same time there is something to be said for the idea that by and large the same features of art find favour with most people; broadly speaking, most people like and admire the same great masterpieces in music, painting, literature, or architecture. Despite this and contrary to Hume, we cannot move from patterns of *common* taste to a *standard* of taste. The fact that a belief or feeling is shared by many people does not of itself mean that everyone is rationally obliged to adhere to it. If someone does have extremely peculiar musical tastes, say, we may regard them as odd, but if Hume is right that aesthetics is all a matter of feeling, we have no good reason to call them 'absurd and ridiculous'; they are merely different. If we want to say that some views about art are mistaken, we cannot make the mistake rest on human *feeling* about art – it just is what it is – but on something about the art itself.

It follows that the connection between art and pleasure is not a necessary one; to say that a work of art is good or valuable is not the same as saying that we find it enjoyable. Nevertheless it can still be argued that art is to be valued chiefly *because of* the pleasure or enjoyment it gives, and this is, I think, what most people who connect art and enjoyment mean to say.

Mill and pleasure

It is worth recording, however, that it is not altogether natural to speak of enjoyment uniformly for all the arts. People quite naturally speak of enjoying novels, plays, films, and pieces of music. But it is odd to speak of enjoying paintings, sculptures, and buildings, as opposed to liking or loving them. It follows that even if we were to agree that 'enjoyment' were the principal value of art, some further explanation would still be needed to show just what this might mean in the case of some of the principal art forms.

But the main problem with 'enjoyment' is not this. It is rather that in asserting that art offers enjoyment, we have said almost nothing. People who enjoy their work can be asked to explain what it is they find enjoyable, and in their answers that they reveal what they find of *value* in it. 'Enjoyment' merely signals that they do find it so. Similarly, with art the initial claim that art is a source of enjoyment is not in itself informative. It means little more than that it is worth attending to; what we need to know is, what *makes* it worth attending to.

People who offer the explanation 'enjoyment' often have something more precise in mind, namely, pleasure. The notion of 'pleasure' also requires examination and clarification, because it too can be used in such a general fashion as to mean nothing more than 'enjoyment' in the sense just described. Moreover, mistaken notions of pleasure abound: those which treat pleasure and happiness as synonymous for instance, or which define pleasure as the psychological opposite of pain, as in the writings of the nineteenth-century British philosophers John Stuart Mill and Jeremy Bentham, classically representative authors of philosophical utilitarianism. These misconceptions are understandable because most thinking about pleasure and happiness is caught up from the outset in a network of ideas which includes the contrasts between 'work and leisure', 'toil and rest', 'anxiety and contentment'. The sense of 'pleasure' we want to examine here is something like 'entertainment value' which, following R. G. Collingwood in *The Principles of Art*, we might call 'amusement'.

Collingwood is partly engaged in the traditional task of philosophical aesthetics – that is, defining what art is – but the way he approaches it embodies a normative or evaluative theory of art as well, an explanation of what is to count as 'true art'. Collingwood wants to show that art as amusement (along with art as craft and art as magic) falls short of art 'proper' and that those who turn to the arts for their amusement have made a certain sort of mistake. It may indeed be the case that they find their amusement in plays, novels, and so on. This is an important point to stress. No one need deny that there is indeed recreational amusement to be obtained from the arts. But Collingwood's contention is that if this is *all* we find there, we have missed the thing most worth finding. His strictures on art as amusement will be examined more closely in the next chapter. Here we need only register a doubt he raises about the facts of the case. The thesis that art is valuable for the pleasure or amusement we derive from it depends, among other things, on its being the case that we do indeed derive pleasure from it.

Is this in fact true? What is undoubtedly true is that people profess to enjoy works of art and many will expand upon this by recording the pleasure they get from them. Whether if we asked them to substitute the word 'amusement' for pleasure they would happily do so is much less certain. This is because the pursuit of pleasure in the sense of amusement does not explain the social estimation of art in a wider context. People generally think that great art is more important than as a mere source of amusement. Nor does it accord with the distinction that is commonly made between art and non-art, or the discriminations that are made between better and less good works (and forms) of art, between, say, pantomime and Shakespearean tragedy.

These points need to be considered one by one. It is widely accepted that art is a respectable object for the devotion of large amounts of time and considerable quantities of financial and other resources. Few people find it improper for schools and universities to encourage their students to devote themselves to intensive study of the arts (though some may query the content of the curriculum), nor do they call for special justification when governments, companies, and foundations spend large sums of money on galleries and orchestras. But they might well object if they were told that in teaching art, schools aimed to *amuse* their pupils, and would probably have serious doubts if similar sums were spent on extravagant parties or other occasions, whose much more obvious purpose is pleasure or amusement. Similarly it is acceptable, even admirable, for artists and critics to make a lifetime commitment to their work. By contrast any talk of commitment to a life of amusement would inevitably carry the same kind of jocular overtones as the phrase 'serious drinking'.

These estimations may be erroneous of course. This is a possibility that we ought not to rule out. It would prejudge many of the questions pertinent to normative philosophy of art if we were to *assume* that art has a value other and greater than amusement value. The point here, however, is that, if we identify pleasure with amusement, it is far from clear that the pleasure theory of art is as commonplace as it may have seemed at the start. It may be generally acceptable to say that people turn to Beethoven largely for pleasure, but less acceptable to suggest that they find his music amusing.

It might be said that this only shows that pleasure is not the same as amusement. However, once we shift our attention from what people are inclined to *say*, to the beliefs reflected in their social practices, it is not at all clear that most people do find most of what we call art pleasurable in *any* straightforward sense. Those in pursuit of pleasure who are faced with a choice between a detective story by Rex Stout or a novel by William Faulkner are almost certain to choose the former, just as they will prefer a Marx Brothers film to *film noir* or the work of Jean Luc Godard, though Faulkner and Godard are evidently artistically more significant. This need not be the case universally for the general point to hold; great novels can also be diverting and amusing. But the fact that pleasure and significance in art can be divorced in this way gives us reason to observe, along with Collingwood, that the prevalence of the belief that art is pleasurable may itself distort people's ability to ask honestly whether anybody is much amused by it. Indeed, Collingwood thinks there is often a measure of self-deception in people's attitudes, and if we are honest we will have to agree that the entertainment value of high art is for most people quite low compared to other amusements.

> The masses of cinema goers and magazine readers cannot be elevated by offering them . . . the aristocratic amusements of a past age. This is called bringing art to the people, but that is clap-trap; what is brought is still amusement, very cleverly designed by a Shakespeare or a Purcell to please an Elizabethan or a Restoration audience, but now, for all its genius, far less amusing than Mickey Mouse or jazz, except to people laboriously trained to enjoy it.
>
> (Collingwood 1938: 103)

These social facts about art and the status it is usually accorded raise doubts about the depth of allegiance to the commonplace pleasure theory of art. There is thus a serious question whether it is true that art is for most people a source of pleasure, and it seems the answer is, 'probably not'. But even if we were to agree, contrary to what has been said, that all art can be relied upon to amuse, a further question arises as to whether, on this ground alone, we would have any special reason to pursue it. There are many other cheaper and less taxing forms of amusement – games, picnics, crossword puzzles, for example. If simple pleasure is what is at issue, on the surface at any rate art can at best be a contender for value and in all probability a rather weak one.

It is tempting to reply to this point by claiming that an enjoyable life does not consist in large quantities of 'pleasure' in the abstract, but a variety of different kinds of pleasure. This may be true – we can easily become surfeited by just one sort of pleasure – but it does not overcome the philosophical difficulty. Even if we concede that painting, drama, and so on are distinctive types of pleasure, this fact alone generates no reason to think that a pleasurable life must contain any of them. If the good life is defined as the life of pleasure, then provided that such a life has a variety of pleasures in it, art need play no part in it. This might be the correct view for a hedonist (someone who believes that the best life is the most pleasurable one) though hardly for an aesthete (a lover of the arts), but the point to be emphasized here is that an appeal to the value of pleasure does not generate any reason to value *art* above any of the many other ways in which amusement and diversion may be found.

In response to this line of thought, it is tempting to try to establish a difference between higher and lower pleasures and argue that art provides a kind of pleasure higher than that generated by the more mundane recreations listed above. This move is closely related to the third objection to be considered, the distinction most art lovers would draw between the light and the serious in art. This is a distinction hard to dispense with, and one worth examining at some length. Almost everyone wants to draw an evaluative distinction between both styles and works of art in terms of the serious and the light: between for instance tragedies and farces, Beethoven symphonies and Strauss waltzes, the poetry of T.S. Eliot and that of Edward Lear, the novels of Jane Austen and those of P.G. Wodehouse. In each case while the latter has many merits and is genuinely amusing, it is the former which is regarded as more significant or profound.

It should be noted here that the distinction between serious and light is not the same as that between high and low art. Some writers have thought that the 'bourgeois' elevation of the art of the gallery and the concert hall, and the corresponding denigration of folk art are part of the ideological underwriting of a certain social structure. But as far as our present concerns go, much folk art can be regarded as serious and much high art as frivolous; it still remains to explain this difference.

Can such a difference be explained in terms of higher and lower pleasures? John Stuart Mill's attempt to draw this distinction, which appears in the essay entitled *Utilitarianism*, is not expressly directed at the question of the value of art. But it is hard to see how any such distinction could be drawn other than in the ways he suggests. There appear to be two possibilities only. Either we say that higher pleasures hold out the possibility of a greater *quantity* of pleasure, or we say that a higher pleasure is of a different *quality*. The first of these alternatives is plainly inadequate because it makes the value of art strictly commensurable with that of other pleasures. If the only difference is that pleasure in art is more concentrated, it can be substituted without loss by more items affording a lower pleasure. Thus, if what Tolstoy's *Anna Karenina* has over *Melrose Place* or *Neighbours* is *quantity* of pleasure, we can make up the difference simply by watching more episodes of *Melrose Place*. The implication of this line of thought is that people who have never acquired any familiarity with any of the things that pass for serious art, including the serious elements in folk art, are in no way impoverished, provided only that they have had a sufficient quantity of more mundane pleasures. Most of us would want to dissent from such a judgment, but whether we do or not, the fact of this implication is enough to show that the pleasure theory of art understood in this way is inadequate, since it cannot show art to have any special value at all.

Mill thinks that 'it is absurd that . . . the estimation of pleasures should be supposed to depend on quantity alone' (Mill 1985: 12). Instead he appeals to the respective quality of different pleasures.

If I am asked, what I mean by difference of quality in pleasures, or what makes one pleasure more valuable than another, merely as a pleasure, except its being greater in amount, there is but one possible answer. Of two pleasures, if there be one to which all or almost all who have experience of both give a decided preference, irrespective of any feeling of moral obligation to prefer it, that is the more desirable pleasure. If one of the two is, by those who are competently acquainted with both, placed so far above the other that they prefer it . . . we are justified in ascribing to the preferred enjoyment a superiority in quality. . . . On a question which is the best worth having of two pleasures . . . the judgment of those who are qualified by knowledge of both, or, if they differ, that of the majority among them, must be admitted as final.

(ibid.: 14–15)

According to Mill, this higher quality of pleasure more than compensates for any diminution in quantity and will in fact offset a good deal of pain and discontent. In a famous passage he concludes:

It is better to be a human being dissatisfied than a pig satisfied; better to be Socrates dissatisfied than a fool satisfied. And if the pig, or the fool, is of a different opinion, it is because they only know their own side of the question.

(ibid.: 14)

Whether Mill's account of higher and lower pleasures is adequate for his purposes in *Utilitarianism* is not the question here. Rather we want to ask whether the same strategy can be used to explain the difference in value that is attached to light and serious art. And the answer plainly seems to be that it does not. This is chiefly because, as we know, tastes differ in art, and consequently the test he proposes cannot be used to adjudicate between competing responses to works of art. Suppose for instance that a dispute arises about the relative quality of pleasure to be obtained from *The Good, the Bad, and the Ugly* and *King Lear*. Mill is obviously correct in his assertion that someone who has seen only the former is not qualified to give judgment. Consequently it is his majority test that must do the work. Assuming, almost certainly without foundation, that majority opinion among those who have seen both favours Shakespeare, we have no reason to infer from this that Shakespearean tragedy generates a higher quality of pleasure than a good western. The judgment that it does may signal no more than a difference of taste between the majority and the minority. We cannot show that beer is *better* than wine simply by showing that more people prefer it. Since it is possible for an individual to prefer a worse thing to a better thing, it is also possible that the majority of people will do so.

It might be said that construing Mill's test in terms of taste ignores an important suggestion: higher pleasures involve the higher faculties; this is what makes them of a higher quality. Such seems certainly to be Mill's view, and it is what justifies him in discounting the opinions of the fool and the pig. Their experience is of a lower order and hence their pleasures are too. Applied to the subject of art what this implies is that serious art engages aspects of mind that lighter art does not address. Now this may, in general, be true, but it is unclear whether this would make a difference to the relative value of the two in terms of pleasure. Most people will accept Mill's claim that there is more to human life than eating, sleeping, and procreating. We might also agree that human beings can expect to enjoy pleasures which are closed to pigs because of innate endowments of mind and emotional capacity. But these evident differences give us no reason to think that the engagement of a higher capacity brings a higher pleasure. Pigs cannot do crosswords, and fools cannot while away the time with mathematical 'brainteasers'. Such activities undoubtedly engage higher faculties, but this of itself does not give us reason to think that the pleasure we derive from them is of a more valuable kind than the pleasure to be found in more simple pastimes. We can stipulatively define 'higher' pleasures as those which involve the higher faculties if we choose, but this will not give us reason to rank crosswords and the like as more signficant or important than any other pleasurable pastime.

More importantly still, even if, despite this point, majority judgments of the sort Mill describes could be consistently aligned with 'serious' art (which is doubtful), his account *assumes* that the explanation of this lies in the pleasure that is generated by different experiences. But why should artistic preference be based upon pleasure rather than some other value, yet to be fully disclosed? It is logically consistent (whether true or not) to maintain the following three propositions.

1 Over the ages majority opinion has found there to be greater value in serious than in light art.
2 People customarily speak of this value in the language of enjoyment.
3 This greater value is *not* adequately explained in terms of pleasure or enjoyment.

But if these three propositions are consistent, this shows that nothing has yet been said to substantiate the pleasure theory of art, and the objections we have considered imply that the value of art does indeed lie elsewhere.

Kant and beauty

So far we have been operating with a uniform notion of pleasure as just one kind of experience. But it has sometimes been argued that what we find in art is not a higher grade of everyday pleasure but a distinctive kind of 'aesthetic pleasure'. The Polish philosopher Roman Ingarden, for instance, urges us to recognize that aesthetic pleasures 'have a special character of their own and exist in a different manner from the pleasures deriving from a good meal or fresh air or a good bath' (Ingarden 1972: 43). (It should be added that Ingarden thinks this recognition to be just a small first step in arriving at a

11

proper understanding of aesthetic value.) Whether there is such a thing as a distinctively aesthetic pleasure is obviously an important question in itself. But still more important for present purposes is another question. Can it give a satisfactory explanation of the value of art? An appeal to 'aesthetic' pleasure will accomplish very little if we mean by this nothing more than 'the special kind of pleasure art gives'. To avoid this sort of emptiness what is needed is another term for aesthetic pleasure. Then we need to establish a relation between this new term and some value other than everyday pleasure or amusement.

One possible term which is to be found frequently in writing about art, is 'beauty'. The idea that the reward for the art lover is 'delight in the contemplation of the beautiful' is an old and familiar theme, an idea probably given its fullest expression by the great eighteenth-century German philosopher Immanuel Kant. The introduction of beauty allows us to say that the impoverishment of the pig or the fool, whose pleasure is of rather an earthy kind, is not to be explained in terms of ordinary pleasure at all but in terms of the absence of beauty.

The idea of the beautiful is a recurrent topic in the philosophy of art. Its merits have usually been discussed as a defining characteristic of art and, as we shall see in Chapter 8, definitions of art encounter serious difficulties. However, it is not difficult to construe the connection with art and beauty as a normative thesis, that is, beauty is something valuable and art is valuable because it consists primarily in the creation and contemplation of beauty. Something of this thesis is to be found in Kant, and his ideas can usefully be considered in this context.

Kant locates aesthetic judgment halfway between the logically necessary (an example would be mathematical theorems) and the purely subjective (expressions of personal taste). Though the proposition 'this is beautiful' has the appearance of a cognitive judgment, that is, a judgment about how things are, in the *Critique of Judgment*, his great work on aesthetics, Kant says expressing such a judgment 'cannot be other than subjective', that is, arising from a feeling of approval (§1 [These numbers refer to sections of the *Critique*]). On the other hand, it is not *merely* subjective since like a judgment about fact or necessity, the person who makes it

> can find as reason for his delight no personal conditions to which his own subjective self might alone be party ... [and therefore] ... must believe that he has reason for demanding a similar delight from every one. Accordingly he will speak of the beautiful as if beauty were a quality of the object and the judgment logical ... although it is only aesthetic and contains merely a reference of the representation of the object to the subject.
>
> (§6)

In plainer language the idea is this: beauty needs to be appreciated, sub-

12

jectively. It is not just a property of an object that we might dispassionately record, such as being fifty years old. To call something beautiful is not just to describe it but to react to it. On the other hand, our reaction is not merely personal, as it might be when we refer to something of which we happen to be especially fond. In declaring an object to be beautiful, we also mean to say that there is something about it which will make other people like it as well.

But can the special delight that is here located in the aesthetic offer an explanation of the value that is usually attributed to art? Kant has more to say about this. He contrasts the sort of approval which expresses a delight in the beautiful with that which declares something to be agreeable and that which declares it to be good. The mark of the agreeable is that it is purely a matter of personal taste (Kant gives the example of a preference for Canary-wine), and those who make such appraisals have no reason to expect others to share their preference. By 'the good' Kant here means what is useful and accordingly holds that judgments of this sort arise 'from the concept' of the end that is to be served; given an end in view, whether something is good (i.e., useful to that end) is not a matter of taste but a matter of fact. It follows that the peculiar value of aesthetic delight lies in this: it is composed of a judgment that is disinterestedly free, free that is to say, from both practical and cognitive determination. It is not a judgment of either personal liking or general usefulness but a judgment arising from the 'free play of the imagination'.

How is such a judgment possible? If it really is to be free and yet a judgment, it must command universal assent just as a claim to knowledge does, while at the same time, if it is not to be determined by objective properties, it must arise from subjective feeling. To explain this curious double nature, Kant postulates a *sensus communis* or 'shared sense' among humans, which is invoked when a judgment of taste is made (§§22 and 40). If this shared sense is not to be converted into objective common agreement about classes of things and thereby lose what is distinctive to the judgment of taste, judgments of taste must be 'invariably laid down as a singular judgment upon the Object'. This is why 'delight' in the beautiful is fixed upon an object; it takes the form not of an intellectual classification but contemplation of the object itself.

Kant's aesthetics is notoriously difficult to understand. For present purposes however we can make the following relevant observations. Suppose that Kant is correct in thinking that a peculiar delight arises from the free play of the imagination on some object: a picture, a poem, or a piece of music for instance. The connection between this and the activity of art remains somewhat obscure. Kant has a philosophy of art as well as an account of the aesthetic judgment. That is to say, he is concerned both with the artifacts of art and the attitudes we bring to them. But on the strength of what he says in the third *Critique*, the relation between the two is very hard to determine. If judgments of taste are as he says they are, then presumably

13

they may freely play where they choose, provided only that they express themselves as singular judgments upon an object. If finding something beautiful is a subjective matter, though one which commits us to believing that others will also find the object in question beautiful, there is no obvious restriction on what we can find beautiful. One acknowledged result of this is that natural beauty seems as fitting an object for aesthetic delight as anything an artist might create, but so too are scientific theories and geometrical proofs.

Second, at best Kant has shown that judgments of taste constitute a distinctive activity of mind, namely, the free play of imagination. Allowing that there is the common sense of which he speaks, we may add that this is an activity of mind in which human beings characteristically engage. But its being distinctive and its being engaged in, taken together, do not imply that it has any special value, even though Kant's way of speaking continually suggests it does. Why should it not be that here we have something wholly idle, however widely engaged in? There is a parallel in humour. When I say a joke is funny, I do not simply mean that I am amused by it, but imply that others will be amused as well. But this does not mean that I have isolated the essence of *comedy* – people find all sorts of things funny – and for this reason it does not show that I have explained what is especially valuable about comedy. Similarly, the free play of imagination in judgments of taste, as described by Kant, has neither been shown to have any special connection with the activity of art, nor has its value been explained.

Of course it might be asserted that beauty's value lies in nothing but itself. This, leaving aside Kantian aesthetics, reflects a simpler and more widespread claim, that beauty is to be valued for its own sake. 'Beauty for beauty's sake' is a familiar artistic slogan, similar in spirit to Oscar Wilde's celebrated remark that all art is quite useless. Yet to accept, as most people probably would, that the value of beauty is not to be reduced to or explained in terms of something else such as usefulness, still leaves a gap in the argument. We cannot make the jump from the value of *beauty* to the value of *art* without some additional explanation. Kant does have something to say about the 'genius' of the artist and its relation to the beautiful, but the fact is we can value the beautiful simply by contemplating it, and perhaps preserving it. Since the world already has beauty in it without any creative activity on our part, why do we need art as well? It is for this reason that the appeal to beauty as an irreducible value leaves unexplained the value, if there is any, in artistic activity. It also leaves unexplained the multiplicity of art forms. If we already have music, why do we need poetry?

An attempt to overcome this difficulty has been made by the contemporary German philosopher Hans-Georg Gadamer. In an essay (the title in English translation is 'The relevance of the beautiful') Gadamer aims to explain the value of art by building upon Kant's conception of the beautiful. At the same time, he attempts to refute the suggestion that there is a radical discontinuity between classical and modern art and does so by explaining the value of artistic activity in terms of the value of play.

Gadamer and art as play

Gadamer acknowledges the points just made about Kant's aesthetic. As he puts it, 'The approach to art through the experience of aesthetic taste is a relatively external one and . . . somewhat diminishing' (Gadamer 1986: 19). Nevertheless, Kant's great advance is to see first, that aesthetic taste is not a *purely* subjective matter but something which claims universal assent; second, that it arises not from any concept of the understanding but from the free play of the imagination; and third, that the ability to play freely is the peculiarity of artistic 'genius'. This is where Kant's philosophy of art joins his aesthetic. Taste, according to Kant, is merely a critical, not a productive faculty. While 'a natural beauty is a *beautiful thing*; artistic beauty is a *beautiful representation* of a thing' (§48, emphasis original) and it is the special task of genius to make beautiful representations. The problem is that on Kant's account there seems no more than a contingent, one might almost say accidental, connection between the exercise of taste and the production of beauty.

In contrast, Gadamer thinks that we can make a much closer connection than Kant does if we attend more carefully to the idea of genius. As Kant explains it, the mark of genius lies in productive activity which does not subserve some purpose that makes it useful, and which cannot be captured in set rules or formulas. Even the genius does not know the rules by which his free creative activity is determined. What Gadamer observes is that 'the creation of genius can never really be divorced from the con-geniality of the one who experiences it' (Gadamer 1986: 21), which is to say that appreciating a work of art requires imaginative activity on the part of the observer no less than the maker. The mind of the artist and the mind of the audience, we might say, must be mutually engaged in creative activity.

> A work of art . . . demands to be constructed by the viewer to whom it is presented. It is . . . not something we can simply use for a particular purpose, not a material thing from which we might fabricate some other thing. On the contrary, it is something that only manifests and displays itself when it is constituted by the viewer.
>
> (*ibid*.: 126)

This is why aesthetic judgment and artistic production go hand in hand. The artist's creativity needs its audience, and for the audience, creative art provides 'the experiences that best fulfil the ideal of "free" and disinterested delight' (*ibid*.: 20). An artist who cannot capture the attention of an audience is a failure, whatever merits may be thought to lie in the work, but a

15

great work of art stimulates and directs the perceptions of the audience, and is not only passively subject to appreciation.

Granted all this, we may nevertheless ask why experiences of this kind are to be valued. Gadamer thinks we must look at what he calls 'the anthropological basis of our experience of art', and this turns out to be play. It is a fact about human beings (and some other animals) that they engage in play. In thinking about play we readily contrast it with work and are thus disposed to accept its characterization as purposeless activity. But in Gadamer's view it is a deep mistake to suppose that this is a contrast between 'serious activity' and 'mere diversion'. What is significant about play is that, although in an important sense it is indeed activity without a purpose, it is not aimless but *structured*. In play we can discern rules and goals which are established within the play itself, and this is true even in the simple games of small children. So for instance the aim in soccer is to put the ball in the net. Viewed extrinsically, such an accomplishment is valueless and accomplishes nothing. What is there to value about a leather ball crossing a line? This is the sense in which the game is purposeless. But viewed intrinsically, that is, within the terms of the game itself, the achievement is not to be described in these terms, but as a *goal*. And a goal *is* an accomplishment, something that lends focus and point to the rules of play and to the skill that may be exhibited in it.

Play can be serious, not in the sense that it is professionalized, but in the sense that it demands, solely for its own purposes, the best temperaments and the finest skills of which human beings are capable. Now Gadamer thinks that art is a kind of play, in which together artist and audience join. What is distinctive about great art is the challenge it presents to the viewer to discern a meaning within it. This is not a meaning which can be conceptualized or explicated in language (to this extent Gadamer follows Kant closely) but is rather symbolic, that is, a work of art is something which (in words of Austin Farrer) aims to *be* that which it represents. The artist's challenge to the audience is to engage in a creative free play of images whereby a self-representation is realized.

This is a communal activity. Since the realization of symbol requires cooperative activity, this same activity is something in which all and any may engage. (This is Gadamer's interpretation of Kant's *sensus communis*.) His explanation of the value that attaches to the cooperative activity is novel and interesting. We discover in art, according to Gadamer, the same kind of universality we discover in festivals. The important thing about festivals in Gadamer's analysis, is that they punctuate the flow of time, so to speak.

> We do not describe a festival as a recurring one because we can assign a specific place in time to it, but rather the reverse: the time in which it occurs only arises through the recurrrence of the festival itself.
>
> (*ibid.*: 41).

Thus, everyday events are located before or after Christmas, for instance, not the other way around. Christmas is the 'marker' relative to which other days take their significance. One consequence is that festivals are 'not subject to the abstract calculation of temporal duration'(*ibid.*) Gadamer thinks that we have two fundamental ways of experiencing time and in festival time we get, as it were, a taste of eternity. In an elegant summary he says this:

> [I]n the experience of art we must learn how to dwell upon the work in a specific way. When we dwell upon the work, there is no tedium involved, for the longer we allow ourselves, the more it displays its manifold riches to us. The essence of our temporal experience is learning how to tarry in this way. And perhaps it is the only way that is granted to us finite beings to relate to what we call eternity.
>
> (*ibid.*: 45)

This compelling final sentence reveals where the value of great art ultimately lies. The observation has however a certain vagueness, for we have not been told what the nature of this form of 'relating' is. As I hope to show, despite the many merits of Gadamer's analysis, this is a crucial omission.

Plainly Gadamer is correct to resist the correlation between 'play' and pleasurable diversion and to stress that 'play' can be as serious as anything else in human experience. For this reason, it seems to me, in identifying art as a form of play, he endorses a view of art importantly different from the commonplace pleasure view, whatever superficial similarities there may be. Moreover, in stressing the *creative* participation of audience as well as artist, and hence the necessary unity of what Kant would call the estimation and production of the work, he has bridged the gap that appears to exist in Kant's aesthetic. Nor is his account of art as symbol to be treated as yet another attempt at 'necessary and sufficient conditions'. Since his principal interest is in showing the importance of art, we can reasonably construe him to be giving an account of the value that resides in art at its best, even if his manner of speaking does not always bear this interpretation. Finally, by attempting to show art to be 'perhaps the only way' of relating to eternity, he has, I think, given the right *sort* of answer. That is to say, he has shown how art contributes to the human pursuit of significance.

There are of course important questions about the meaning of 'eternity'. Is there such a dimension? Philosophers have often argued that eternity is an incoherent idea, that we can attach no sense to it, and a theory which relies on it is to that degree weakened. We might however preserve the major elements of Gadamer's theory of art as play with something less ambitious. Another philosopher who has pursued the idea of art as play is the American Kendall Walton. In his book *Mimesis as Make-Believe*, he develops and applies the idea that many art works are what he calls 'props' in a game of make-believe, and he finds the value of art rests in the value of playing this game.

17

Make-believe – the use of (external) props in imaginative activities – is a truly remarkable invention. . . . We can make people turn into pumpkins, or make sure the good guys win, or see what it is like for the bad guys to win. . . . There is a price to pay in real life when the bad guys win, even if we learn from experience. Make-believe provides the experience – something like it anyway – for free. The divergence between fictionality and truth spares us pain and suffering we would have to expect in the real world. We realize some of the benefits of hard experience without having to undergo it.

(Walton 1990: 68)

Walton's theory, which will be mentioned again in a later chapter, rests its case for the value of art on an idea that is less elusive (if also more pedestrian) than that of 'relating to eternity'. Works of art provide benefits without the cost that would normally attach to them. But he shares Gadamer's basic contention, that art is a kind of play, a suggestion we have seen has important virtues. Still, to refer to art as a game is to employ a metaphor, and one way of asking whether the metaphor is adequate is to look at a literal use of 'game', namely sport.

Art and sport

Sport is a variety of play, and for this reason it is wrong to think of sport as mere diversion or entertainment. Some sport is lighthearted, some is serious, and what creates the possibility of serious sport is the fact that sport can provide a structured but self-contained activity in which human virtues and vices can display themselves. Moreover this display is not for the sake of something else but for its own sake. Thus sporting contests require prowess and stamina, intelligence and ingenuity, courage, integrity, forbearance, determination, and so on. Different games require different skills and mentalities, but all provide, not merely occasions for, but vehicles for, the realization of these distinctly human capacities.

It is because of its connection with this sort of achievement and expression that sport has a value greater than the pleasure which arises from amusing diversion. As with art, this feature of sport justifies expenditure of time and money on a scale which, if devoted to more mundane pleasures, would be regarded as indulgence. Of course people can overestimate the importance of sport, and perhaps they often do, but someone who tries to remind us that 'it's only a game' has, on at least some occasions, failed to see just what role sport can have in the realization of human excellence. In short, sport is free play of the sort that Gadamer isolates and analyses. What then is the relevant difference between sport and art?

Following Gadamer's analysis, we might be inclined to argue that,

18

whereas art involves a cooperative act of creation on the part of both artists and audience, sport is participant-centred, and the audience mere spectators. But, as Gadamer himself implies, this is not so. The significance of a sporting occasion is often determined by spectator participation as much as by sporting endeavour. What makes a win into a victory or a loss into a defeat is a function of spectator expectation and involvement. Moreover, sporting occasions have that character of festival that Gadamer finds in art, and hence the underlying universality that Kant's common sense possesses. It is precisely because the individual can get swept up in a communal involvement which cannot be articulated in words that the appeal of sport crosses almost every boundary. It is for this reason too that sporting events can have the character of national contests, triumphs, and defeats.

The self-contained and universal character of sport allows it to provide the experience of 'eternity in time' that Gadamer attributes to art, though 'eternity in time' is an expression not of Gadamer's but of the Danish religious thinker Kierkegaard. Wimbledon, the Superbowl, or the Cup Final, provide occasions similar to Christmas and Easter in just this respect that ordinary events can be related in terms of them and not the other way about.

But if all this is true, if sport no less than art can allow us to 'tarry' and thereby taste eternity, why is art to be valued distinctly from sport, or even as better than sport? One answer would be that we have so far ignored the symbolic character of art. The importance of symbol is that it is a form, perhaps the highest form, of self-representation. A symbol, although it represents, does not direct us beyond itself, as do other forms of representation. It contains all that is needed to structure the free play of imagination and understanding. Because it is self-representative, it is self-contained.

Now it is true that as far as common speech goes, the symbolic is to be associated with art rather than sport. What is not so clear is whether this makes any significant difference to their respective values. It is not clear that the presence of symbol in art and its absence in sport gives us any reason, following Gadamer's analysis, to value art more highly than sport. The value of art seems to arise through the self-containment of symbol: the free play of creative activity is invoked and directed entirely within the work of art and we need not look beyond the work. Surely the same is true of sport. The game itself provides for the engagement of all our faculties; we need not look beyond it.

It is clear that Gadamer means us to regard art as an especially valuable form of play, but we have found nothing in his analysis that gives us reason to discriminate between art and sport in this regard. If both Gadamer's analysis and the subsequent argument are convincing, there is a conflict here with the widespread belief that art is of higher value than sport. That this belief is indeed widespread can hardly be doubted. Though sportsmen and women are often fêted as much as artists and performers, in the longer term the great figures of sport are not ranked alongside the great figures of art. Although there are sports equivalents of Maria Callas and David Hockney – Jesse Owens or Sugar Ray Robinson perhaps – there are no sporting equivalents of Shakespeare or Mozart. Great creative artists such as these take their place beside historically significant philosophers, scientists, religious figures, and political heroes; great sportsmen and women do not. We could dismiss this and conclude that there is no difference in value between art and sport, and that any general belief to the contrary is a cultural prejudice. Or we can endorse this evaluation and seek some explanatory justification of it. This is just what Gadamer's theory of art does not supply, because by his account the two come out on a par. The same is true of Kendall Walton. He believes that art is literally a game, but if so it enjoys no special advantages over other games, except possibly in terms of quantitative rather than qualitative involvement, which raises again the problems we found in Mill.

We ought not to suppose, however, that this is a conclusive objection to the theory (though Gadamer's way of speaking suggests that he himself might regard it as such). The relative estimation of art and sport could indeed be erroneous, and arguably some widely held estimations of this sort *are* erroneous. One of the attractions of normative theory of art is that it can generate social criticism of just this sort. Since how we value art and the relative importance attributed to different kinds and forms of art are distinguishing features of our cultural life, a critical investigation of the true value of art is at the same time an examination of the rationality of our culture. Collingwood regards philosophy of art as having this social dimension also, and he is not sparing in his social criticism.

> The cliques of artists and writers consist for the most part of a racket selling amusement to people who at all costs must be prevented from thinking themselves vulgar, and a conspiracy to call it not amusement but art.
>
> (Collingwood 1938: 90)

Just as the relative estimation of so-called high art and folk art may be based on nothing more than custom and prejudice, so the relative standing accorded to art and to sport may not reflect real differences in value. This and similar possibilities must for the moment remain open.

Most people will object to the analysis of art as play because it cannot attribute to Shakespeare or Mozart any greater significance than to the leading sporting figures of the day. We may strengthen the objection by adding the observation of a striking difference between art and sport which the 'play' theory does not seem able to accommodate. Art can have content whereas sport cannot. That is to say, a play or a book or a painting can be *about* something, but it would be senseless to speak of a game of tennis or football's being about anything. Moreover, it is in the meaning or content of a work of art, what it communicates, that the value is often supposed to lie, a meaning which may be examined again and again.

Having content and having meaning are not synonymous. There are important differences between them. The point here however is that to draw a parallel between art and sport is to omit an important ingredient of art. Just what this missing ingredient is has to be explained further, but for the moment I shall refer to that ingredient as the 'content' of art and observe that this element of 'content' is not to be explained by the contingent fact that most artistic activity results in an abiding work of art, while games do not. Even in the age of video recorders, when games can be recorded for posterity, there is relatively little to be gained from repeated viewing of them, leaving aside external gains like acquiring a better mastery of the techniques of the game. Nor could a game be played again in the way that a drama can. The difference is that the drama has a meaning that can be explored; the game, however compelling to watch, has none.

Walton, in the omitted parts of the passage quoted previously, speaks of exploration and of insight.

> The excitement of exploring the unknown will be lost to the extent that we construct the worlds ourselves. But if we let others (artists) construct them for us, we can enjoy not only the excitement but also the benefits of any special talent and insight they may bring to the task.
> (Walton 1990: 67–8)

Exploration and insight are not terms that naturally apply to games, just as it would be odd to speak of games as profound, shallow, or sentimental, descriptions which are readily applied to works of art. The more apposite use of all these terms is in contexts where it makes sense to speak of content or subject matter, and this implies once more that art, unlike sport, has communicative import. Whether this important fact can be made to justify the differing estimates of each depends upon the content of the communication. Here we encounter another important area of debate in the philosophy of art, namely the communicative nature of art. Of the rival theories on this point, one has dominated thinking about the arts for over a hundred years. This is the view that art communicates emotion or has emotional impact. It is to this theory that the next chapter is devoted. Before that, it is useful to retrace our steps by way of summary.

Summary

The commonplace view that the value of art lies in the pleasure we get from it has been found to be deficient on a number of grounds. First, it is not clear that what is commonly regarded as the finest in art is, except for those 'laboriously trained to enjoy it', a real source of amusement. Second, if art's value is pleasure, this makes it nearly impossible to explain the various discriminations that are made within and between forms and works of art. Third, it is hard to see how the pleasure theory could sustain the sorts of evaluative distinctions that are made between art and non-art in the cultural and educational institutions of our society. We might try to amend the pleasure theory by speaking of higher or distinctively aesthetic pleasures. But in fact no such distinction seems to be sustainable. Even if we replace aesthetic pleasure with a Kantian conception of beauty, we are pulled in the wrong direction, namely, towards the mental state of the audience, and we thus appear to lose any possibility of explaining the peculiar value of art *works* themselves.

It should be noted that nothing in the argument against the pleasure theory implies that art cannot be entertaining, or that people are never entertained by it, or that some things that are commonly regarded as works of art are not valued chiefly because of the pleasure they give. Nor does the argument deny that paintings and pieces of music are beautiful and are partly valued for this reason. All that the argument so far has shown is that if the chief value of art were to reside in the pleasure that is to be derived from it, or in its being an occasion for judgments of beauty, art cannot be given the high estimation we commonly give it.

Gadamer, building upon Kant's aesthetic, offers us a more sophisticated version of a similiar theory according to which art is to be valued as play. The advantage of 'play' over amusement reveals a mistake in regarding play as mere diversion. Play is a serious and important part of human life, and in Gadamer's analysis may even be shown to have a semi-religious significance. By Walton's account it is a game which has the benefits of experience without the usual costs.

But for all this it remains play, and this means that we cannot, as we customarily do, draw a distinction between the importance of art and the importance of sport. Sport can be no less 'serious' than art in Gadamer's theory. In itself this is no refutation, but combined with the further observation that art, unlike sport, can communicate something, that it can mean something, there does seem to be reason to look further and to ask whether this element of communication might not justify the attribution of greater value to art. One familiar suggestion is that art communicates emotion, and this is the idea we examine next.

Suggestions for further reading

As far as possible, suggestions for further reading are taking from Neill and Ridley (eds), *The Philosophy of Art: Readings Ancient and Modern*, hereafter referred to as *N&R*.

R.G. Collingwood, *The Principles of Art*, chap. 5.
Hans-Georg Gadamer, 'The play of art', *N&R* p. 75.
David Hume, 'Of the standard of taste', *N&R* p. 254.
Immanuel Kant, 'Analytic of the beautiful' *N&R* p. 269.

2

———∘⊙∘———

Art and emotion

It is frequently said that what matters in art is emotion, both the feeling of the artist and the emotional impact of a work on its audience. If pleasure is the commonplace explanation of the value of art, expression of emotion is the commonplace view of its nature. This is a view to which we can usefully give the label 'expressivism'. This distinguishes it from 'Expressionism', a term widely used for a school of painting which held that painting ought to contain emotion. The two terms and the ideas they invoke are obviously connected, but expressivism is a theory that applies to art in general, and not merely to the visual arts. It is a view closely allied with nineteenth-century Romanticism – the belief that true art always embodies sincere feeling – and the extensive influence of Romanticism subsequently explains, at least in part, the widespread acceptance of aesthetic expressivism. In this chapter, the connection which expressivism makes between art and emotion will be explored, first in what might be called an everyday version, and then in the more sophisticated version that is to be found in R.G. Collingwood's *The Principles of Art*. In both cases, the crucial question will be taken to be: 'Can the appeal to emotion explain what is valuable about art?'

Tolstoy and everyday expressivism

Not infrequently, great artists theorize about their work. This is unsurprising, but what is more surprising is that even the greatest of creative artists can take a very simpleminded view of art. One of the best known instances of this is Leo Tolstoy, the Russian literary giant. As well as his many novels, Tolstoy wrote a short book called *What is Art?* and in it the everyday conception of expressivism is set out with striking naiveté.

> Art is a human activity consisting in this, that one man consciously by means of certain external signs, hands on to others feelings he has lived through, and that others are infected by these feelings and also experience them.
>
> (Tolstoy, in *N&R* 1995: 511)

24

In a few words, Tolstoy here captures a picture of artistic activity which is very widely shared: artists are people inspired by an experience of deep emotion, and they use their skill with words, or paint, or music, or marble, or movement, to embody that emotion in a work of art. The mark of its successful embodiment is that it stimulates the same emotion in its audience. It is in this way that artists may be said to communicate emotional experience.

This picture of the relation between artist and audience is widely accepted. Even more famously than Tolstoy, the poet Wordsworth (in the Preface to the *Lyrical Ballads*) held that 'Poetry is the spontaneous overflow of powerful feeling'. Yet we do not have to think very long about this view before serious difficulties arise. Many of these were lucidly catalogued by the American philosopher John Hospers in an essay entitled 'The concept of artistic expression'. First, in attributing the origins of artistic production to emotional experience we appear to be determining *a priori* – by definition – what can only be determined *a posteriori* – by experience and investigation, namely the causal conditions under which works of art come to be. That is to say, the expression theory appears to announce in advance of considering the facts that it was emotional experience which caused Shakespeare, Haydn, Leonardo, Christopher Wren and countless others to create in the way that they did. Of course, in response to this objection, the claim can be construed as an empirical one. But then it appears to be false; many celebrated artists have expressly denied that emotion lay at the heart of their endeavours.

Besides this, by focussing upon the *origins* of the work as a way of classifying it as art, where such classification is meant to attribute some sort of status, the expression theory seems to involve a version of what is called the 'genetic fallacy'. This is the fallacy of assessing the merits (more usually the demerits) of something by referring to its cause. Hospers puts the point in this way:

> Even if all artists did in fact go through the process described by the expression theory, and even if nobody but artists did this, would it be true to say that the work of art was a good one because the artist in creating it, went through this or that series of experiences in plying his medium? Once the issue is put thus baldly, I cannot believe that anyone could easily reply in the affirmative; it seems much too plain that the merits of a work of art must be judged by what we find in the work of art, quite regardless of the conditions under which the work of art came into being.
>
> (Hospers 1955: 147)

Thirdly, in looking for an originating emotion we appear to ignore the difference between simple and complex works of art. In some cases the attribution of an overriding emotion, or set of them, to a work of art is not implausible. Mahler's *Songs of a Wayfarer*, for example, for which Mahler wrote both words and music, can easily be thought of as the outpouring of emotion, and it is not hard to suggest an emotion of which each song is the expression. But any move from simple cases to more complex ones brings with it a loss in plausibility. A simple love song may be said to express love, but in a complex work with, say, a great array of characters in a variety of relationships, so wide a range of emotions and attitudes is represented that it is impossible to say that any single one, or even straightforward set of emotions, is that which the work expresses. What emotion lies at the heart of, or is expressed by, a novel such as George Eliot's *Middlemarch* for instance?

This question is not easy to answer, but this does not mean that it is unanswerable. It might be claimed with some plausibility, for example, that Conrad's *Nostromo* is an expression of his deep pessimism. Yet it is a novel with a complex plot and a wide range of disparate characters, and thus it certainly seems possible to regard a complex work of art as the expression of a single emotion. But, it is no accident that examples have to be chosen with care here. The ease with which we may answer the question with respect to *Nostromo*, does not make it any easier to answer with respect to *Middlemarch*. Moreover, it is doubtful that we can give any easy answer for any really major work of art. Though there is much emotion in the drama, there is not, it seems to me, any one emotion which may said to be expressed in any of Shakespeare's tragedies. Indeed, in calling them tragedies, we partly focus attention not on their emotional content but on the structure of their events. Whatever the range and degree of emotion to be found in a tragedy, and there is usually a good deal, the truly tragic element is to be found in the ineluctible interplay of character and event. It is the interplay of forces beyond his control which makes Oedipus, despite his best intentions, commit the horrible acts of parricide and incest. The horror he feels is the outcome of the tragedy, not its source.

So too with other art forms, music for instance: we are sometimes misled about the plausibility of expressivism in music by the impact of Romanticism on its composition. Romantic music can mistakenly be assumed to be the paradigm of all music. But think of the music of Bach. We would miss the importance of the complex mathematical structure of a toccata and fugue, something which requires understanding if it is to be appreciated, were we to scan it for an expression of some deep emotion. On the surface at any rate, most Baroque music has nothing to do with emotion. Yet it would be absurd to dismiss it as valueless or less than artistic.

Fourthly, doubts can be raised about the emotional content, not merely of specific works of art, but of *forms* of art. Possible examples of emotional expression are easy to find in poetry, opera, and the theatre. But is it plausible to suggest that works of architecture express emotion? Emotion (and other things) on a grand scale may feature in Rubens, but this gives us no reason whatever to extend the theory of Expressionism to abstract paintings (despite the school known as Abstract Expressionism). And, as over a century of extended debate and discussion has shown, there are serious philosophical difficulties in attributing an expressive capacity to 'absolute music', a topic to be addressed more fully in Chapter 4.

Hospers' doubts about expressivism have gained such currency that they are sometimes regarded as elementary. But even if they could be laid aside, there are further more substantial difficulties. How is emotion supposed to be embodied in a work of art, exactly? It is clearly a requirement of the expressivist theory that it must be embodied in some way or other. This is because for any given work, it could be true (1) that the occasion of its creation was an emotional experience, (2) that its reception engendered emotion on the part of the audience, and yet (3) still be false that emotion was the content of the work. For instance, a singer past his prime might, in a mood of despondency, try to recapture some of the vigorous jollity of his singing, and failing to do so, engender a similar despondency on the part of his admirers. But neither fact would by itself make the song he chose a sad one. So it must be the case, if expressivism is to be true, that the emotion is not merely in the artist and in the audience, but also in the work itself. Yet, if we say of a song or a painting, not merely that it caused or was caused by sadness, but that it is *itself* feeling sad, this seems unintelligible. Unless of course, sadness here does not mean what it usually means. But then emotion does not mean what it usually means, and expressivism is called in doubt in another way.

In reply, the proponent of expressivism might draw a distinction between 'being *an expression of* sadness' and 'being *expressive* of sadness'. Expressivism then becomes the view that works of art are expressive of emotion, rather than actual expressions of emotion. This is an important distinction, which will have to be looked at further in a subsequent section. For the moment however, we can note that drawing it constitutes a major modification of the commonplace understanding of expressivism. Indeed, the need to draw some such distinction is only the first of a number of refinements upon Tolstoy's picture of art and emotion, and others will emerge as we proceed to find further difficulties in it.

Those we have identified so far have to do with expressivism's conception of the artist and the work, but there are also problems about the role assigned to the audience. Is it true that we are guilty of a failure of appreciation if at the end of Mahler's songs we are not filled with *Weltschmerz* (world-weariness)? Must we grieve to the degree that Leontes does in *A Winter's Tale* if we are to understand the remorse that follows his jealousy? Must we in fact feel jealous ourselves during the first part of the play? Unlike the previous question about associating a single overriding emotion with a complex work of art, these *are*, it seems to me, rhetorical questions; the answer to them is plain. It may be true that sad and solemn poetry tends to .

27

induce sadness, and that laughter and gaiety portrayed on stage or in a story engender lightheartedness in the audience (though this isn't obviously true; it is jokes, usually, not the dramatic representation of being amused by them, that induce mirth). It is certainly often the case that horror and fear are induced in an audience by plays and films. (Who can fail to be shocked when Giovanni appears holding a human heart and covered in blood in John Ford's *'Tis Pity She's a Whore*?) Perhaps it is the truth of these generalizations that inclines people to expressivism, but once the generalizations are extended to cover not only all works, but all emotions – jealousy, despair, romantic love, hatred, patriotism, contempt, spite, and so on – expressivism's account of an audience's involvement in art loses whatever plausibility it had. It may be true that people cannot usually be said to appreciate, say, nostalgia in a work unless they have felt themselves touched by it, but the same is obviously not true of other feelings. Can we only be said to understand and appreciate a portrayal of racist loathing if we have felt slightly racist ourselves? In short, the successful portrayal of an emotion in a work of art does not depend on generating that emotion in the audience.

It might be replied that an artistic portrayal of any of these emotions, even those of a violent or evil nature, must certainly be counted a failure if it leaves an audience as uncomprehending as before. But this reply signals another move away from expressivism, because it relies upon the idea that a work of art might alter our *understanding* of emotions, not that it makes us *feel* them. Since understanding often breeds sympathy, it can be true that those who come to a better understanding of an emotion come to feel differently about it, but if and when this is the case, the change in feeling is brought about through the intermediary of the understanding; it is not induced directly.

A third reason for moving away from the commonplace version of expressivism arises not from its descriptive paucity but its implausibility as an explanation of the value of art. What is so good, we might ask, about the outpouring of emotion? One does not need to subscribe to the virtue of austere reserve, said to be the mark of the Englishman, in order to wonder why, taken in isolation, there is something to be valued in the expression of emotion. If someone screams his hatred of another race in a skilful display of vitriolic language, this does not, of itself, give us any reason to admire him or dwell upon his utterances. Of course, songs like Mahler's are markedly different from this, but if it is right to call them outpourings of the composer's emotion, their value seems to lie *in the way this is done*, not in the mere fact of its *being* done.

Indeed, expressivism's explanation of the value of art is worse than this. To regard the expression of emotion as the mark of art properly so called, robs it of a value it might otherwise be thought to have – imaginativeness. If it is a requirement of an emotion's being expressed in a work that it should be the artist's own, this removes from artistic endeavour just what makes so many works of art remarkable, their being major feats of imagination. Hospers remarks in this connection:

> Shakespeare could hardly have gone through the experiences of Hamlet, Macbeth, Iago, Cleopatra, Lear, Goneril, Prospero and Coriolanus in one lifetime, but what difference does this make as long as he could present us with a series of vivid, powerful, convincing characterizations?
>
> (Hospers 1955: 149)

But to make the point in this way understates the case. It is not merely that expressivism ignores the value of imagination; it actually eliminates it. An emotion that is imagined need not be felt, and the absence of feeling is a mark of real artistic creativity. But we cannot accommodate this kind of creativity on the expressivist model.

A similar question arises about the value of arousing emotion in an audience. To begin with, the general picture seems to fit preaching and speech-making better than it does art. But even ignoring this we can ask, why should greater success in the arousal of emotion count as the mark of higher art? Perhaps the most obvious works of art (if for the moment we may call them that) whose aim is to arouse a specific emotion in the audience, and which are often highly successful in doing so, are horror films. The point of these is to induce fear, and that is what they usually do. Moreover, in the main they do it with greater success than more celebrated works of art. The horror aroused in most audiences by the gouging out of Gloucester's eyes in *Lear*, is weak compared to that aroused by *Nightmare on Elm Street*. But no one would regard the latter as a greater work than the former, or put horror films, as a *genre*, on a higher level than Shakespearean tragedy. Even within the *genre* itself, discrimination in terms of quality is not generally made on relative capacity to arouse fear or the strength of the fear aroused. Alfred Hitchcock's films (or some of them) stand out because of the subtlety with which the audience is made fearful, rather than because they are made *more* fearful than they are by other films. In so far as we consider the arousal of emotion important, this seems to have more to do with the ways in which it is aroused than with the mere fact of its arousal.

A further important point is this. It is very plausible to think that the value of arousing emotion is a function of the value of the emotion aroused. Thus, if Dickens's *Hard Times* arouses pity for the downtrodden and righteous anger at heartless oppressors, this is good because these are good emotions to arouse in people. If, by contrast, Trollope's *The Eustace Diamonds* leaves us with loathing and contempt for Jews as a race (because of its portrayal of Mr Julius), this does not redound to the novelist's credit. (The ability of poets and artists to arouse dangerous emotions was one of the factors that inclined Plato to ban them from the Republic.) Viewed in this way, the arousal of emotion in itself is neutral, neither a good thing nor a bad. There is thus no reason to encourage or discourage it in and for itself. It follows that expressivism's understanding of art can attribute no intrinsic value to it at all.

Tolstoy himself, despite the generality of the remarks in the passage quoted, did not think that the communication of emotion in itself had value, but only the communication of *good* emotion. What made it good on his account was its connection with Christian ideals, but expressivism properly so called does have to show that there is something intrisically valuable about the arousal of emotion. One suggestion appeals to the Aristotelian doctrine of 'katharsis'. This is the theory that by arousing emotions in us and giving us objects upon which to vent them, the artist purges us of emotional disturbances which might otherwise erupt inconveniently in ordinary life. Aristotle applied something of this view to tragedy, and to a greater extent music. The precise interpretation of his account of katharsis is a matter of some dispute, but if we leave the interpretation of Aristotle aside and consider just the general idea of emotional purging, and extend it to art in general, the value of art appears to lie in the contribution it makes to our mental health. Now, even if there is some truth in this, the imputation of value must surely work in two ways. If art can purge us of harmful emotions, it can equally purge us of beneficial ones, with the result that if we don't hurt as many people as we might, we don't help as many either. The net effect of the theory of katharsis, in short, is not to alter the moral neutrality of arousing emotion; it merely reverses the respective evaluations. Good art will be that which arouses (and expels) bad emotions and vice versa.

If all these points are granted it will be evident that as a description of the nature of artistic creation and appreciation, Tolstoy's simple version of expressivism, even though it is widely shared, is seriously flawed. Why then is it a theory that attracts so much support? Expressivism derives some of its appeal from the fact that people do find many works of art moving, and further, that they enjoy being moved by them. But just why this should be so is, as Arnold Heisenberg once remarked, a matter for psychology not philosophy – it is fact about the mentality of people, not about the intrinsic nature of art. What our examination of expressivism has shown is that there is nothing in art as such, or in its special value, that makes this psychological fact philosophically significant. We can record that people like being moved, and attach a value to works that move them solely in virtue of this fact. But in so doing we have not arrived at an *explanation* of the value of art.

The version of expressivism we have been working with so far, though rather crude, has been worth exploring for two reasons. First, since it is widely held and informs a common understanding of art, it is important to make its errors plain. Second, its errors having been made plain, we are in a better position to see what difficulties a more sophisticated version must overcome.

Essay

Collingwood's expressivism

In *The Principles of Art*, Collingwood repudiates most of the features of the everyday version of expressivism. Art, on his view, is not concerned with the arousal of emotion at all. Indeed he expressly distinguishes between art proper and art as amusement on the one hand, which by his account arouses emotion for the sake of enjoyment, and art as magic on the other, which arouses and focusses emotions which may then be directed at concerns in ordinary life. Neither of these is art proper for the reason that both use the medium (of paint or poetry or whatever) as means to end. This places them both in the camp of technology or craft, something which Collingwood wishes to distinguish sharply from art.

[Collingwood uses the word 'magic' in a slightly uncommon way. He means the arousal of emotion for practical purposes. He suggests, for example, that art as magic is exemplified in many of Kipling's poems which, on his reading at least, are intended to arouse political emotions as a means to stimulating political loyalties. By 'amusement' he means the sort of thing discussed in the last chapter. His main point, however, is that if either emotional stimulation or entertainment is the sum of what art has to offer, it may be replaced by other forms of magic and amusement without significant loss. The value of a craft, a means to an end, resides entirely in its products, so that other means to the same end will do just as well – machines can replace carpenters for instance – and if art's value is as a means to an end, it too can be dispensed with. But it is a presupposition of Collingwood's philosophy of art that the nature and value of art has to be explained in a way that makes it distinctive, and this is a presupposition that the arguments about pleasure and play have given us reason to accept: entertainment value may be found in many other ways and so cannot be an explanation of what is distinctively valuable about art. Similar arguments can be made about what Collingwood calls magic – the use of the power of emotion to practical ends.

The simple version of expressivism, Collingwood thinks, is also mistaken in its supposition that the emotion that is to be found in a work of art pre-exists the work. That is to say, it is wrong to imagine that a work of art is merely the translation into paint or music or words of an emotion the artist feels before ever the work of creation has begun. According to Collingwood, the original emotion is nothing more than an indeterminate 'psychic disturbance' which is gradually identified and refined in the process of creating the work until the artist can recognize it as the emotion it is. An example might be a general uneasiness which the artist gradually identifies as anger rather than anxiety, say. It is wrong to suppose that even this vague 'psychic disturbance' must be temporally prior to artistic activity. It is rather the case that the activity of feeling and the activity of creating, though 'not identical . . . are connected in such a way that . . . each is conditional upon the other' (Collingwood 1938: 304), which is to say that neither can be isolated or identified without the other. In other words, we can only identify the emotion when it has come to realization through the work of art.

Towards the end of *The Principles of Art*, Collingwood adapts to his own use the terminology of 'impressions and ideas' made famous by David Hume. An 'impression' is a sense experience of any kind – a sound, a sight, a smell – and an 'idea' is a concept which has intellectual but not sensual content. According to Collingwood, each act of imagination has an impression, or sensuous experience, at its base, which by mental activity is converted into an idea. 'Every imaginative experience is a sensuous experience raised to the imaginative level by an act of consciousness' (Collingwood 1938: 306). He means by this that the sensual and emotional experience contained in a work of art is not 'raw', felt experience, but experience mediated by the thought and imagination of the artist.

Tolstoy's version of expressivism, we saw, is seriously deficient in that it excludes the importance of imagination. In Collingwood's aesthetic, by contrast, imagination plays a central role. In fact, art proper as he describes it has two equally important elements, expression and imagination. It is by imaginative construction that the artist transforms vague and uncertain emotion into an articulate expression. The process of artistic creation is thus not a matter of making external what already exists internally, which is how the simple model construes it, but a process of imaginative discovery. And since the psychic disturbance with which it begins is the artist's, art is a process of *self*-discovery. Herein, in fact, lies its peculiar value: self-knowledge.

> Art is not a luxury, and bad art is not a thing we can afford to tolerate. To know ourselves is the foundation of all life that develops beyond the mere psychical level of experience. . . . Every utterance and every gesture that each one of us makes is a work of art. It is important to each one of us that in making them, however much he deceives others, he should not deceive himself. If he deceives himself in this matter, he has sown in himself a seed which, unless he roots it up again, may grow into any kind of wickedness, any kind of mental disease, any kind of stupidity and folly and insanity. Bad art, the corrupt consciousness, is the true *radix malorum* [root of evil].
>
> (*ibid.*: 284–5)

This is a striking panegyric to the value of art, and attributes very great importance to it. Two thoughts spring to mind, however. If 'every utterance and every gesture' is a work of art, this, on the face of it, leaves 'art' in the more restricted sense in which it is commonly understood, of no special interest or value; anyone and everyone is an artist. Furthermore, if the end of art is self-knowledge, knowledge of our own emotional states, artistic creation seems to be of consequence only to its creator and art becomes a form of introspection. The implication of both points is that we

32

no longer seem to have any reason to devote special attention to a Leonardo or a Shakespeare. Their works are not uniquely expressions of emotion, and in any case, as such, they are primarily of value to the artists themselves.

Both these inferences are natural, but nonetheless mistaken. Collingwood is aware that his account of art and the artist may easily be construed in this way, and as a result he devotes a whole chapter to the relation between artist and community. In it he argues that it is not 'what *I* feel' that the artist identifies and articulates, but 'what *we* feel'.

> The artist's business is to express emotions; and the only emotions he can express are those which he feels, namely his own. . . . If he attaches any importance to the judgment of his audience, it can only be because he thinks that the emotions he has tried to express are . . . shared by his audience. . . . In other words he undertakes his artistic labour not as a personal effort on his own private behalf, but as a public labour on behalf of the community to which he belongs.
>
> (*ibid.*: 314–15)

To this extent Collingwood shares Kant's supposition of a *sensus communis*, and it is for this reason that art is socially important. It is not merely artists, but also the whole community of which they are a part, that come to self-knowledge in their work. This is why 'Art is the community's medicine for the worst disease of mind, the corruption of consciousness' (*ibid.*: 336). Secondly, it is wrong to think that the work of art consists in a material object such as a painting or a book. This is not because some works of art are not obviously material at all – a dance for instance – though that is an important objection, but because, being acts of imagination, works of art must be recreated in the minds of their audience. This claim has sometimes been interpreted in rather startling ways, as though it implied that art is all in the mind. But Collingwood is making the point that since, for instance, the same poem can appear in many different books, and the same piece of music can be played at different times and on different instruments, the work of art cannot be identified with its physical manifestation. It can only be said to exist if it exists in the active apprehension of a work by an audience. Collingwood expressly rejects any conception of audience as passive spectator: 'Art is not contemplation, it is action' (*ibid.*: 332), and the function of the audience is 'not a merely receptive one, but collaborative' (*ibid.*: 324). This is one of the very few points in which he concurs with Gadamer, whose theory otherwise he must regard as mistaking art proper for art as amusement.

Expression versus expressiveness

The Principles of Art advances beyond the commonplace version of expressivism. Even so, there is reason to inquire more closely into how far

33

Collingwood really overcomes its defects. At least one of the objections set out earlier – the difficulty of attributing an emotion or even set of emotions to many works and some forms of art – is no less an objection to Collingwood's theory, despite its sophistication. But let us leave that difficulty aside, because there *are* substantial objections to the Tolstoyan view which Collingwood's theory can be made to answer. It is clear, for instance, that his version of expressivism does not attribute to artists independent, identifiable emotional states of which their art is the expression. What it attributes, if anything, is an undifferentiated 'psychic disturbance', and we can only take an interest in this in so far as it is realized in the work of art. This is why Collingwood thinks art criticism must be centred on the work rather than the artist. Whereas the commonplace version invites us to scrutinize the artist's history and psychology, Collingwood is scathing about criticism that has been reduced to nothing more than grubbing around for historical titbits about painters and poets.

Still, if there is no way the emotion of an artist expressed in the work can be specified or even apprehended independently of that work, what reason is there to call the work an expression of emotion? Why reason back from the work to the artist's emotions at all? And if, with Collingwood, we acknowledge that what we find in a work of art is 'wholly and entirely imaginative' (Collingwood 1938: 306), why not conclude that the emotion presented to us is presented indifferently as to ownership? It is not *anyone's* and hence not the artist's. This is the line of thought that leads the eminent English literary critic Helen Gardner, in a slightly different context, to reject similar reasoning about Shakespeare's religious beliefs.

> No other dramatist shows, I think, such imaginative response to the quintessentially Christian concept of forgiveness, or gives such memorable expression to it. But . . . one cannot argue from this [to any conclusion about Shakespeare's own religious beliefs]. Shakespeare is our greatest poet of human nature, and all we can say is that if his play requires that a character should speak as a Christian he enters imaginatively into Christian experience and feeling with characteristic understanding and sympathy.
>
> (Gardner 1983: 72, material in brackets added)

The point can be generalized. Emrys Jones, another critic, writes: 'Shakespeare's wholehearted submission to the principle of rhetorical dialectic – his willingness to lend a voice of the utmost eloquence to every point of view – is his dramatic secret' (Jones 1978: 15).

It is worth observing that this 'apersonal' view of poetic imagination is not open to refutation by appealing to the 'depth' of the emotion to be found in a work. Depth of this sort can just as plausibly be construed as evidence of the imaginative power revealed in the work, as it can be taken to be evidence of the poet's having sincerely felt the emotion in question.

34

There is much to be said for making the imaginative treatment of emotion, rather than personal expression, the hallmark of art, and it has important consequences for expressivism. Collingwood argues that a specific emotion cannot be attributed to the artist independently of the work, and that imaginative power is an indispensable part of the artist's endeavour. This implies that the artist's peculiar gift is not a special capacity to feel, but a special capacity to imagine. To accept this view of art, however, Collingwood must abandon an important element of expressivism, one to which he holds throughout, namely, that 'the artist's business is to express emotions; and the only emotions he can express are those which he feels, . . . his own'.

In a similar fashion, the audience's emotional experience also ceases to be important once we examine Collingwood's expressivism closely. The everyday version, it will be recalled, holds that emotion is transmitted from artist to audience by being aroused in the audience. Collingwood argues vigorously that to try to arouse emotion through the medium of art is a profound mistake. Nevertheless, given that the artist's expression of emotion itself derives from an experience of emotion, and given further that audience participation is a collaborative realization of that experience on the part of both artist and audience, it seems to follow that the artist's emotion is aroused in the audience. In order to avoid this apparently inevitable conclusion, Collingwood must argue that the audience's collaborative activity, like the artist's own, is 'wholly and entirely imaginative'. It follows that what anyone actually feels on reading a poem or watching a play is as wholly irrelevant to a proper appreciation of it as the psychological history of the author. If imagination rather than feeling is what matters, it is as much a mistake to try to determine the merits of a work of art by audience 'reaction' as it is to judge the work on the author's 'sincerity'.

To understand this point, we have to return to the distinction mentioned earlier between 'being an expression of' and 'being expressive of'. Some writers sympathetic to expressivism have argued that the errors in the everyday theory arise from a confusion between the two. 'Being an expression of emotion' implies that there is someone whose expression it is. 'Being expressive of' does not imply any possessor, either artist or audience. For instance someone can cry 'Aahh' in pain. This is an expression, but being largely inarticulate is not expressive. Later when the pain is gone, it might be described as 'rising to a climax' before the cry. This is expressive of the pain but not an expression of it since the pain is now gone.

Holding this distinction clearly in mind we can see that it is possible to apprehend the peculiar appropriateness of the manner in which an emotion is expressed by a work, without falling into any false 'psychologism' about how the artist or the audience must feel. In short, art can be expressive of an emotion, without being an expression of that emotion. A simple illustration of the point is this. Those who write verses for birthday, sympathy, and other sorts of cards compose lines which are not an expression of what they themselves are feeling, but which are expressive of the relevant emotion, to be called into use whenever anyone happens to have a use for them.

The question now arises as to whether anything properly called expressivism can survive the drawing of this important distinction. Why is a work's being expressive of emotion something to be valued? Recall Collingwood's explanation of the value of art. In acting imaginatively upon emotion we bring it to consciousness, discover thereby what our consciousness contains, and come to self-knowledge. Now if the artist is not expressing emotion, but formulating expressive utterances or representations of it, and if the audience does not need to feel any of these emotions, but only appreciate their imaginative expression, the value of the work cannot consist in self-knowledge on the part of either artist or audience. Since the emotions represented are not *our* emotions, we come to no further knowledge of ourselves by apprehending them. But this still leaves unclear why we should give special attention to the artist's expressive utterances, and why value is to be attached to them.

One response is to say that these are *possible* emotions, with which we may empathize. This is certainly correct, but by implication it divorces audience apprehension from emotion completely because even where the work in question can indeed be said to be expressive of an emotion, it does not matter how the audience *feels* at all, but only what it comes to understand. Collingwood himself seems to make this move in places. He sometimes describes the activity of both artist and audience in the language of cognition rather than feeling. For instance, he imagines a (rightminded) painter declaring, 'One paints a thing in order to see it'. And '[o]nly a person who paints well', he goes on to tell us, 'can see well; and conversely . . . only a person who sees well can paint well'. 'Seeing' here 'refers not to sensation but to awareness. It means noticing what you see. And further: this act of awareness includes the noticing of much that is not visual' (Collingwood 1938: 303–4). On the face of it, this alternative analysis implies that the value of art lies not in its helping us to come to a proper apprehension of personal (or even communal) feeling, but to a greater awareness of the world around us. And this remains the obvious interpretation even where, as in expressive representations, 'the world around us' is the world of emotional experience.

We might put the matter this way. The expressivist theory of art, at least in its commonplace version, holds that where a specific emotion can be assigned to a work of art, the work is an expression of that emotion and appreciation of the work consists in feeling that emotion oneself. If now we say that the work is not *an expression of* but rather is *expressive of* the emotion, appreciating would consist in being brought to a heightened awareness of that emotion. Being brought to a heightened awareness of an emotion does not imply undergoing any element of that emotion. For example I may to date be unaware of the intensity of your jealousy until one day you hit upon an especially expressive word or gesture. Then I appreciate your jealousy, but I do not share any of it. The expressiveness of your gesture can make me aware of your emotional state without engendering any emotion whatever in me. It is equally possible of course that my being made aware of your feelings gives rise to an emotional response on my part, but any such emotion has only a causal connection with yours; my having the emotion is neither a necessary nor a sufficient condition of being made aware how you feel. Conversely your gesture may arouse an emotion in me (fear, perhaps), and yet I remain unaware of your true emotional state. What these various possibilities show is that the initally innocent substitution of 'being expressive of' for 'being an expression of' brings about the abandonment of expressivism. If the function of art is to heighten awareness, the special connection between art and emotion which all forms of expressivism try to articulate and maintain is broken, because art can heighten our awareness of much in human experience besides emotion.

Collingwood would probably not deny this. His most extended discussion of a work of art is of T.S. Eliot's *The Waste Land*, and what he says about it is instructive, for he sees Eliot as presenting us with a prophetic vision.

> This poem is not in the least amusing. Nor is it in the least magical. The reader who expects it to be satire, or an entertaining description of vices, is as disappointed with it as the reader who expects it to be propaganda, or an exhortation to get up and do something. To the annoyance of both parties, it contains no indictments and no proposals. To the amateurs of literature, brought up on the idea of poetry as a genteel amusement, the thing is an affront. To the little neo-Kiplings who think of poetry as an incitement to political virtue, it is even worse; for it describes an evil where no one and nothing is to blame, an evil not curable by shooting capitalists or destroying a social system, a disease which has so eaten into civilization that political remedies are about as useful as poulticing a cancer.
>
> (*ibid.*: 335)

In *The Waste Land* Eliot shows 'what poetry can be', for 'the artist must prophesy not in the sense that he foretells things to come but in the sense that he tells his audience, at risk of their displeasure, the secrets of their own hearts' (*ibid.*: 336).

What should concern us here is not the justice of Collingwood's estimate of Eliot's achievement but the language he uses to make that estimate. Eliot is said to describe, not feel, the present evil, and to tell, not express, for the audience the secrets of their hearts. This is the language of cognition, not emotion. Collingwood would claim that the world the artist describes and tells his audience about is the world as charged with emotion and that talk of 'describing' and 'prophesying' is compatible with expressivism, provided we do not confuse consciousness and intellect. It is the intellect, in

Collingwood's view, which orders and organizes the data of consciousness and establishes relations between them. But it is art which brings those data to consciousness in the first place by realizing the sensuous impact of experience in a form in which consciousness can grasp it. This is the fundamental function of language in Collingwood's theory, and that is why he regards every linguistic act as a work of art. The works for which the term 'art' is usually reserved exercise this function to perfection or at least to the highest degree. There are thus two kinds of truth: the truth of intellect and the truth of consciousness. Science broadly understood is concerned with the former; it is pure thought and has no experiential element. Art, on the other hand, is concerned with consciousness, because real experience is essential to it. We must actually hear music or see a play in person. It is not enough merely to understand their structure or content. (Collingwood struggles, it seems to me, with the relation between philosophy and poetry, and in the end appears to conclude that they are the same.) Thus art may indeed be said to describe, to tell, to prophesy, but since its concern is with the truth of consciousness none of this removes it from the world of emotional experience, or so Collingwood contends.

Two observations are pertinent here. First, if one is to speak of truth in art, some such distinction as Collingwood draws is needed, because whatever we learn from artists is not what we learn from the laboratory. This is a subject that will be dealt with more fully in the next chapter, 'Art and understanding'. At the same time, it is only a lingering loyalty to expressivism that causes Collingwood to go on speaking of emotion in the way he does. For 'emotion' at the end of his analysis means nothing more than sensuous experience brought to consciousness. Even this formulation might be misleading, for the term 'sensuous' is not to be understood as feeling or perceiving in any very restricted sense – it includes feelings of anxiety or loneliness for instance, and a sense of mystery or foreboding – and he allows that the bringing of an experience to consciousness (i.e., being made aware of it) is intimately tied to having the experience.

Collingwood is here employing a notion of 'experience' which is to be found in other philosophers in the British Idealist tradition. Now to say that artists give voice to experience, where this is to be contrasted with scientific (or other) abstraction from experience, may well be correct. But to insist that this is *emotional* experience is to extend the idea of emotion until it loses its usefulness. Collingwood says the world of the artist is charged with emotion. He also says that the artist's province is sensuous experience brought to consciousness. He might as easily say that artists are concerned with the imaginative presentation of immediate experience rather than the construction of abstract reflections upon experience. This last formulation leaves out all mention of emotion and the sensuous, and if it does so without significant loss, this is proof that Collingwood's theory of art has been driven beyond expressivism.

That there *is* no significant loss in describing art and the aesthetic in terms of imagination rather than feeling is shown by the following example. Consider this poem:

> I see His blood upon the rose
> And in the stars the glory of His eyes.
> His body gleams amid eternal snows,
> His tears fall from the skies.
>
> All pathways by His feet are trod,
> His strong heart stirs the everbeating sea,
> His crown of thorns is twined with every thorn,
> His Cross is every tree.

These are the first and last stanzas of a poem by Joseph Plunkett, an Irish nationalist revolutionary executed by the British for his part in the Easter uprising of 1916. A literary critic would no doubt find faults in this poem (though I have omitted the weakest verse), but it is one of the plainest examples I have found of a work which could be said to reveal a *charged* world. Another might be Salvador Dali's picture 'Christ of St John of the Cross', which could be thought of as a pictorial equivalent of Plunkett's poem. But with what is either work charged? The obvious answer is 'with religious significance'. In acknowledgement of important differences between science and the arts, we can agree that 'significance' here cannot mean just what it means in the case of an experimental result or a statistical correlation that is said to be 'significant'. To this degree Collingwood is correct in supposing that the contents of mind fall into different kinds. But what does it add if we say 'charged with religious *emotion*'? We could mean by this the kind of experience that leads people to talk in religious ways; either this means no more than 'religious significance' already says, or it refers us to a specific emotional state such as Rudolf Otto's *mysterium tremens*, fear of the divine and awe in its presence, for instance. If we suppose that the poem is an expression of such a feeling, we face all the objections rehearsed against Tolstoy's expressivism; the poem itself gives us no evidence for supposing that Plunkett was in such an emotional state or that we will (or have to) feel awe or dread in reading and appreciating it.

What we get from the poem, whatever the state of mind in writing it, is an idea of how a Christian belief in the omnipresence of Christ can enter experience of the natural world. If this is conveyed, it is not by the transference of an emotional state but by the point by point correlation between *traditionally important* features of Christ – his body and blood for instance – and the features of the natural world. (This is why the blood and the rose, the crown and the thorns, the cross and the tree are strong correlations, while the eyes and the stars (and those in the omitted verse) are weak). To call the world that Plunkett describes 'charged with religious emotion' is harmless enough, provided we understand that this means nothing more than an invocation of the world of religion.

It may be said of course that the poem ought to allow us not merely to observe that world, but to enter it imaginatively and thereby in some measure come to understand it. This is correct, but the key words here are imagination and understanding, and the key question is, 'What kind of understanding is this?' If with Collingwood we want to talk about a distinctive truth in art we need to ask not how art stimulates emotion, but how it directs consciousness. This is to ask about art as a source of understanding, and it shows that feeling or emotion, ordinarily understood, has been left behind. So the next topic for us to consider is art as understanding.

Summary

We have now explored two accounts of the value that is to be found in art in both commonplace and sophisticated versions. It is true that works of art can give pleasure and can be valued precisely because they give pleasure. To value them solely for this reason, however, is to give art no special status over other sources of pleasure and to rank its importance rather lower on the scale of human values than most writers on art are apt to do. Gadamer's thesis – that art is to be understood as a form of play – overcomes something of this difficulty because play may be serious, even solemn, as well as light-hearted and pleasurable. This modified version of the pleasure theory also has its drawbacks, however, since it gives us no reason to rank art higher than sport. In itself this may not be an objection; perhaps they are equally valuable, unpalatable though this conclusion would be to many art enthusiasts. What it fails to explain is a difference between all sport and some art, namely, that although art, like sport, consists in structured activity, unlike sport, art can also have content, *be about* something. Any theory of the value of art which does not take account of this important difference must be regarded as to some degree defective.

It was concerning this question of content that expressivism was considered. It has to be acknowledged that, as a matter of fact many works of art *do* arouse emotion, and this seems to be one of the ways in which art can give audiences pleasure. Perhaps it is this fact that sustains the more generally widespread belief in Romanticism and expressivism. But the expressivist holds more than this, namely that the content of art is emotion. A number of problems confront this contention. First, it is difficult to locate the expression of emotion in a relevant and plausible account of the relation between artist, work, and audience. Second, an emphasis on the artist's emotion robs artistic activity of what would seem to make it special, namely imagination. Third, there is nothing valuable in the expression or arousal of emotion for its own sake. Collingwood offers us a more sophisticated version of expressivism which has the great merit of avoiding what we might call 'psychologism', and which proves as good an explanation of the value of art as one could want. But on closer investigation we saw that these advantages are won through an effective abandonment of the essentials of expressivism. What we end up with, if we follow Collingwood's theory to its logical conclusion, is an account of art as a distinctive way of understanding human experience. And this is the suggestion that is to be investigated in the chapter that follows.

Suggestions for further reading

R.G. Collingwood, 'From *The Principles of Art*', *N&R* p. 117.
John Hospers, 'The concept of artistic expression', in Hospers, *Introductory Readings*.
Leo Tolstoy, 'From *What is Art?*' *N&R* p. 506.

3

—◦◎◦—

Art and understanding

The preceding two chapters have shown that pleasure, beauty, play, and emotional stimulation are all closely connected with art and our experience of it and all of considerable value, yet none of them adequately explains the value of art at its finest. The arguments that have shown this have brought us now to the idea that art is valuable as a source of understanding. Among prominent modern philosopers of art the best known exponent of this belief is the American philosopher Nelson Goodman. In an influential book entitled *Ways of World Making* he says, '[a] major thesis of this book is that the arts must be taken no less seriously than the sciences as modes of discovery, creation, and enlargement of knowledge in the broad sense of advancement of the understanding' (Goodman 1968: 102).

The aim of this chapter is to ask whether and in what sense we can learn from art. In one way it is obvious that we can. Information of all sorts can be picked up from novels and paintings. But this does not capture the essence of learning from art because the information we pick up is incidental to the work of art that contains it; we might as easily pick up the same information from a newspaper or a history book. In other words, the information is not an integral, but a coincidental part of the work. A more integral relationship between artistry and understanding exists in those works of art, of which there are many, especially literary ones, which contain self-conscious statements and elaborations of doctrines and propositions. Artists often have 'messages' that they intend to convey. We need to distinguish between works of art which merely display or assert and those which lead us to a better understanding. Art with a 'message' can be nothing more than propaganda, the skillful promotion of a point of view. Propaganda endeavours to secure belief and assent by whatever means is most effective, whereas modes of teaching seek belief through reflective understanding. The interesting version of the claim that we learn from art, then, is that paintings, poems, plays, and so on, do not provide us with information or even propagate opinions in attractive ways, but that they advance our understanding.

Showing this latter claim to be correct would increase the importance of art in most people's estimation because knowledge and understanding are generally given a greater status than entertainment, or even the expression of emotion. This greater status explains in part the high standing in which science is normally held, and this is why Goodman draws the parallel he does. And as we shall see, if it is true that art is a source of understanding, it would indeed be of greater consequence than either of the theories of art discussed in the preceding two chapters is able to establish.

Art and knowledge

The theory that art is valuable because of what we learn from it is sometimes called 'cognitivism,' a label derived from the Latin for knowing, and one we will use here. In the opinion of some philosophers, however, advancing our knowledge is just what art ought not to do. They hold that to entertain cognitivism with respect to art is to give in to a certain sort of prejudice against art proper. In a well known essay with the title 'Must art tell the truth?', Douglas Morgan argues that trying to construe art as a source of understanding is not only forcing it into a mould it will not fit, but is over-estimating the relative value of knowledge.

> To the question of the 'cognitive significance of art' I say directly that although many works in many arts can and do give us knowledge of many kinds, nonetheless if this knowledge were the key and limit to the love of art, the world would be even sorrier than it now is.
>
> (Morgan, in Hospers 1969: 231)

In Morgan's view we are driven, unfortunately, to explain the value of art in terms of 'cognitive significance' first because of an 'absurd alternative which offers us only a specious choice between art as a diversion or decoration, on the one hand, or as a peculiar second rate substitute for true-blue empirical knowledge on the other', and second because of a slavish adulation of science.

Now the temptation to think in this way may indeed be a local peculiarity, something that is true of twentieth-century Western thinking but not true of other periods and places. In fact in times past, the parallel between art and intellect was invoked the other way around; it was deemed a convincing way of justifying philosophy, for instance, to view it as a kind of music. So Morgan is right to be cautious lest the attempt to see art as a source of understanding is not just the result of a cultural prejudice we have. He is also right in his concern to resist reductionism in art, that is, any explanation of the value of art which does not preserve its *distinctive* value. There is a danger that the theory of art as understanding, by construing art as containing important truths, should come to think the *truths* are central, while the *art* which conveys them remains secondary; however, any satisfactory explanation of the value of art must make seeing or hearing the work itself indispensible. Morgan asks, 'Who among us would exchange the Sistine Ceiling for one more monograph, however learned, on Pauline theology?' in confident expectation of what answer any serious theory of art must give.

Even if the answer to this question is plain – no one wants to replace the Sistine Ceiling with a scholarly treatise, and no adequate theory of art can allow such replacements – this does not in fact establish as much as we might think. To suppose that the Sistine Ceiling could be replaced by a theological monograph is like supposing that anyone who has read the history of Henry V does not need to see the Shakespeare play. This is certainly an absurd supposition, but the fact that the play cannot be replaced by straightforward history does not carry the implication that Shakespeare cannot enhance our understanding of English history (though this is not, I would say, the principal way in which we can learn from it). Similarly to agree that the value of the Sistine Ceiling is *sui generis* (something unique) does not imply that this value cannot lie in its ability to enhance our understanding of, say, the theology of St Paul.

One of Morgan's mistakes which misleads him on this point is to think that the 'cognitive significance' theory must be spelled out in terms of propositional truth, that is, singular or universal claims about how things are. At least one of his arguments against the cognitivist theory relies very heavily upon this idea that cognitive significance must take the form of true propositions. This argument goes as follows:

> Any truth must be contradictable;
> One art work cannot contradict another;
> Therefore, art works cannot be a source of truths of some sort.

This argument is a good one, but it is effective against the cognitive theory of art only so long as it is expressed in terms of truths. In fact in the passage with which this chapter of our study began, Goodman speaks of art in terms of *understanding* rather than truth, and while it is correct that any proposition can be negated, an *understanding* of something may be defective or deficient, but it is odd to speak of its being negated. For example, the physical mechanics developed by Sir Isaac Newton offers an understanding of the laws of matter in motion quite different from and more fruitful than the physics of Aristotle, which dominated science before Newton. But it just is not true that one contradicts the other in any straightforward sense. And in spite of all Morgan shows to the contrary, as much can be said of artistic understanding.

Having offered some general considerations against the 'cognitive significance' view, Morgan goes on to consider its application in specific art forms: music, painting, and literature. He thinks it patently absurd that the importance of that 'breathless final moment when you have moved intensively with heart and mind through a quartet of Brahms or Bartok' should be explained by 'what you learned'.

Learning, knowledge, and truth are no less valuable because their value is not exclusive. There really are other goods in the world than these, and there really is no need to confect such bogus kinds of truth as poetic or pictorial or musical truth for works of art to wear as certificates of legitimacy.

(Morgan, in Hospers 1969: 232)

The weakness in this line of argument however is that no one, not even cognitive theorists of art, need deny it. Pleasure – what Morgan dismissively speaks of as 'diversion or decoration' – is certainly *a* value. The problem for a normative philosophy of art which appeals to it as the essential value in art is, as we have seen, that the value of pleasure cannot ultimately explain the significance of art satisfactorily. It *can* be made to explain the value of *some* art, the sort of art Collingwood identifies and unwarrantedly condemns as amusement art. But it fails as a general theory of the value of art because it cannot capture the full range of evaluative distinctions that there is reason to make. It cannot, for instance, explain satisfactorily the difference between light and serious art; we can often say light art is better than serious art from the point of view of pleasure and entertainment. Now a cognitive theory of art need not claim that *everything* that is commonly called a work of art is valuable because of its ability to enhance our understanding. This would obviously be false; some works are valuable primarily because they are beautiful, and others are to be valued chiefly for the pleasure they give us. Cognitivism is an explanation of the substance or significance of major works of art, and its contention is that these are not simply pleasurable or beautiful, but in some sense they contribute to our understanding of experience. The remainder of this chapter is devoted to exploring this idea.

In fact Morgan has difficulty resisting this contention altogether. He, no less than others, wants to speak of art enriching us, and when he refers to being 'moved intensively with heart and mind through a quartet of Brahms or Bartok', it is difficult not to give this a cognitivist twist: what else could an intense movement of the mind be, if not something to do with greater understanding? It is precisely the inclination to talk in this and many similar ways that lends plausibility to the thesis that we learn from art. And provided we remember always that it is best regarded as a claim about *understanding* rather than *truth*, nothing said so far shows that we cannot learn from art.

However it must be acknowledged that cognitivism about art has had far fewer supporters among either philosophers or artists than expressivism. This is because it undoubtedly faces several important difficulties which have to be examined carefully if cognitivism is to be plausible. Before doing so, it is worth reviewing the advantages cognitivism enjoys as an explanation of the value and importance of serious art because these show that there is good reason to persist in trying to solve the problems that it encounters.

Aesthetic cognitivism

The thesis that serious art presents us with a means by which human understanding may be advanced makes it relatively easy to explain its place in our culture. The role and status of art in the curricula of schools and universities is immediately intelligible. Given that the purpose of education is to develop the mind and promote understanding, and if it is true that art is one form of this understanding, the study of art clearly has a proper place in education. The fact that private time and public resources are devoted to it in greater quantities than to the pursuit of amusement or even the development of sport is now no more puzzling than that the devotion of time and resources to study of the sciences also exceeds these. Furthermore, in contrast to the other explanations of the value of art we have considered, cognitivism has little difficulty making sense of someone's undertaking a lifetime commitment to art, as a painter, poet, or composer. This is now to be understood simply as another instance of devotion to the old Delphic ideal 'Man, know thyself!' rather than an excessive pursuit of pleasure, an effete absorption with beautiful objects (aestheticism), or an unintelligible wallowing in emotional turbulence (expressivism).

If art is a source of understanding this also enables us, in principle at any rate, to explain the discriminations that we make between works of art. A work may be said to have substance and seriousness to the degree that it enhances our understanding and be relatively undistinguished to the extent that it does not, in just the same way that the importance of one experiment or mathematical proof is judged greater than that of another in accordance with its contribution to wider intellectual concerns.

Cognitivism also helps us explain an important range of critical vocabulary which is widely used. If greater understanding is what art offers us, we can describe a work as the *exploration* of a theme in a straightforward sense and without any conceptual or linguistic oddity. It also makes sense, if cognitivism is true, to speak of insight and profundity, superficiality and distortion in art, and it will be appropriate to describe a portrayal of something as convincing or unconvincing, just as we would describe an argument. Since people often speak of works of art in precisely these ways and since, in contrast to both aestheticism and expressivism, cognitivism can make sense of them, this is a substantial point in its favour. All such assessments are either impossible or puzzling if aestheticism is true, and contrary to what some have supposed, expressivism cannot make much sense of such assessments either. If art is the expression of an artist's emotion, then it can have an effect upon an audience but it cannot direct the mind, either superficially or toward insight and illumination. Emotion can be expressed strongly or weakly, but not with insight or profundity.

A principal virtue of cognitivism, then, is its ability to explain and sustain a number of ways in which people actually think and talk about art. It is important to note immediately, however, that not all attempts to speak of art in this way will be well-founded. The world of art criticism is notorious for the pretension of its language, and whether it really makes sense to speak of *all* forms of art as sources of understanding capable of generating insight as well as illusion is an open question. Can we for instance apply cognitive language to music, or to architecture? These are questions which, in the end, can be resolved only by looking at individual art forms in detail, something which chapters 4 to 7 aim to do. What we can say in general is that wherever the idea of understanding can be applied in art, cognitivism can offer a better explanation of its value and significance than either the pleasure-cum-beauty theory or expressivism can supply.

So much for cognitivism's advantages. It is time now to consider more closely its difficulties. Two of these are crucial. *How* does art advance our understanding, and *of what* does it do this?

Art as understanding

To appreciate the force of these questions it is instructive to examine in greater detail Goodman's original parallel between art and science. We have to understand 'science' here as a general term, encompassing more than the natural sciences and including a wide variety of intellectual inquiries: history, mathematics, philosophy, and so on, as well as physics, chemistry, economics, and so on. In all these disciplines, we can characterize inquiry as a movement of thought from an established original basis to a yet to be established conclusion via a logic or set of rules of reasoning. In empirical studies the established base is usually called evidence, and the conclusion is called a hypothesis or a theory. In mathematics the equivalents to these are axioms and theorems, in philosophy they are premises and conclusions. The terminology differs from subject to subject, but all these forms of intellectual inquiry share the same basic structure: an effort is made to show (in the sense of demonstrate) a progression from base to terminus. Since an established terminus becomes the base for the next chain of reasoning, successful inquiry moves progressively from terminus to terminus.

There are important differences between disciplines, of course, but the abstract analysis of the structure of intellectual inquiry allows us to pose some important difficulties in the idea of art as a source of understanding. The first of these is that in a work of art there does not appear to be any obvious parallel to the distinction between the established ground upon which we begin and the terminus to which we are being led. Nor is there anything very obvious that might parallel a 'logic' of inquiry. This is partly because works of art are, as Collingwood observes, works of imagination. Unlike scientific or historical theories, they have no ground outside themselves. Consider, for instance, this example: Arnold Bennett's novel *Lord*

Raingo tells the story of an imaginary British politician in the early years of this century. If we think of literature as a source of understanding we might say that it is a study of the interplay of principle and ambition in politics. We could say the same of Stephen Oates's biography of Abraham Lincoln, *With Malice Toward None*. But to speak of both of them as studies or explorations disguises an important difference between the two. Oates is constrained in what he writes by history, by what actually happened. He presents the facts of Lincoln's career and leads us by argument and inter-pretation to take a certain view of his political life. Bennett on the other hand has no such constraint; he can make the 'facts' of Raingo's career whatever he wishes. Lincoln is recorded as being assassinated. That his life and career should end in this way is a matter over which Oates has no choice. In Bennett's novel Raingo's career suffers a serious setback. Just when his political fortunes begin to rise again, he contracts an illness which proves fatal. That his life and career should end in this way is a matter wholly of Bennett's choosing. The 'logic' of historical inquiry, the rules by which it proceeds, are in part laid down by the need to present evidence and adhere to the facts. Imaginative storytelling seems free from such constraint.

The same point can be made about many other contrasting works of fact and fiction, and indeed it can be extended to other forms of art as well. John Constable's famous picture of Salisbury Cathedral is not any less a wonder-ful painting if in fact the cathedral cannot and never could be seen from the angle chosen by Constable. A similar misrepresentation in a guidebook however would be a serious fault. What seems to follow is this: however novelists or other artists might direct our thoughts, they cannot direct them from truth to truth since at the base of their activity lies not truth but imagination.

A second major difficulty with cognitivism about the arts is this. In his-tory, philosophy, or natural science, the evidence, argument, and ideas that are employed, the hypotheses advanced and the conclusions defended can almost always be expressed or explained in widely differing ways. There can be better and less good formulations; some explanations are better because they are more simply expressed than others for instance, and sometimes physics employs mathematical formulae that cannot be substituted. In gen-eral however the precise wording of an argument or hypothesis or the order in which evidence is presented is not essential to their truth and validity. It appears that the contrary is true in art. It has long been held that one of the peculiarities of art is its unity of form and content. It is impossible for a work of art to say or to show what it does in any other form without significant loss of content. The normal way of expressing this is to say that works of art are 'organic unities', that is, entities so integrated that the alteration of a single item within them – a line in a poem or a colour in a painting – destroys the whole work. Such a view has been current among philosophers of art at least since Aristotle, and though it may often be an exaggeration to say that not one item, however small, can be altered without altering the whole, it is true that the form of the presentation is of great importance in art.

If this claim about the necessary unity of form and content in art is true, it is evident that artistic insight and understanding cannot be paraphrased. For as soon as we attempt to paraphrase the content of a work, that is, present in any other form, we destroy it. Thus the 'truth' in art eludes us every time we try to explain it. Despite the ease and regularity with which it is quoted, Pope's well known line, 'What oft was thought but ne'er so well express'd', *cannot* properly describe the nature of poetry, since in poetry there is no way of isolating the thought or idea other than in its expression. Again this is something of an exaggeration, but what does seem to be true is that apprehension of the work itself is crucial, and no paraphrase or summary, however good, can substitute for this. How then is truth in art to be tested, refined, and revised? More importantly, what reason have we for employing the ideas of truth and understanding in art at all? It can certainly be *claimed* that there is a great truth to be learned from some work of art or that it reveals great insight into aspects of human experience. But if it is the sort of truth that cannot be independently stated, and cannot therefore be tested outside the artistic medium, we have no reason to think of it as a truth in the ordinary sense at all.

It is worth noticing that this difficulty cannot be overcome by appeal to a special sort of 'poetic' truth. Even if we allow that not all truth is scientific truth (the sort of truth that is established by evidence or experiment), we can still see that science provides us with a method of arriving at truth and understanding, whatever 'kind' of truth that may be. The problem is not that there is no such thing as 'poetic' truth, but that it is difficult to see how art can be conceived as a way of ascertaining it.

Third, there is the difficulty of particularity in art. Cognition, Aristotle tells us, trades in universals. He means that the acquisition of knowledge always involves a measure of abstraction and generalization. We learn not about this or that vine leaf but about vine leaves; we learn not about this person here and now but about the person in general. It is this that allows us to transcend the peculiarities of the particular case and arrive at a greater understanding of a range of cases. Even where it is inappropriate to speak of anything as precise as a theory, there is nonetheless always a measure of abstraction, however modest this may be. Now, though Aristotle himself thought that art deals in universals and thus is something akin to philosophy, this is not a view that is easy to accept. Paintings, plays, sculptures and so on portray, and must portray, particulars. We can say of a face in a painting that it is the face of human distress, but the fact remains that it is *a* face, and how we move from a judgment about this one face to a judgment about humanity seems something of a mystery.

Some philosophers have tried to get around the difficulty by saying that art is concerned with 'concrete universals', but on the face of it, the curious hybrid 'concrete universal' seems to function more as a label for the problem than a solution to it. Alternatively, we might question Aristotle's dictum about universals. And there is reason to do so. History is an important mode of human understanding which nonetheless deals in particulars. Yet it does seem correct that there are the makings of an important difficulty here. Mr Woodhouse in Jane Austen's *Emma* might be said to be an image of hypochondria, but once we regard him as a 'universal', a 'type' with standardized or generalized character traits and patterns of behaviour mirroring those to be found elsewhere, we seem to move away from the 'concrete', the particularity of her imaginative creation – a character rather than a stereotype. Yet it is in the creation of characters that her genius is correctly thought to lie.

These, then are the three major difficulties that the theory of art as understanding most obviously encounters. First, art is through and through a matter of imagination. How then can it direct us to the truth? Second, unity of form and content seems an ideal in art, but if so, this excludes the possibility of putting the understanding it conveys to the test. Third, art deals in particulars, understanding in universals. How then can art be a source of understanding?

Imagination and experience

Works of art – let us agree with Collingwood – are works of imagination. Does this fact remove them from a concern with reality? More needs to be said about the imaginative character of art, because it is natural to think that some forms of painting, such as portraiture, and still life are a sort of copying (a topic to be taken up again in Chapter 5). In whatever sense it is true that imagination is essential to art, it must be made to square with a distinction between types of art, namely, the distinction between the realistic and the fantastic. In *A History of Tom Jones* Henry Fielding prefaces each book with some remarks on the art of writing novels. In the course of these reflections, he eschews all fantastic mechanisms whereby the problematic action of a story may be resolved – magic spells, witches, good fairies, and the like. So when it appears that Tom Jones has been to bed with his own mother and that this fact will present insuperable difficulties for him, we know that Fielding has to find a non-fantastic way of getting him out of them. He has to *imagine* some resolution to the plot, but his imagination is constrained by the realities of human experience. This does not imply that fantastic works cannot deal with the content of human experience. Nor is it to deny that *Tom Jones* is a work of imagination. The distinction between the realistic and the fantastic in art is important because it shows that imagination can operate in different genres. Because this is so, it does not operate without constraint. Imagination then is to be distinguished from mere fancy or whimsy. It is in fact a deliberative act of mind.

Conversely, to come back to the parallel with science, it is a mistake to think of scientists or historians as passively 'tracking' the truth on the basis of empirical data which just present themselves. At every stage, intellectual inquiry employs imagination. Hypotheses in science and history have to be checked against the facts, but scientists also 'float' ideas, engage in guesswork, and follow up lines of thought according to their sense of the problem. All these are acts of imagination and the hypotheses are themselves imaginative conjectures. Indeed, the 'facts' may need imaginative treatment before they yield much in the way of a test, and often imagination has to be employed in rooting out the facts in the first place.

To appreciate these observations and to see a little more clearly the similarities and differences between art and science, we can usefully compare a map and a photograph. Maps aim faithfully to represent the landscape whose features they record. Because they aim to do nothing more than this, it might be supposed that mapmaking involves the complete suppression of imagination, the soulless recording of fact. However, geographical features are represented on maps by symbols, and the clarity of the representation, and hence the usefulness of the map, depends upon the imagination with which symbols are devised. To see this one need only look at old maps. The difficulty in reading them is often caused not by the unfamiliarity of their symbols but by their clumsiness. By our present stage in the history of mapmaking representation is largely governed by conventional symbols that are universally agreed. Even here however, the imagination with which these are employed on the map makes a great difference to its utility. One has only to compare maps constructed for special purposes to see that imagination in the devising of symbols is of the first importance. Yet the purpose of every map remains the same – the representation of things as they are.

Compare now a photograph of a landscape with its represention on a map. The very comparison shows the mistake in Morgan's remark about Pauline theology and the Sistine Ceiling, for despite the fact that both map and photograph may give us knowledge of the area, no one supposes that either could replace the other. Occasionally it has been thought that photography, since it cannot but 'represent what is there', is not an art. Such a view however is impossible to sustain, since it is evident that photographs can have focus, composition and use of colour, no less than a painting. The photograph gives us a knowledge of the area. Unlike the map, it does not do so by supplying information in the form of conventional notation but by letting us see the landscape itself. Imagination enters into the taking of the photograph, if only by the choice of a point of view, which then becomes the point of view of those who look at the photograph. But imagination can enter into the photograph more deeply than it can into the mapmaking. It is true that maps of the same area can differ precisely according to the purposes for which they are drawn – land use maps and geological maps for instance – but the business of the map maker is nonetheless to record information in a neutral way. The photographer by contrast can choose a point of view precisely in order to give the landscape a particular focus of interest. Furthermore, the more imaginative a photographer is, the more he or she is likely to select a point of view which, left to our own devices, we would not have chosen. In this way the photographer gets us to see what we would not otherwise have seen. Imagination chooses a point of view and the photograph directs our perception accordingly. It is not fanciful to speak of a photograph's revealing new, and hitherto unimagined aspects of a landscape. All this of course is to be contrasted with doctoring the photograph. A photograph of a landscape, however imaginative, is to be distinguished from the celebrated 'photograph' of fairies at the bottom of the garden. It is at one and the same time a work of imagination *and* concerned with what is really there.

The sharp contrast between reality and imagination upon which the first objection depends can thus be seen to be less clearly drawn. However, there is the second difficulty to be considered. Where is the 'logic' in art which we might test, if each work is sufficient unto itself? Even if imagination is involved in ascertaining truth in history or in science, there still seems to be an important difference between a work of art and a work of inquiry, namely, that the latter has a structure of reasoning by which it moves from premise to conclusion, whereas the former does not. To put the same point another way: history, science, and philosophy are disciplines, organized systems of knowledge and not merely collections of isolated facts or propositions. A piece of experimental science, an historical narrative, a philosophical argument does not just confront the mind with fact or hypothesis but *directs* the mind through a progression of thought. It is this capacity to direct the mind which allows us to call these modes *of understanding*. In contrast, it seems, the best that art can do is to present a point of view. Even writers sympathetic to the idea of truth in art have generally supposed that art merely expresses truth, not that it argues for it. If it does not argue for it, however, it cannot be said to *show* anything, and if it cannot show its audience the truth of what it contains, it can at best be a mode of expression or representation, not of understanding.

But is this correct? Though there are undoubtedly important differences between art making and intellectual inquiry, to contrast them in quite this way is misleading. The life of the human mind should not be construed as consisting only in thought; the activity of the senses is as much mental as is intellectual reflection. The content of my mind is made up of visual, auditory, tactile, and other sensations as well as the intelligible. Moreover this sensual experience, as an aspect of mind, is not a matter of passive seeing and hearing but of active looking and listening. When I look and listen my mind is engaged no less than when I think or calculate. Now while it may be true that works of art, even works of literature, do not direct abstract thought (though there is more to be said about this), it may nonetheless be true that they direct the mind, that is direct the perception of the audience. The example of the photograph makes this plain. In looking at a photograph we are *given* a point of view. Something similar may be said about painting; the painter *determines* how we see the objects in the picture. This is most obviously true at the basic level of perspective; foreground and background are essential elements of our visual experience, and in a picture it is the painter, not the spectator, who determines what is in the foreground and in the background. Whereas when I look about me I determine what I focus on, in a photograph or a painting this is largely (though obviously never wholly) determined for me by the person who took the photograph or painted the painting.

If this is correct, we can indeed speak of works of art directing the mind, while acknowledging that they do not accomplish this by proof, or demonstration, or even by the presentation of propositions. Examples of the ways in which works of art may thus direct our minds are legion. Rhythm in poetry, for instance, may be more than a linguistic counterpart to music. By determining how we hear the line, and where the emphasis falls, rhythm can determine what the sense is. Or again, composers determine how music is heard: which sound predominates over others both acoustically and harmonically. It is the fact that the performer has a certain licence here that allows us to think of them as creative artists also. An architect can determine the order in which shapes and materials are seen by those who walk through a building, and so on.

Of course how and with what degree of success these methods of directing the mind can be used to bring us to an apprehension of the truth of something are questions yet to be investigated. Moreover it should be added that the answers to these questions are unlikely to be the same for different forms and works of art. Nevertheless enough has been said to show that at least some forms of art have resources which imagination may employ in directing the minds of the audience, and as yet we have seen no reason in principle against the idea that this can be to the end of greater understanding.

There is still the third difficulty to be dealt with: art uses particulars, understanding requires universals. For the moment, however, we will leave this to one side, since the solution to it is best rehearsed at a later stage in the argument, near the end of the section 'Art and the world'.

The objects of imagination

Aesthetic cognitivism must answer two questions: 'How does art enrich our understanding?' and 'Of what does it enrich our understanding?' The three difficulties we have been concerned with so far relate to the first of these questions. But the second is no less important. What could artistic understanding be about? What is its object? To tackle this question, consider again the parallel of the photograph and the map. The argument was that the photograph, no less than the map, can give us information about a landscape and that a good photograph does so by presenting us with imaginative ways of looking at the landscape. Now it seems to be confirmation of this thought that we can speak of a deceptive photograph, one which gives us mistaken ideas about the object photographed. But in fact this possibility counts against the suggestion that photography *as an art* is a source of understanding because, considered as an object of aesthetic interest, the deceptive character of a photograph is of no consequence. In order to decide whether a photograph is worth exhibiting or not, we do not need to inspect the original subject of the photograph. We need not go beyond the photograph; its aesthetic merits and demerits are wholly within the work itself.

The irrelevance of the independent subject is one consequence of the view that in art the ideal is unity of form and content. In the imagined photograph what matters is not the accuracy of beliefs about the subject that the photograph generates, but the internal harmony between the subject and the way the photograph, deceptively or not, presents it; in other words, the harmony of form and content matters.

Similarly, in a poem what matters is not the truth or falsehood of the sentiment expressed, but the apt or inapt manner of its expression. Macbeth says,

> Life's but a walking shadow, a poor player
> That struts and frets his hour upon the stage
> And then is heard no more.
> (*Macbeth*, Act V. Sc 5. ll24–6)

It is irrelevant to assess the merits of Shakespeare by asking whether life *is* a walking shadow. Someone who said that life is not as bad as Shakespeare here claims would rightly be thought to be making a foolishly irrelevant remark. What matters is whether despair of the sort Macbeth is imagined as undergoing is or is not aptly expressed in the line. The ideal poem is one in which there is a perfect match between thought and expression, content and form. Once more, then, the substance of the 'message' in Macbeth's speech is of no interest from the aesthetic point of view.

What both these examples purport to show is that though photographers, poets, and painters can direct the mind, the point of their direction does not lie beyond but wholly within the work of art. And it seems it must be so. Collingwood makes this point in connection with portraiture.

> A portrait . . . is a work of representation. What the patron demands is a good likeness; and that is what the painter aims, and successfully, if he is a competent painter, at producing. It is not a difficult thing to do; and we may reasonably assume that in portraits by great painters such

as Raphael, Titian, Velazquez, or Rembrandt it has been done. But, however reasonable the assumption may be, it is an assumption and nothing more. The sitters are dead and gone, and we cannot check the likeness for ourselves. If, therefore, the only kind of merit a portrait could have were its likeness to the sitter, we could not possibly distinguish, except where the sitter is still alive and unchanged, between a good portrait and a bad.

(Collingwood 1938: 44)

This argument may be regarded as a conclusive refutation of the idea that what is valuable in portraiture is what philosophers of art often refer to as *mimesis* (imitation) or its capacity for producing a convincing resemblance. (It is important to distinguish the view of 'art as *mimesis*' from 'representationalism'. The difference will be discussed in Chapter 5.) Collingwood assumes correctly that we can tell the difference between good and bad portraits even when we do not know what the sitter looked like, from which it follows that what matters is not faithful copying of the original. This argument can be generalized to other branches of painting and the arts; we can profitably read Tolstoy's *War and Peace* without knowing whether he has accurately represented the history of the Napoleonic Wars, we can watch Eisenstein's *Oktober* without worrying about the actual course of the Russian Revolution.

Clearly there is something correct in this line of thought, but what is right about it tends to be misconstrued. It is true that we ought not to think of Macbeth's speech as a short treatise on despair by Shakespeare. Similarly, we ought not to regard a picture like Gainsborough's portrait of Mr and Mrs Andrewes, say, as primarily a record of the appearance of the couple in question, and we ought not to judge *War and Peace* by its historical accuracy. Nevertheless, it does not follow that these works do not point beyond themselves in any way whatever because, while not being chiefly concerned with these or those objects, they may still be related to more general aspects of human experience. So while it is not the immediate content of Macbeth's speech that an audience should focus on, his speaking it at that point in the play may constitute an image, not just of one man's mood but of despair itself. Similarly, though we know nothing about what the originals looked like, it is possible to see in Gainsborough's portrait of the Andrewes, something that they themselves may not have been able to see, a visual image of proprietorship. *War and Peace* is wrongly regarded as a record of the impact the Napoleonic Wars had on Russia, but not wrongly regarded as in part an image of the impact of war in general.

There is of course an important question about what exactly makes the image in any of these examples a convincing one. If the relation between a work of art and the things to which it points is not direct or immediate, what can it be? The relation between art and anything beyond it cannot be construed as one of correspondence. It *may* also follow from this that the merits of a work of art can only be looked for within the elements of the work itself and that these are to be found in the degree to which form and content are unified. What does not follow is that there can therefore be no relation between a work of art and an external reality. Indeed the insistence upon unity of form and content as an artistic ideal may be turned to advantage for the theory of art as understanding. Granted that the relation between art and 'reality' is not one of correspondence, there is no reason to suppose that the merits of a work of art are to be judged in the light of such relation between the two as there may be. Perhaps the relation between a work of art and the world of human experience is only a matter of interest *after* the merits of the work in question have been decided.

Art and the world

What then is this relation? Formulating an answer brings us back to an objection to cognitivism only partially answered. How could a work of art teach us anything, the argument runs, when what matters about art is the internal relation between form and content, not any external relation it bears to its subject matter? This reference to an external relation between the work of art and something else can be interpreted in two ways. The assumption behind such an objection is that if art is to enhance our understanding of the world, the two must stand in some sort of correspondence relation. That is to say, if there is to be any sort of check upon the understanding a work of art offers us, we have to be able to look independently at reality and then at art in order to see how well the latter has represented or understood the former. But the problem is that a work of art seems to be sufficient unto itself. This is what the argument about portraiture established.

However, in thinking about the relation of art to the world, we do not need to be bound by the idea of correspondence. Indeed we may as easily, and to greater advantage, the relation as the other way around. Why should we not look first, and independently, at art in order to see reality afresh and even sometimes in this way become properly aware of it for the first time? The poet Robert Browning expresses this thought in *Fra Lippo Lippi*:

> nature is complete
> Suppose you reproduce her – (which you can't)
> There's no advantage! You must beat her then
> For, don't you mark, we're made so that we love
> First when we see them painted, things we have passed
> Perhaps a hundred times nor cared to see;
> And so they are better, painted . . .
>
> (lines 297–303)

In short, the 'unity of form and content' objection to cognitivism fails, once we think about the the role of artistic understanding bearing upon the world in this way, rather than in terms of resemblance or correspondence.

Aesthetic cognitivism is most plausible if we think about bringing art to the world, rather than checking art against the world. To appreciate the extent of the alteration in thinking about art that this reversal brings about, something more needs to be said about the abstract metaphysical notion of 'the world' that this way of speaking employs.

'The world' here is best understood not as a set of objects like furniture in a room which we might or might not occupy, but as the things we experience. 'Experience' too is an abstract term which needs some elucidation, but though philosophers have used it in obscure ways, for present purposes we can employ an everyday understanding of it. We speak quite happily of having or lacking experience, of being experienced and inexperienced. Usually when we do so, some specific context is understood – military experience, say, or experience of mountain climbing. But as far as the word itself goes, the contexts in which 'experience' may be used are broad. We may talk of experience in highly restricted contexts as in the examples just given, or more broadly in emotional contexts – experience of fear or love – or most broadly of all perhaps – sense experience. In this last use some writers have thought that the sense of the word changes, but if, as we saw earlier, the mental life of a human being is comprised of many different kinds of elements, there is no reason to think this.

Understood in this way, we may say that the life of any human being, as opposed to a mere organism, is largely, though not exclusively, a matter of experience. It is not exclusively so because, if the word experience is not to become too general, we must distinguish it from memory, from imagination, from anticipation of the future, and from intellectual abstraction. All of these play important parts in the life of a human being, and each of them may inform experience, but they are not identical with it. In attending to what is happening around us and to us, these other aspects of mind allow us to make interconnections – with past events, with hoped for outcomes, with true generalizations. What is of most interest to present concerns is imagination. Human beings have the ability to manipulate their experience imaginatively, and this is one of the ways in which they can bring it more sharply into focus and find greater significance in it.

To repeat: this is a highly abstract way of describing something already familiar. A lot of our everyday experience is made up of encounters with the words and actions and gestures of other people. The meaning of these is not always plain; the same words can indicate anger, or upset, or anxiety. We can interpret other people's behaviour with more or with less imagination, and the result is a greater or lesser degree of understanding of its meaning and significance.

Now individuals are not all possessed of imagination to the same degree, any more than they have equally good memories. Some are sensitive to nuances, in speech, appearance, gesture, and so on. Others are less so, and it is for this reason that we can find a significant role for art and artists. This may make it sound as though art is important because it can help us understand our friends and acquaintances better, but we need to remember that what is in view here is human experience in its widest sense – visual, aural, tactile, emotional, mental. Works of art can supply the imaginative apprehension of experience in all these respects, and their value derives from the fact that we may ourselves be deficient in this regard. This is the sense in which art is a source of understanding.

To appreciate this possibility properly, it is essential to see that first and foremost the process involves moving from art to experience, not from experience to art, though in both creation and appreciation of art, there is often something of a dialogue between the two. Even if the power of art to illuminate in this way is accepted, something still needs to be said about the third problem identified (but set aside) earlier, the problem about particulars and universals. The images by which we are confronted in art are always images of particulars. In order to illuminate the experience of others, of anyone and everyone in fact, we need generality. How then can particular images illuminate universal experience? This residual problem is not hard to dispel, however. To begin with, as Aristotle pointed out, images and characters can be generalized images and characters. Bruegel's celebrated picture can be of a country wedding, for example, can depict *a* country wedding, without being the picture of any particular country wedding. It will not alter its subject to discover that the faces and objects collected in it were never assembled together at any one time or even that they never existed. The value of a picture lies not in its supplying an accurate record of an event but in the way it enables us to look at the people, circumstances, and relationships in our own experience. The question to be asked of such a work is not, 'Is this how it really was?' but rather, 'Does this make us alive to new aspects of this sort of occasion?'

The same point may be made about the example we used earlier to state the problem, Jane Austen's Mr Woodhouse. The problem was, however convincing a portrait of a hypochondriac he may be, he is one particular character. How then can he summarize general truths about hypochondriacs? But once we reverse the relation between art and reality, it becomes apparent that what there is to be learned from Jane Austen in this regard is not to be obtained by seeing in Mr Woodhouse bits of real hypochondriacs, but seeing in real hypochondriacs aspects of Mr Woodhouse. Our experience is not summarized in the character, but illuminated, perhaps awakened by it.

Understanding as a norm

We have now seen what sense can be attached to the idea that art is a source of understanding and how once this is understood correctly, the problems philosophers have identified for the theory of aesthetic cognitivism can be resolved. It is important to understand, however, that the claim that art can illuminate experience by making us more sensitively aware of what it contains, and that this is a reason for valuing it, is much more plausible as a normative than a descriptive doctrine. As a normative doctrine it says that in so far as the arts have the capacity to enhance our understanding of experience they are to be valued more highly for this than for any other reason. It does not carry the implication that art always does this, or that this is the *only* reason for valuing it. Both claims are false, in fact, but they follow only if we construe cognitivism descriptively, as a definition of art of the sort that has marked philosophical aesthetics since Kant. Definitions of art will be discussed at length in the final chapter of this book. Here it is sufficient to note that there are obvious objections to cognitivism as a definition of or a descriptive generalization about art. It must be evident to anyone that a huge number of poems and pictures and pieces of music, statuettes, stories, plays, tapestries, and items of jewellery which have been held in high regard as works of art, cannot be thought to have a cognitive dimension. This means that aesthetic cognitivism taken as a *definition* of what is to count as art is susceptible to straightforward empirical refutation.

So it is crucial to remember that we should regard cognitivism as a normative theory, a theory about the value rather than the essence of art. Even with respect to the explanation of value something more needs to be said. The belief that the most significant art is to be valued as a source of understanding does not imply that all that is called art is either to be valued for this reason or not at all, for this too is false. Nor does it imply that the art that can be thought of in this way is to be valued for this reason only. There is nothing odd or inconsistent in someone's reading a novel, learning from it, and enjoying it as well.

More than this, those who are skilled in language or music or painting may resolve *not* to employ their art in this way, and yet produce much that is to be valued. The comic songwriter Michael Flanders once remarked that while the point of satire is to 'strip away the veneer of half-truth and comforting illusion' the point of his songs was to put it back again. The wit and verbal dexterity shown in his lyrics is good enough reason to value them. Why should we want more? Similarly the hugely amusing comic novelist P.G. Wodehouse thought that the writing of great literature was beyond him. He rightly regarded the stories he wrote as of no profundity whatever. Yet Wodehouse displays a cleverness with language and a perceptiveness that is to be envied highly, and it was not absurd for another writer, Richard Gordon, to describe him as 'our greatest writer' (though not, of course, our greatest novelist).

It is judgments of this sort that incline people to claim and others to deny that the work of people like Flanders or Wodehouse is art. But once all the relevant facts and distinctions have been set out, nothing very much turns on this dispute. Whether we call it art or not, it is to be valued for certain sorts of reasons and not others. It is not deep and serious, but it was not meant to be. There are no great truths to be learned from it, but it can be clever and entertaining. Once all this has been said, there is no point to the further question 'Is it art?'

What cognitivism about art explains is the sense in which some creative works of imagination are more profound than others and why this matters. Talk of art as having depth and profundity often implies a denigration of more obvious values such as wit, entertainment, and enjoyment in art. But this is an unwarranted implication. However enthusiastically we greet the suggestion that there is more to art than the pleasure we derive from it, we need not deny that pleasure is sometimes one of the things that makes it valuable. The point to be emphasized is that a normative theory of art, as it has been elaborated here, is not intended to demarcate 'true art' or 'art proper' to the detriment of 'art' which does not or cannot fit this description. It is meant to justify rationally certain discriminations between works and forms of art, discriminations that show themselves not only in express judgments but in status accorded.

Nor does a normative theory carry any implications about personal taste. Whether anyone prefers the novels of D.H. Lawrence to those of P.G. Wodehouse, or thinks more highly of the music of Michael Tippett than Scott Joplin is not to the point. What the theory explains is why there is reason to include the former in curricula of study rather than the latter, or why the different status accorded to these different artistic productions is not the result of mere social prejudice and cultural illusion. If it is true, as aesthetic cognitivism claims, that some works of art can supply us with a deeper understanding of human nature and the human condition by imaginatively illuminating our experience, then it is no more puzzling that we lend greater importance to them than to works of entertainment than it is to discriminate between significant scientific experiments and amusing or fascinating tricks that exploit a knowledge of optics or magnetism. Science no less than art can be entertaining; it can require very high levels of expertise; it can have practical uses. But the greatest scientific achievements are those that have made fundamental contributions to human understanding.

Art and human nature

It is this parallel with science with which, following Goodman, we began. But despite all that has been said, there might appear to be something of a disanalogy remaining. Scientific understanding has an object: the natural world. This is what the scientist's theories are about. But we have yet to state clearly what artistic understanding is about. What is its object? The preceding paragraph gave one answer, namely, human nature and the human condition. Great works of art enable us to understand what it is to be a human being not as physiology and pschology do but by providing images which illuminate our experience.

Here, however, another possible objection arises, that of sociohistorical relativism. Just as the sociologist of art, whose views will also be discussed in detail in the final chapter, holds that the concept of art changes over time and place, it can be argued that the concepts of human nature and the human condition are not fixed. 'Human nature', this argument goes, is not one thing for all humans at all times; neither is 'the human condition'. Different cultures understand these ideas differently. Consequently, they are concepts that cannot be given universal content, nor can they be construed as boundaries or fixed points of reference which we might hope to know or understand better.

Whether this is true or not, it is worth observing that there are nonetheless elements in human existence which obtrude upon all human beings – mortality, susceptibility to cold, hunger, and pain, interest in sexual relations, humour, sorrow, and so on – and these supply many of the major themes of artistic endeavour. The treatment of these themes is always in a socialized context, but even if the relativist's general point is sound, it does not undermine the cognitivist theory of art that this chapter has given us reason to accept. For the theory to hold, it is enough that there are indeed concepts of human nature and the human condition because, relative or not, they may still provide us with the subjects of artistic understanding, whose force is to illuminate some of the primary features of human experience. Whether illuminating human nature and the human condition as these are conceived in one culture can illuminate the experience of all human beings everywhere is another question, and one with which we need not be concerned here. We can conclude that the sociohistorical relativist's objection, whether sound or unsound, does not undermine the claim that art can be valued for its illumination of human experience.

Up to this point in our study we have been thinking about art in general. To make good the claims of cognitivism it is not enough to show in the abstract that something of this sort is *possible*, which is all that the argument of this chapter has done. We must show that it is *actual*. It is not hard to believe that this could be done easily. Literature seems to provide many likely examples. Almost any major Shakespeare play – *Othello*, *King Lear*, *Henry V* – could be interpreted as providing insight and illumination on the themes of human nature and the human condition, as could novels like George Eliot's *Middlemarch* and Joseph Conrad's *Lord Jim*. What is much more difficult is to show that aesthetic cognitivism applies not only to specific works of art such as these but to the different forms of art. For instance, can we sensibly maintain that absolute music (music without words) can illuminate human experience? And if it cannot, are we reduced to explanations of its value only in terms of pleasure or the expression of emotion? And what about architecture? Is the construction of a building the construction of an image? And if so, an image of what? In any case, do we need to give this explanation of its value when it so obviously has another value, namely, usefulness? Even in the case of the visual and literary arts, from which all the illustrations so far have been drawn, there are problems for cognitivism. Some visual art, abstract painting for instance, does not seem to be composed of images at all. And if images can be constructed in straightforward prose, why do we need poetry or narrative?

These are all important questions which need to be dealt with at length before even a normative theory of art as a source of understanding can be given credence. This is why the next four chapters of the book leave behind questions about art in general and examine specific forms of art in some detail.

Summary

This chapter has explained and defended a version of aesthetic cognitivism, the view that art is most valuable when it serves as a source of understanding. Though there are evident differences between art on the one hand and science or history on the other, the former, no less than the latter, can be seen to contribute significantly to human understanding. In appreciating how it does this, it is essential to see that works of art do not expound theories, or consist in summaries of facts. They take the form of imaginative creations which can be brought to everyday experience as a way of ordering and illuminating it.

Aesthetic cognitivism can explain more successfully than other theories why we attribute to great works of art the value we do. Although there is pleasure to be gained from the arts and beauty to be found in them, and though they are often moving, these features alone cannot explain the value of art at its finest. The idea that we come away from art with a better understanding of human experience is able to make sense of this, but it is unclear whether this explanation of value can be applied to all the arts. So we need now to look in more detail at specific art forms – music, painting, literature, and architecture.

Suggestions for further reading

R.G. Collingwood, *The Principles of Art*, chap. 13.
Nelson Goodman, *Ways of Worldmaking*.
Douglas Morgan, 'Must art tell the truth?', in Hospers, *Introductory Readings*.
Morris Weitz, 'Truth in literature', in Hospers, *Introductory Readings*.

4

—•◎•—

Music and meaning

We have considered in general the various explanations that might be offered for the value we attach to art. One conclusion to emerge is that different explanations allow us to attribute different *degrees* of value to art. If we think of art in one way – as a source of pleasure for instance – we will have reason to value it differently than if we think of it in another – as a play of beautiful symbols, a source of emotional stimulation, or as a form of imaginative understanding. That different explanations generate different degrees of value allows us to adjudicate between them. Some will explain better than others both the social status of art and the discriminations we make between works.

No philosophical theory of art can slavishly take social status and critical evaluation as data which it *must* accommodate; there is considerable scope for the critical revision of common beliefs and preferences. A normative philosophy of art may well produce surprising results. It leaves open the possibility that we are mistaken about the basis and degree of value of even very prestigious arts. Opera is generally regarded as one of the greatest forms of high art. But it is possible in principal that critical philosophy might show this to be a groundless prejudice.

There are some facts about art, however, that any explanation of its value has to respect. These are the facts about different art *forms*. Music is a different medium from paint, architecture different from drama, and so on. So different are they that the value of art is an issue which has to be investigated in a more detailed way in relation to the variety of art forms and the features that differentiate them. Perhaps some forms of art have a value that others do not or even cannot have. This is why it is appropriate to move at this point to an examination of four principal forms of art – music, the visual arts, literature, and architecture – and, in the light of the arguments of the last three chapters, to ascertain what can be said about their value.

Music and pleasure

There are several reasons for beginning with music. Music itself, sometimes called by philosophers 'absolute music' (as opposed to music with words – songs, arias, chorales, and so on), is often regarded as the purest and most unmistakable form of art. Consequently anything which purports to explain the value of art must explain the value of music satisfactorily. Second, absolute music very quickly calls into play the arguments of the last few chapters. It seems beyond doubt, for instance, that absolute music can and does give pleasure; it is often valued for this reason. It is also widely regarded as a powerful vehicle for the expression of emotion. Though it is problematic how and whether music can 'say' anything, many composers and musicians have attributed to it a power to reveal something about human life and experience. (In musical analysis, music for which this claim is made is often called 'programme music' and is contrasted with 'absolute music' in a pure sense.)

The aim of this chapter is to explore these three dimensions of music, beginning with pleasure. That music can and does give pleasure is beyond doubt. Is this the sole explanation for its value? If it is beyond doubt that music gives pleasure, it is no less beyond doubt that many musicians and music lovers claim to find more in music than simple pleasure. For instance, in a book significantly entitled *The Language of Music*, Deryck Cooke says this:

> to put it in the contemporary way, [the writer on music] is expected to concentrate entirely on the 'form', which is not regarded as 'saying' anything at all. . . . Instead of responding to music as what it is – the expression of man's deepest self – we tend to regard it more and more as a purely decorative art; and by analysing the great works of musical expression purely as pieces of decoration, we misapprehend their true nature, purpose and value. By regarding form as an end in itself, instead of a means of expression, we make evaluations of composers' achievements which are largely irrelevant and worthless.
>
> (Cooke 1957: 5, brackets added)

Cooke and the many other music theorists who speak in this way could be mistaken. Perhaps the depth they purport to find in music and which they think goes beyond mere pleasure is in fact only pleasure of a special sort, one which is enjoyed exclusively by those with a high degree of musical refinement. Since people have a tendency to objectify their personal preferences and thus elevate them to a higher status, it could be that when musicians and critics talk in these terms they are presenting their likes and dislikes in the form of judgments, and a similar prejudice might explain the relative inattention given to jazz or heavy metal music.

In Chapter 1 we considered the relation of pleasure to aesthetic judgment, in particular Hume's attempt to found a standard of taste on preferences widely shared among human beings. The argument there showed that mere taste however common cannot be made the foundation of good and bad. In any case the language people use to appraise music goes beyond talk of pleasure and enjoyment. It is certainly natural for people to say of almost any concert, whatever kind of music it may have contained, that they 'enjoyed it', and less common for them to speak in the high-flown language of Cooke. Nonetheless most people apply a wider range of other terms once they start identifying what it was about the music that they enjoyed. Music is easily described as 'moving' or 'exciting', and probably it is more often described in this way than as pleasurable. More importantly, 'pleasant' and 'nice' can be used in ways that *contrast* them with terms of praise. To describe a piece of music as 'pleasant' can be to damn it with faint praise. Nor when used in an adulatory way, do these terms readily fit those pieces of music upon which we want to heap the greatest praise. No one would describe Beethoven's *Quartets* or Bach's *Double Violin Concerto* as only pleasant.

However, to show that the vocabulary people use about music is wider than Hume suggests does not of itself show anything about the basis of music's value. This is because there is no necessary conflict between being 'agreeable' and being 'moving' – why should music not be pleasurable precisely because it moves us emotionally? To point out that the vocabulary we use to describe music includes many terms besides 'pleasant' shows nothing. Indeed it even shows nothing to observe that people often employ terms sharply contrasted with pleasure; a melody can be 'haunting' for instance, and music can be used to alarm, because human beings, somewhat surprisingly perhaps, can gain pleasure from activities that at one level are unpleasant. Horror movies are instances of the same phenomenon, as indeed are sad stories. People enjoy being terrified, and they often 'love a good cry'.

This attempt to combine pleasure and emotion in an explanation of the value of music has considerable plausibility. It is certainly true that we can derive pleasure from the emotional impact that music has upon us, and it is also true that the differences between the way we customarily describe music and the nature of our interest in it may be superficial only. Nevertheless there are some differences between pieces of music which cannot be accommodated in this way. Chief among these differences is complexity. There is more to Beethoven's *Fifth Symphony* than there is to *Greensleeves*. At least some of the difference must lie with their relative complexity. Beethoven's symphonies have a scope and scale which the average popular song does not begin to aspire to. This difference in scale is of considerable importance in assessing the merits of a piece of music, yet from the point of view of pleasure there does not seem any reason to prefer one to the other since greater complexity in a piece of music does not in and of itself lead to greater pleasure on the part of the listener. On the contrary, since a large-scale piece of music demands a great deal from us in the way of concentrated attention, simple harmonies with a catchy tune are usually easier to enjoy.

Complexity is an intrinsic feature of the music. By locating the principal value of music in the pleasure it gives, we focus attention upon the listener rather than the music itself, and by doing so we naturally come to regard its affective capacity as its most important property. But of course music also has a structure. Every piece of music of any sophistication is a construction out of certain variables – harmony, rhythm, timbre, form, and texture, chiefly. A great composer is one who can combine some or all of these variables in ways which have sufficient novelty and complexity to admit of analysis and understanding.

To see that any assessment of a musical composition must take account of its intrinsic structure as well as its effect upon the listener is at the same time to see how we might make sense of a difference in value between different composers and pieces of music, one which even the most sophisticated account of degrees of pleasure cannot accommodate. A piece of music such as Elgar's *Cello Concerto* or Brahms's *Violin Concerto*, is not only worth listening to but *requires* listening to over and over again because there is more and more to discover in it. It may also be performed again and again in markedly differing ways because it allows considerable variety of interpretation. A musician can use an instrument or an orchestra to explore a piece of music and to reveal the results of that exploration to the audience. From both the point of view of the listener and the performer, then, either of the musical examples just given may be described as richer, in the sense of containing more of interest, than simpler and initially more attractive and indeed more pleasurable pieces. Were we to restrict ourselves to talk of pleasure, or even to degrees of pleasure, we could not capture the relative structural wealth or paucity that people rightly see in different styles and pieces of music, and upon which they base critical judgments. The tunes that Abba produced are genuinely pleasurable in a way that most symphonic music is not. But this does not make them better music. Boccerini's *Minuet* is a very pleasing sound; Beethoven's *Kreutzer Sonata* is not. Nevertheless the second is obviously a superior piece of music. We can only consistently hold both these judgments if we can explain the value of the Kreutzer without having, openly or surreptitiously, to appeal to 'deeper' or 'higher' pleasures. The most straightforward way of doing this is to appeal to relative intellectual complexity. Music is not just undifferentiated sound which may or may not please. It has a structure, which lends it interest and consequently value, and great music exploits structural possibilities to a degree that puts it far beyond the level of simple pleasant melodies. It does not merely have an effect upon us, as the melody does, but provides us with material for our minds.

Music and emotion

One might reply that to counter the simple, perhaps naïve view that music is valuable chiefly as a source of pleasure by appealing to structural complexity is to construe music *too* abstractly, as a matter chiefly of form and intellect, ignoring altogether its affective properties. To make structure the principal focus of critical attention is to leave out precisely what most people would suppose to be an essential element in music appreciation, namely, the ability to be moved by it. It seems possible that someone could analyse the form and structure of a piece of music and at the same time feel no sympathetic response to it. Such a person might have some understanding of the piece as an artificial construct but could not be said to appreciate it as music. Moreover, what is missing from such an analytic understanding is the very thing that most musicians and music lovers hold to be peculiarly valuable in music, namely, its emotional content.

Thus, it may be argued, to reject the pleasure view on the ground that good music offers us a complex construction of which we may hope to attain an intellectual grasp, and to argue that the value of much music lies chiefly in this is to make a mistake about where the importance of form and structure lies. It is certainly true that part of the difference in value between, say, a Bruckner Mass and a simple hymn is the sophistication and complexity of the former. It is also true that the respective value of each is in part due to this difference in complexity. But it is wrong to draw the conclusion that structural complexity in itself is to be valued. Rather, what is valued is what that complexity enables a musician to achieve, namely musical effect. By itself no formal property in music can be held to have value, and indeed undue complexity of structure may destroy the very emotional experience aimed at, as arguably it does in some of the music of Telemann.

Now in this line of thought there is plainly something correct. The idea that mere complexity increases value is indeed mistaken (though whether *mere* complexity is possible in music is debatable), and it is a topic to which we shall have to return. Even if it is true that complexity in music, if it is to be valuable, must serve some further end, it is not at all evident that the end must have something to do with emotion, with affective properties that move us. Or rather it is far from clear how construing emotional content as the end at which musical complexity aims could help us explain the value of great music. This is partly because of the general difficulties about art and emotion rehearsed in Chapter 2. But there is a further difficulty in the case of music; it is hard to see how there could be any connection between emotion and music at all.

People often and easily say that music is filled with or expresses or arouses emotion. The main support for speaking in this way lies in the undoubted fact that we can use emotional terms to describe pieces of music. Indeed some pieces of music are such that it seems impossible to avoid the language of emotion if we are to say anything at all about them. Elgar's *Cello Concerto* is one particularly marked example. Michael Hurd, Elgar's biographer, describes it as 'filled with sadness and regret' and 'shot through with melancholy' and these are descriptions which anyone who has listened to the piece, especially the third movement, will find it hard to resist. Conversely it seems entirely appropriate to describe the *Rondo* in Mozart's *Fifth Violin Concerto* as irrepressibly happy in tone; there is just no better way of describing it.

It is the ability to apply emotional terms to music compositions and performances and the established practice among critics of doing so that inclines people to generalize about music and the expression of emotion. But we should observe that in doing so they move from the level of facts about linguistic behaviour to a theory about music, and it is just this move that needs some explanation and defence. Expressivism in music cannot rest its case simply on this fact about linguistic usage, for the philosophical question is, 'What are we to make of it?' Does the ease and regularity with which emotional terms are applied to music imply that music can express emotion? There are a number of reasons for thinking that it does not.

To begin with, when asked to specify the emotions with which a piece of music may be filled or which it may arouse or express, the list turns out to be surprisingly short. Music is said to be 'sad' or 'happy' (or some variation of these general terms – 'sombre' and 'joyful', for instance), but very few other emotional states or conditions can be ascribed to music without a measure of absurdity creeping into the discussion. Perhaps it is right to say that music can arouse or even express fear and pride as well as sadness and happiness, but could a piece of music express shame, or embarrassment, or envy or hatred or love? (It is important to remember here that we are talking about absolute music in the broad sense. Music with words will be considered later.) In the general discussion of expressivism we saw that there seems no reason to regard the expression or arousal of emotion in itself as either a good or a bad thing, but even if that argument were to be called into question here and the expression of emotion come to be regarded as something valuable, we would have to conclude that the value of music is therefore severely limited since the range of emotions it can express and arouse is itself so limited.

But there is a further and more damaging point to be made against musical expressivism. The recourse to emotion, it will be recalled, was made in the attempt to escape pure formalism about music and to explain why complexity is to be valued. In the expressivist view, it is to be valued presumably because greater complexity of construction facilitates greater emotional expression. But is this true? A simple minor chord repeated in common 4/4 time can effectively evoke sadness, while a complex of melody and harmony with a relatively complicated time signature (Dave Brubeck's *Take Five* for instance), may not clearly express or evoke any emotion at all.

If now we combine these two points – that the range of emotions that it is possible for music to express or evoke is extremely limited and that the ability of music to evoke even this limited range of emotions does not seem to have any obvious connection with complexity – and add them to the earlier argument about art and emotion in general, then music will seem of little real value. That is to say, if what is important about music is its ability to express or arouse emotion, and it is this end that complexity of structure must serve if it is to be valuable, music cannot attain much of importance. And music as we know it, we must conclude, contains a great deal of idle complexity.

This is a rather damning conclusion to arrive at. But in arriving at it we have not really abandoned expressivism, for we have been assuming throughout that music can indeed express emotion. This assumption is unwarranted. The mere fact that the same terms are applied to music as are applied to human moods and attitudes does not show that those terms share the same meaning in both contexts, that they both describe or point to emotional states. This is a point that Roger Scruton makes: 'The ways of hearing sound that we consider to be ways of hearing music are based on concepts extended by metaphorical transference' (Scruton 1983: 79). The use of emotion terms may be a case of what is usually called 'analogical extension'. We can see this possibility at work in another range of vocabulary commonly employed. Music, though a strictly aural medium, is often, perhaps surprisingly, described in terms that have their home in strictly visual contexts. Brass may be said to be 'bright' for example, the stops on an organ may be said to give its 'colour', and a cello or an alto voice be said to have 'dark' tone. And vice versa – colours are commonly said to be 'loud' or 'soft'. But there is nothing in either fact about language use which allows us to conclude that the visual and the aural, despite being wholly different media, have common properties. On the contrary, just because they are wholly different we have reason to think that the terms do *not* mean the same when applied in such different contexts.

Similarly, though tunes and harmonies are frequently described in emotional terms – sad, happy, and so on – there is nothing in this fact alone which supports the idea that music has emotional content. The fact that music and states of mind are so very different gives us reason to accept that the use of emotional terms in music is indeed a case of analogical extension. Such extension reaches back into the description of emotional states themselves. The American philosopher Arnold Isenberg once pointed out that it is often assumed that a puzzle only arises over whether 'light-hearted' can be applied literally to a piece of music, whereas it is no less puzzling what its literal application to a human being could be. The terms we use to describe emotion are often metaphorical extensions without any obvious literal meaning.

Expressivism in music might be rescued and a firmer connection with emotion established if we could give an account of emotional origins. That is to say, so far we have been thinking of emotion as the *content* of music. An alternative is to think of music as expressing the emotions of those who compose or play it. However, in the earlier discussion of emotion a point of some importance emerged which is relevant here. This relates to the distinction between 'expressing' and 'being expressive of'. The capacity of a work of art to be expressive of something gives it greater significance than any mere emotional 'letting off of steam' would do. Expressiveness, as opposed to expression, is artistic imagination providing us with a way of articulating something. What is important about expressiveness, however, is not that it has emotional content, because words and gestures and so on can be expressive of more than emotion, but that it enhances awareness. In a sense it is misleading to use the term 'express' at all, just as it would be somewhat misleading (as well as odd) to describe an observational statement as an 'expression of perception'. So in appealing to a theory of expressiveness, we are really leaving any special concern with emotion behind and asking whether we can use art to say things. But to put it like this is to raise a major difficulty in the case of music: can absolute music *say* anything?

Music as language

Many people believe that it can indeed convey a meaning or message. Some of the most reputable students of music have not hesitated to assert that music is a special sort of language, one in which composers may tell us things and in which statements can be made. Moreover, and this accords with the general tenor and direction of the argument, some of them have made this claim expressly in order to establish the value and importance of music and to show it to be on a par with other artistic and intellectual endeavours. The passage from Deryck Cooke's book quoted earlier continues:

> If man is ever to fulfil the mission he undertook at the very start – when he first began to philosophize, as a Greek, and evolved the slogan 'Know thyself' – he will have to understand his unconscious self; and the most articulate language of the unconscious is music. But we musicians, instead of trying to understand this language, preach the virtues of refusing to consider it a language at all; when we should be attempting, as literary critics do, to expound and interpret the great masterpieces of our art for the benefit of humanity at large, we concern ourselves more and more with parochial matters – technical analyses and musicological minutiae – and pride ourselves on our detached de-humanized approach.
>
> (Cooke 1957: 5)

We need not here be concerned either with the justice of Cooke's complaint about fellow musicians or with his view of the unconscious and its language. The point to emphasize is that his attempt to establish the importance of music consists in allying it with philosophical reflection and literary criticism, both of which are intellectual endeavours much concerned with meaning and meaningfulness. He is not alone in this. Throughout his monumental work, *Man and His Music*, the English musicologist Wilfred Mellers consistently tries to establish the relative importance of composers and their work by appealing to what they have to say, the magnificence of their 'statements' and 'visions'. All Haydn's later music, he tells us, 'reflects the beliefs that had meaning for him – an ethical humanism based upon reason and the love of created nature' (Mellers, Part 3, *The Sonata Principle* 1962: 606). With equal confidence he asserts that Mozart 'transformed the symphony from rococo entertainment into a personal testament' (*ibid*.: 626). In a similar vein Karl Barth is recorded as saying that Mozart could cause his listeners to hear 'the whole context of providence'.

Some commentators have thought that Mellers' ready appeal to this sort of interpretation is excessive. Be this as it may, he is expressing more clearly than most something that has been a constant theme in the writings of musicians and their interpreters. Asked about the significance of his cello concerto, Elgar described it as 'a man's attitude to life', and Beethoven himself evidently held a view of this sort when he declared that 'music is a greater revelation than the whole of philosophy'. Nor is it hard to see just why the thoughts of composers and musicians have moved so easily in this direction. Johann Christian Bach is said to have remarked of his brother C.P.E. Bach, 'My brother lives to compose, I compose to live'. The remark was intended merely to reflect a difference of attitude towards the relative value of music on the part of each of them no doubt, but others have been quick to see in it an explanation of the relative merits of the music each composed: Carl Phillipe's is of serious interest, Johann Christian's merely light and amusing. To live for the sake of composition, if it is to make sense as a human ideal, requires that what is composed can be properly described in terms like 'affirmation' and by adjectives like 'profound'. Even the exponents of minimalist music, who might be supposed least likely to think in terms of cognitive content, can be found employing the idea in order to justify evaluative judgments. In a programme note on *Litania*, a piece by the minimalist composer Somei Satoh, the pianist Margaret Lee Teng finds in it a 'dance of the dark soul'.

These examples illustrate that the importance of one type or piece of music over another seems most easily explained by reference to what each has to 'say' to us. This is why composers and performers are often led to speak in this way. Their doing so is consonant with a good deal of the language of musical criticism. Critics and interpreters readily speak of musical 'statements', of what a particular passage 'signifies' or 'conveys', and they pass judgments which would be difficult to understand unless music can be thought of in this way. For instance, Beethoven's music has sometimes been said to be witty rather than funny, Lizst's piano music described as structurally clever but thematically banal, and Bruckner accused of long-windedness and being inconsequential. In short, both musicians and critics have sought to explain the importance of music in terms of its communicative import, and this implies that music has communicative power.

Once more it needs to be remembered that common ways of speaking do not of themselves settle philosophical questions. The fact that critics and even composers speak and write in this way is important, but is not itself proof or even evidence that music is a form of communication. To begin with we need to allow the possibility here, as much as in the application to music of the language of emotion, that these discursive terms used in connection with music may systematically differ in meaning from that which they have elsewhere and that analogical extension is at work here also. Certainly it is plausible to think that this is true of the expression 'musical statement' because for many writers on music it means nothing more pretentious than a relatively plain rendering of the central motif or melody around which subsequent variations and developments are built.

Still, both composers and interpreters have also striven for more than this and used these communicative terms of music with the intention that they should retain the cognitive import they have in other contexts. In short they have wanted to say that music is a language. But as Mellers himself says, this raises a fundamental question.

> [I]f music 'conveys' experience as a language does, what kind of language is it? The language of poetry is basically the same as the normal means of communication between human beings. The poet may use words with a precision, a cogency and a range of emotional reference which we do not normally find in a conversation. Yet though the order he achieves from his counters may be more significant than the desultory patterns achieved by Tom, Dick and Harry, at least the counters (words) are the same in both cases. Even with the visual arts there is usually some relationship between the order of forms and colours which the artist achieves and the shapes and colours of the external world. The relation between the formal and the representational elements is extremely complex and not easily susceptible to analysis; but it is at least usually clear that some such relationship exists.
>
> With music, the relationship between the forms of art and the phenomena of the external world is much less readily apprehensible.
>
> (*ibid.*: vii).

Music and representation

Sometimes the answer to the problem of music's meaning is thought to lie with the ability of music to represent. Musicologists often draw a contrast between 'absolute' music and 'programme' music, the latter a term coined by Lizst to describe music which conjures up literary or visual images. The idea is that programme music can 'say' things because it can be used to represent to us aspects of nature and human experience. And surely, it might be said, there can be no doubt that music *can* represent – birdsong, battles, storms, armies, royal processions, pastoral countryside – as well as a range of emotions – grief, jollity, excitement, and so on. Certainly music sometimes seems to represent; we can say very easily of some point in a piece of music, 'This is the wind blowing, the storm gathering', and so on. But it is important to be precise about what is actually going on on such occasions, if we are to be clear about the place of representation in the character and value of music.

The first point about representation in music is that some of the things that pass for representation are more properly described as imitation or replication. Replication of the sound of a bell is not properly called representation of the bell, at least not in the way that it might be the representation of a summons or a visitor arriving. Similarly more sophisticated replications and imitations of the sort found in music are not properly described as representations. Birdsong is an obvious case. A composer may use instruments to imitate the song of a bird and successfully get us to think of birds at that point in the music, but it does not follow that he has represented the bird or said anything about it. Indeed this need not be his purpose. The French composer Olivier Messïaen, for instance, wrote music much of which consisted (he said) in the transcription of sounds made by birds. He regarded birdsong as a very pure form of music that human beings can hardly hope to surpass. Consequently, though his music may rightly be described as imitative of birds and may prompt us to think of birds, he is not representing, but copying them. And representation is not imitation.

What then is representation proper? We might define it as the use of music, not to replicate the sound of something, but to prompt the idea of that thing in the minds of those who listen to the music. The example of the bell illustrates the difference. The sound of a triangle might *imitate* or replicate a bell, but thereby *represent* the arrival of a visitor. It is this sort of example, rather than birdsong or the howling of the wind, that ought to be under discussion when we speak of representation in music. Better examples are the grief that is conveyed by a slow rhythm in a minor key, the fury suggested by violins as they rush up a scale, the regal character of trumpet fanfares, or the melancholy of a solo cello.

That composers do use such devices to convey ideas to the minds of their listeners can hardly be denied, given the express intention of many composers, and that they succeed is equally well attested by the recorded reaction of listeners. No serious listener for instance has failed to identify some pastoral representations in Beethoven's *Pastoral Symphony*. But before drawing the conclusion that music does have power to communicate, we must note that there is an important distinction to be drawn between a form of communication and a means of prompting ideas.

When I write or speak a natural language such as English or French, I am possessed of a means by which I can not merely prompt or stimulate thoughts and ideas in the minds of others but direct and manipulate them. If you understand the words I use, you are compelled to have the thought that I express (though not of course, to accept it, approve of it, or anything of that sort; if I say 'This is a cup of tea', pointing to a flowerpot, your mind will entertain the thought 'This is a cup of tea', but not believe it to be true). A natural language is thus a powerful instrument of communication because it allows us to constrain the thoughts of others; it allows us to *make* them think things (though not to make them believe those things) and to do so in a certain way. In contrast are many other ways in which we can merely *prompt* thoughts in others. The least interesting are accidental ways in which other people are merely caused to have thoughts by chance actions of mine. For instance I might by my chance gestures remind you of your child-hood, or of a play you once attended. To do so however would not properly be described as communicating the idea of these things, since at the very least there was nothing intentional in what I did. Of course I might know that such-and-such a gesture would cause you to be reminded of an episode in childhood, and might intentionally make the gesture. It would still not be plausible to speak of this as a form of communication. A single effect brought about thanks to my knowledge of facts peculiar to you, even if it can be repeated, does not have the degree of generality which the idea of a *form* of communication requires.

It is not difficult to imagine the same sort of thing expanded both in extent and complexity and across individuals. A group of children, for instance, might invent a system of signs and gestures which they used to convey information and warnings to each other. Such a system need not be deliberately or consciously learned. Other children might simply acquire their knowledge of the system in the course of play and thereby become receptive to messages received in this form and adept at sending them. Accordingly, we could say that we have here a form of communication that rests upon widely shared conventions. A similar story might be told for music. Over the years a shared understanding has arisen amongst those who compose and listen to music by which it is possible for composers to prompt in the minds of listeners certain ideas, that include both ideas of objects and of feelings; in this way music has become a form of communication in its own right, just as a sign language like semaphore is a form of communication.

That the principal basis of musical communication is indeed conventional is born out by the fact that the music of different parts of the world does not readily transcend the cultures that have grown up there. People sometimes, and somewhat romantically, speak of music as a universal language, but it is obvious that Indian or Arabic music is difficult for those brought up on Western music to understand and appreciate, initially at least (and vice versa, perhaps). This is not hard to explain. Take for instance the example of a peal of bells used to convey the idea of a wedding, or a tolling bell to convey the idea of death. In both cases the sound of the bell gets its 'meaning' from certain social practices at weddings and funerals, and in the absence of those practices or in the ears of one unfamiliar with them, the sound of the bell cannot convey those ideas. Mosques do not have peals of bells and consequently the sound of bells does not have the same associations in Islamic countries.

This is not to imply that the resources deployed by music in the conveying of ideas are entirely conventional. There are also natural associations between sounds and rhythms around which conventions may be built; it is no accident that the ringing of bells at weddings takes the form of a peal – loud and jangling – whereas that for funerals takes the form of a toll – slow and solitary – and each seems 'naturally' fitting to the occasion. A rapidly rising sequence of notes has an unmistakable association with physical upward movement, and it seems to have an equally natural association with excitement. Thus almost every setting of the Mass makes the music of the line 'Et resurrexit tertiam die' ('and on the third day he rose again') move vigorously upwards. Similarly with sombre moments, with the expression of happiness, and with countless other examples there appear to be natural associations which composers can exploit. Talk of musical 'jokes' is often rather strained, but there is no doubt that there are musical sequences which actually do make people laugh, just as there are musical sequences which make them pensive.

There are, then, a number of resources which composers may use to convey ideas in their music. There are conventional devices embedded in the practice of learning music, socially acquired connotations (such as the association of royalty with trumpets), and natural associations. Taken together they comprise a complex and sophisticated set of devices for the stimulation and/or provocation of feelings and ideas. But is this enough to allow us to declare music to be a language with all the power, and hence the (potential) value, that Cooke and Mellers attribute to it?

Musical vocabulary and musical grammar

We now need to return to the distinction between a means of promoting ideas and a form of communication. Take again the case in which some chance gesture of mine awakens in you a memory of childhood. That I have caused you to think of your childhood is indisputable, but we cannot on the strength of that alone infer that I have conveyed that idea to you. Nor does it become correct to speak in this way even if we extend the example and imagine a fairly complex sequence of gestures on my part which causes you to have a sequence of images or thoughts. Why not? The answer is that by causing this sequence of thoughts in you. I have relied not upon your understanding, but upon certain contingent connections between my gestures and your early childhood experience. I have no more communicated an idea to you than has a dog whose barking reminds you to lock the door at night. In both cases, you have merely been caused to have the idea.

Something of the same sort might now be said about the representational use of music. I might use the sound of a triangle to prompt in you the thought 'a visitor', but if I succeed, this is not because you have, in any proper sense, *understood* the sound, as you might a word, but that you have come to associate the sound of a bell with the arrival of visitors. What is missing is the idea that my music has *constrained* your thoughts. When a bell caused Pavlov's dogs to salivate, it may not be fanciful to suppose that the idea of meat was prompted in them. But it would be fanciful to suppose that they understood the bell to be saying 'meat'.

Consider a parallel with painting. A painter might so arrange abstract colours and shapes on his canvas as to cause you to think of a tree that once grew in front of the house in which you lived. This case may usefully be contrasted with one in which the painter reminds you of a tree and a house with which you are familiar but has so painted them that perspective *obliges* you to see the tree in front of the house. This ability of painting to use perspective not merely to *prompt* but to *constrain* perception is what makes painting a form of communication. The question is, 'Is there a parallel to perspective in music?'

In view of the considerable representational resources of music listed above – all its natural and conventional associations – it is important here to observe that the distinction between a means of communicating thoughts to others (best exemplified in a natural language), and a means of prompting ideas in others (which we will call a representational system), allows us to imagine representational systems of considerable complexity which nevertheless fall far short of being a 'natural language'. Their deficiency might be expressed thus: they have a vocabulary but no grammar.

Music can be interpreted as having a vocabulary. It is not hard to find many simple examples in which some musical phrase can plausibly be said to indicate or represent some object, emotion, or event. But even if we agree that music has a vocabulary in this sense, it is hard to discern in music any facility for directing our thoughts about what is represented. Consider once more the simple case of the sound of a triangle imitating a bell and thus representing the arrival of a visitor. If this is all the music does, it cannot tell us what to think *about* the object represented. Thus far described, 'Oh good!

a visitor' is as suitable an interpretation of the music in the first case as 'Oh no! a visitor'. This is true of more sophisticated cases also. Deryck Cooke in *The Language of Music* interprets 'the descending minor 5–3–1 progression' as the expression of a 'falling away from the joy of life' (Cooke 1957: 137). This is a more controversial example of representation in music, and even if we accept that an interpretation as ambitious as this is possible, there is still an important deficiency in considering music as a form of communication. For the progression might as easily be taken to mean 'Fall away from the joy of life' as to 'Never allow yourself to fall away from the joy of life'. Since these are contradictory injunctions, the music cannot be considered an effective means of communication at all. It prompts ideas and thoughts but cannot constrain them in any particular direction.

Of course ambiguities and uncertainties in music are often resolved when the music has some linguistic accompaniment, either in the form of libretto or in the form of dedication or title. One of the best known pieces of programme music is Mussorgsky's composition *Pictures at an Exhibition*, originally ten piano pieces, but now generally performed in an orchestral arrangement by Ravel. Mussorgsky was inspired to write it by an exhibition of paintings in St Petersburg. Someone who did not know its title would have no reason to describe it in this way, and without the help of programme notes could not identify the objects in the various pictures just by listening to the music. Similarly, in Prokofiev's *Peter and the Wolf* or Saint-Saëns' *Carnival of the Animals*, although the instruments and tunes that represent the different animals are no doubt appropriate in a general way, any one instrument could equally well serve for a number of different animals. We know precisely what animals are represented because we are *told*, in words; the music itself is not enough.

This is not to say that the words do all the work. A musical setting can embellish, illustrate, and illuminate words, and on occasion transform them almost from banality to the sublime (witness parts of Britten's *Saint Nicholas*). It can conversely reduce them to farce (witness parts of Stainer's *Crucifixion*). It can take a thoroughly familiar text and wholly enliven it, indeed give it a definitive interpretation (Handel's *Messiah* is perhaps the clearest example of this). Nevertheless the relationship between words and music is asymmetrical. Words resolve ambiguities in the 'meaning' of the music, but should the words themselves be ambiguous, the music cannot resolve the matter. In short, the music always follows and never leads the words; it lacks the ability to impart a meaning of its own.

This deficiency and the fact that it is a deficiency of the first importance are both illustrated in a well known example. Against the theme of the finale of his last string quartet Beethoven wrote 'Muss es sein? Es muss sein' (Must it be? It must). Most commentators have taken these words as indicative of the meaning of the music and have thus understood the music to be expressing a hard-won mystical or religious acceptance of the human condition which Beethoven only achieved at the end of his life. Beethoven himself said that the words recorded an exchange between him and his housekeeper who was asking for more money. Of course this might have been a joke on his part, but equally it might not. Perhaps he wrote these down as a reminder of the mundane need for money which caused him to compose music he himself regarded as the finest he had ever written. And indeed such an interpretation need do nothing to diminish the value of the music. The philosophical point which the example makes, however, is that appeal to the music – its tunes and harmonies – cannot settle the matter in favour of either interpretation, since the music itself is consonant with both. If the music really did *communicate* the metaphysical or religious ideas that some have found in it, there should be no doubt that Beethoven's own account of the matter is indeed a joke. Since there *is* a doubt here, it follows that the music by itself cannot direct our thoughts in one way rather than another.

This example is especially telling in the context in which we are discussing the issue. Beethoven's late quartets are often cited as examples of the most serious and profound music ever written, music which we therefore have reason to value more than any other. And the explanation of this profundity is given in terms of the ideas about human life and experience that they express. Yet as we have seen, the music taken by itself cannot confirm this explanation. We cannot say that the music shows or teaches us anything, because even if we agree that it regularly prompts or stimulates or even expresses a limited range of moods and ideas, there is nothing in the music that constrains us to think about them in one way or another. If something similar were true of a work of philosophy or science, we would have no hesitation in concluding that it had failed. An argument, conceptual or empirical, which merely prompts those who follow it to think a wide variety of different and incompatible things about the subject in hand cannot be said to add to our understanding of human experience. A philosophical or scientific argument *brings* us to a conclusion, just as the painting imagined earlier obliges us to see the tree in front of the house.

In short, even if we make large concessions to those who believe that music can be said to have content other than harmonious sound and allow that music may be used systematically for the suggestion of ideas and feelings, we still cannot conclude that music constitutes a true form of communication, still less a valuable one.

Resumé

The argument so far has shown this. If we value music solely because of the pleasure it gives us, we cannot explain those differences in value between pieces of music which arise from their complexity and sophistication of structure. The sort of music that is described as serious just has more to it, has more worth listening for, than music which is merely light and pleasant. To attach the difference in value solely to the complexity, however, leaves out precisely what those most attracted to music find in it, namely, its affective content. But if we do suppose that complexity of structure in music is to be valued in so far as it contributes to emotional impact, we are no further forward in explaining its value since, as we saw, the range of emotions that can be expressed or evoked is limited and the value of invoking or expressing them obscure.

It is a desire to explain the difference between serious and light music in the face of the failure of appeals to pleasure and emotion to do so that has led many to the view that music is better thought of as speaking to, and out of, human experience, and that the composer presents us with a view of life and experience. But we have seen that though a measure of representation is possible in music, there is no ground for the more ambitious claim that in Beethoven's words music can give us the sort of revelation aspired to by philosophy. Music has a vocabulary (albeit limited) but no grammar. We can call it a language if we will, but on most things it will have little to say, and on nothing will it have anything of any sophistication to say. To put it bluntly in a best possible showing, the language of music is not much more advanced than a system of monosyllabic grunts.

The uniqueness of music

From some points of view, the conclusion that music is not a language will be regarded as deeply disappointing, but from another it is nothing more than we would expect. There is an old joke among opera goers that Wagner's music is better than it sounds, whereas Puccini's music sounds better than it is. There is a point the joke is making, but its humour arises from the absurdity of the idea that music could be better than it sounds; music just *is* sound. Consequently any attempt to explain the merits of Wagner or demerits of Puccini in terms other than how their music sounds must come to grief. The general lesson to be learned is that all explanations of the value of music which pass beyond the sound itself to pleasure, or emotion, or images, or visionary ideals, must fail. Music has to be listened to and nothing can replace this experience. Sometimes interpreters speak as though what a piece of music 'says' can be explained in other ways. Mellers offers T.S. Eliot's poetry as an explication of Beethoven's late quartets. It is hard to see how one work could be said to correspond exactly to another, but if ever such an explanation were successful, the music would in a sense be redundant; we could read the poem instead.

That there is something inherently right about insisting upon the irreplacability of music seems certain. All attempts to explicate the character or meaning of music in non-musical terms are doomed from the outset, for what we are seeking to explain – music – is unique. Music differs from other art forms. For instance, it is neither unintelligible nor silly (though it may be wrong) to think that photography could replace painting or film replace theatre (and the novel perhaps) without loss or remainder because though we may be uncertain about what exactly it is we get from painting or drama, we are clear enough that the same sort of thing is on offer from photography and film. But what could possibly take the place of music? Those things that we can think of as having a musical dimension of sorts, such as verse, are obviously limited in their 'musical' aspects compared to music itself. This peculiar character of music makes it incomparable and its value cannot therefore be compared with that of anything else. The great twentieth-century philosopher Ludwig Wittgenstein (whose brother was the one-handed pianist Paul Wittgenstein) once remarked, 'It is impossible to say all that music has meant to me'. People have interpreted this remark in different ways, but it is possible to understand it quite literally.

On the other hand, the uniqueness of music in this respect can wrongly be taken to imply that its significance and value cannot be spelled out in any way whatever, hence the slogan 'Music for music's sake'. But such a slogan is open to the same objections as the more general slogan 'Art for art's sake', discussed briefly in Chapter 1. It can only convince the con-verted and obliges us to overlook what plausibly can be said. Faced with a choice between the most ordinary of popular tunes played on a pre-programmed keyboard, or a double harpsichord concerto, the claim that the superiority of the second can be apprehended but cannot be explained looks like a dogmatic assertion on the part of those whose pref-erences are for harpsichords. Besides it gives up the game too quickly since it leaves out of account all the differences between the two that *can* be observed. What is needed then is a way of saying something about the value of music which, while it does not attempt to explicate it in non-musical terms, allows us to consider critically the claims that can be made on its behalf.

Music and beauty

The uniqueness of music is worth exploring further. Sometimes people, even composers, speak as though music is a refinement of things found in nature. They refer us to birdsong, the wind in the grass, the sound of the cataract, and suggest that all our music is an attempt to provide these things for ourselves. The truth is that natural sounds are not musical. The chatter of birds, the sound of wind or waterfall have nothing remotely resembling either the purity, the complexity, or the variety of the simplest composition

81

for the smallest orchestra. The only thing in nature which may be truly musical is the human voice when it sings, and of course singing is itself *making* music, an intentional activity in which human beings uniquely engage.

We cannot find the origins or basis of music in the natural world, then. Nor should we be surprised that this is so. Music making is an accomplishment, something which humankind has achieved only after extensive periods of development. This is true even of singing. To hum or sing a series of notes is a spontaneous activity in human beings, but to turn this series into an extended and developed melody with organized keys and scales is not. Singing even a popular song takes us far beyond the ability and inclination of the baby in the pram to make resonant noises.

The point of stressing the non-natural character of music is this: music is not obtainable anywhere else than in the music-making activities of human beings. Why does this matter? One answer is that the intentional, organized character of music makes it unique as a means by which values can be realized and exemplified in purely aural experience. An obvious suggestion is that only in music is beauty of sound to be found. Since beautiful things are valuable, this means that music is uniquely valuable because it is our only source of one kind of beauty. No one can doubt that music is frequently valued for its beauty. What can be doubted is whether this constitutes the final or most satisfactory explanation of its value. To begin with, the claim that beautiful sound is to be found only in music is too sweeping. It is not plausible (I have claimed) to describe birdsong as music, but it is plausible to claim that some birds make beautiful noise. Similarly, I may properly describe someone as having a beautiful speaking voice, where the beauty is not attributed to anything recognizably musical but only to the sound of the voice.

These sorts of examples can appear questionable because people have a strong tendency to identify beautiful sound with music and are therefore inclined to describe a beautiful speaking voice as 'musical', or to call the beautiful cry of a bird 'song'. But that there is a marked and unmistakable difference between speaking and singing, and that the cry of a bird has no melody and is in no key are important and incontestable facts. Call them what you will, these sounds should be differentiated from music proper. But they are not to be differentiated in terms of beauty, for the whole purpose of denying their musicality is to show that there can be beautiful but non-musical sounds.

In any case, beauty as the source of value in music fares not much better than pleasure. The music of a large-scale and complex symphony is no more (and probably less) likely to be thought beautiful than a simple melody for a single violin. We might usefully contrast here Beethoven's and Bruch's violin concertos. Bruch's, it seems to me, is the more beautiful but Beethoven's the greater work. Certainly melodies and harmonies can be extremely beautiful,

but there is no reason to think that beauty and harshness exhaust the possibilities for assessing harmonic patterns or explaining what makes them
worth hearing. Beethoven's harmonic structures are more frequently interesting than beautiful but nonetheless valuable for that. In short, music may
be our most familiar source of beautiful sound, but it is not our only source,
nor is its being such a source an adequate explanation of the value we attach
to it.

Nevertheless there is something right about this general line of thought.
Music is the sole source of *organized* sound. One end to which it can be used
is the exemplification of beauty, but there are others. The philosopher
Malcolm Budd identifies several of these when he writes:

> One general value exemplified by many fine musical works is the unifi-
> cation of diverse material ... so-called 'unity in diversity' or 'organic
> unity'. . . . Other values that can be exemplified in music include
> beauty, gracefulness, wit, imagination and mastery. Unblemished
> musical works that exemplify these values are paradigms of perfection,
> appreciated as such.
>
> (Budd 1995 : 171)

Is its power to exemplify values such as these a sufficient explanation of
the value of music? Budd obviously thinks so since he concludes by saying
'How could anything more be demanded of music as an abstract art?' But
there is at least one other line of thought that can usefully be investigated,
namely, music as the unique exploration of one aspect of human experience
– aural experience.

Music as the exploration of sound

Music is for listening to as nothing else is. Such an assertion is neither
startling nor novel and may even sound banal. But its truistic character is in
fact a strength, once we see how it allows us to put into place the various
features of music mentioned in the course of this chapter. Suppose that music
is indeed to be valued chiefly as an extension and exploration of aural
experience. In this case we can see how there can be intelligible and demon-
strable differences between the creations and explorations of different composers because it just will be true of some pieces of music that there is more
to be heard in them than in others. This 'more' is not a simple matter of
quantity of notes or instruments. A composer may allow us to discover
among the qualities of sound those that we have to describe in metaphorical
or analogical language. What is interesting about music that is described as
bright, or sorrowful, or architectonic is not that it is in some odd way
connected with lights, or emotions, or buildings, but that sound, pure
sound, can have properties far more sophisticated than simple loud/soft,

fast/slow that are to be described in this way. That they have these properties is demonstrated not in analyses of their 'meaning' by interpreters or attention to the moods induced by them in listeners but by the composer and the performer *in the music*. We discover the existence of interesting and unusual properties by listening. Borrowing an expression from literary theory, we could say that music is the 'foregrounding' of sound. In music, noise-making ceases to be a mere means of expression or communication, and aural experience becomes the focus of interest in its own right.

Contrary to first impressions this ambition can be found even in the most minimalist music. The purpose of John Cage's 4' 33", where a pianist sits at the piano for the prescribed length of time but never plays, is to induce the audience to pay the same sort of attention to surrounding sound as they would to music. It inevitably fails, of course, because the aural experience that is 'foregrounded' (if it is) is wholly unstructured. The work cannot show us how to hear it. But the example illustrates just what it is we get from music which *does* tell us how to listen to what we are hearing.

Reflection and analysis can help us discover the properties of a piece of music. Indeed where the music is of a highly developed sort we may need the vocabulary of technical analysis to isolate and describe the structures of sound to be found within it. Nevertheless, if we are to know that *these* sounds have *that* property, listening is inescapable. And so it should be of course. The problem with the explanations of music's value discussed up to this point is this; even if the explanations work in other respects, they make the music redundant. Other pleasures as good as those derived from music are as readily available; emotional 'highs' are to be had elsewhere; what the music 'says' can be said more intelligibly in words. The values which it exemplifies, such as beauty or gracefulness, are exemplified in other arts. But if we follow this final suggestion and locate the value of music in its unique ability to extend and explore *aural* experience, we cannot have that experience non-aurally, and thus the activity of actually listening to music cannot be eliminated.

A further advantage to the theory of music as aural foregrounding is this. We saw earlier in the chapter that any propositional meanings we are inclined to attach to pieces of absolute music are invariably ambiguous, because there appears to be nothing about the music which directs, as opposed to prompts, our thoughts. But now we can see that, as the painter directs our visual perceptions, so the composer and performer direct our aural perceptions. Listening to music is not just a matter of sound pouring into a receptor, but of the mind being directed through a series of perceptions. We are, so to speak, steered through our experience. It is as though the composer were saying 'It must be heard *this* way' by actually making us hear it that way. An analogy might be this. We enter a series of underground caverns where our journey can take alternative routes through spaces of differing shape, dimension, and atmosphere, lighted by different means.

Each composer is the guide who decides upon the lighting and directs us through the caverns. The shapes and dimensions of the caves are 'there for all to see' of course but they can be seen only this way or that. The way we see them and the ways that are especially worth seeing, are matters for which we rely upon our guides.

If the final answer to the question 'What is the value of music?' is: through music alone can we explore the dimensions of aural experience, someone might then ask, 'What is so important about exploring aural experience?' To this question, the only answer would appear to be that aural experience is part of human experience and that by enlarging and exploring that aspect of experience, music assists us in understanding better what it is to be a human being. It is in this way the aesthetic cognitivism developed in Chapter 3 can be applied to music and hence that the value of great music may be explained as the value of great art.

Summary

It is evident that music gives many people great pleasure, and also true that it is widely believed to be expressive of some of the deepest human emotions. Neither fact properly explains its value however. Pleasure does not explain the distinction between light and profound in music and may even give us reason to prefer less profound music. Although music can properly be described in emotional terms, these terms have an analogical or meta-phorical meaning when extended to music and this makes it questionable whether music can be said to express emotion in its ordinary human sense. Several important writers on music have attributed to music both a power to represent and the properties of a language. Upon examination, however, it can be shown that the power of music to represent is limited and dependent upon conventional associations. At best the analogy with language shows that music has a vocabulary but no grammatical structures. This means that though it may be used to prompt thoughts and impressions, it does not have the capacity of a genuine form of communication.

Nevertheless a connection may be made between music and the cognitivist theory of art. Music is special among art forms because, while in theory photography could replace painting or cinema replace theatre, nothing could replace the experience of hearing music. Furthermore music is unique in providing us with extended structures of organized sound by means of which we may explore human experience. The aspect of human experience we explore with the assistance of great music is not that of the emotional or intellectual life, however, but aural experience, the experience of hearing itself.

Suggestions for further reading

Philip Alperson (ed.), *What is Music?*
P. Kivy, *The Corded Shell.*
Anthony Storr, *Music and the Mind.*

5

—•◦◯◦•—

From painting to film

The previous chapter, the first on a specific art form, was devoted to music, since this has often been thought to be art at its purest. But it is a notable fact that the word 'art' is most naturally associated with another form, namely, painting and while the idea of representation is problematic when applied to music, representationalism, the view that art at its best is a method of representation or that representation is one of the chief functions of art, comes into its own when applied to painting. In its commonest version, representationalism is a normative view, for it leads people to place a high value on very lifelike portraits such as those by Rubens and Velásquez and to wonder whether there really is any art in, for instance, abstract painting and sculpture. It is quite widely believed, in fact, that there is an important connection between lifelike representation and artistic value, and for a long time historical understanding of the development of painting was dominated by a concept of artistic progress which consists precisely in better and better methods of representation. Representationalism is not lacking adherents among philosophers of art. While Plato decried art because it did no more than reproduce the appearance of things, Aristotle makes the activity of representing things the distinguishing character of what we call the arts. Some very famous artists, too, have taken a strongly representational view. The sculptor Rodin, for instance, is recorded as saying 'The only principle in art is to copy what you see. Dealers in aesthetics to the contrary, every other method is fatal' (Goldwater and Treves 1976: 325). Yet, as we shall see, though representation is clearly important in painting, representationalism does not adequately explain its value, and even as a descriptive theory it is false with respect to the visual arts. It is only once we see the errors in representationalism that we can appreciate the sort of value that visual art can have, and the first step in doing so is to look more closely at the idea of representation.

What is representation?

Common ideas about representation, even in the visual arts, tend to be confused, even to the point of being contradictory. To begin with, there is widespread uncertainty about the relation between representation and copying. People praise and admire lifelike portraiture and landscape painting. But they also suppose that great artists do not merely copy what they see, and expect them to offer a personal 'interpretation'. (It is in this 'interpretation' that many people think the art lies.) They have doubts about the merits of abstract painting, while at the same time they doubt whether photography can be an art since it merely reproduces what is 'there' by causal means.

But consider this last supposition. In Chapter 3 (in a different context) we saw that every photograph must have an angle from which it is taken and that the choice of angle is often crucial to the interest of the photograph. Yet this is a choice that must be made by the photographer; it is not and could not be determined by the causal processes used in photography or by what is 'there'. Here is one way then, in which the photographer's art determines just what the resulting picture looks like. And there are many others – experimenting with different exposures and different papers for instance. Notice also that the final photograph, even though representational, need not be lifelike at all. It can be black and white, for example, when the world around us is never seen by most of us in this way. This familiar fact shows that in looking at a black and white photograph, we are either *not* looking at a copy of whatever is represented, or that the very idea of a 'copy' is itself uncertain.

The same is true of painting. We are inclined to think of representation as copying partly because the dominant convention in painting has long been to represent *via* strict resemblance. But this need not be so. Figures in ancient Egyptian art often appear peculiar and somewhat primitive to us, as though the artists were incapable of better. Part of the difference between these and modern representations of human beings however is a result of a different convention in representation. Ancient Egyptian art operated with the principle that each part of the human anatomy should be represented from the angle at which it is best seen. Thus while the face was to be seen in profile, the torso was to be seen from the front, and legs and feet from the side. The resulting body taken as a whole was of a sort that no one had ever seen, but it would be a mistake to conclude that there was some failure of representation. There was merely a different *convention* of representation. Ours may seem to us more 'natural', as perhaps it is, but its naturalness should not deceive us into thinking that it is more representational.

This is not to deny that foreshortening, perspective, and the use of light and shade were all important discoveries which greatly increased the power of the painter. But as the celebrated art historian Ernst Gombrich argued in

Art and Illusion, the power that is given to the painter is not to reproduce what is 'there' but to create a convincing impression that we are seeing the thing represented. Even the most lifelike representations cannot be thought of as mere copies. Their creators follow conventions which determine how things are to be represented and employ techniques which oblige us to look at things in certain ways. Constable, that most 'natural' of painters, whose painting *The Haywain* is one of the best known and best loved pictures in existence, uses blues and greens never to be found in sky or foliage, and as is well known, Stubbs (along with others), depicts the speed of a racing horse very effectively in a way that no horse ever actually galloped, an example of which is the painting of horses in the background of *Gimcrack*. (All the paintings referred to in this chapter can be found in E. H. Gombrich's *The Story of Art*.) Any depiction of nature that tries just to copy must fail, partly because every 'copy' of nature must involve seeing selectively, and partly because the work must reflect the representational resources available to the painter.

The truth of this is so evident if we turn to a popular area of visual art – cartoons – that it is hard to see how anyone could persist with the idea that representation is some sort of copying, the production of a resemblance. No mouse ever looked like Mickey Mouse and no ancient Gaul ever looked like Asterix, yet their representative character cannot be doubted. If it were suggested that cartoons are too mundane a form of art to carry implications for art 'proper', many famous woodcuts, drawings, and engravings could be cited to sustain the same point. It is simply a mistake to think of representation in the visual arts as a simple attempt to 'copy' what is 'seen'.

Representation and artistic value

Mimesis (from which we get the word 'mimic') is the Greek term, variously translated as 'resemblance', 'copy', and 'representation', which philosophers of art often employ. But thinking about *mimesis* must eventually lead us to reject representationalism. The fact that cartoons and engravings can depart so easily and successfully from anything thought of as resemblance without ceasing to be art should make us consider the possibility that art can properly employ visual techniques to depart from representation altogether. People who are under the influence of a naïve representationalism sometimes complain that the faces and figures in so called 'modern' art do not look anything like the real thing. (This is probably not a feature peculiar to the modern period. It seems likely that those brought up on the highly realistic pictures of Dürer and Holbein thought something of the same about El Greco's rather more extravagant paintings.) In response to this sort of complaint Gombrich (in *The Story of Art*) invites us to compare Picasso's *A Hen with Chicks* with his slightly earlier picture *A Cockerel*. The first of these is a charming illustration for Buffon's *Natural History,* the second a rather grotesque caricature. Gombrich makes the point that given the first of these pictures, no one can deny Picasso's ability to make lifelike representations. Knowing this, when we look at the second drawing and see that it looks 'nothing like' a cockerel, we would be foolish to dismiss it and should ask instead what Picasso is trying to do with it. According to Gombrich, 'Picasso was not content with giving a mere rendering of the bird's appearance. He wanted to bring out its aggressiveness, its cheek and its stupidity' (Gombrich 1987: 9). L.S. Lowry supplies us with another illustration of the same point. In his most famous pictures people are generally drawn with a childish simplicity, 'stick' figures in fact, but his early drawings of male nudes show that this manner of depiction was a matter of choice, and we will only appreciate the pictures properly if we look into the reason for that choice.

Gombrich's interpretation of the Picasso caricature brings out an important distinction which representationalism tends to overlook. There is a difference between representing something and giving a rendering of something's appearance. Those who favour representational art usually mean to favour painting that gives a good rendering of the appearance of things. But 'giving a good rendering' cannot be a matter of 'copying' the appearance of things. What the painter does is create a convincing impression of having seen the object. The example from Picasso shows that the creation of a resemblance is only one purpose for representation. The caricature cockerel does not look like a bird we might see. It draws attention to a certain characteristic. But it is still representational. This shows that representation can serve purposes other than creating a resemblance. If this is so, perhaps these other purposes can be served by means other than representation. Furthermore, if these other purposes include some of the things for which the visual arts are to be most valued, we have reason to conclude that however common and important representation may be in the history of visual art, representationalism, the doctrine we are examining, is false.

Consider some further examples of representation. Almost all the painting from the European Middle Ages is religious in inspiration and purpose. The aim of much of it was to provide the illiterate faithful with instruction in Bible stories, Christian doctrine, and the history of the Church, especially the history of its saints and martyrs. It did not aim at *mere* instruction, however, since it sought also to be inspirational, to prompt in those who looked at it a mind receptive of divine grace. An interesting example of this is Dürer's engraving *The Nativity.* (Dürer is a particularly good choice here because his pictures give such obviously excellent 'renderings of the appearance of things'.) The engraving is of a dilapidated farmyard in which Joseph, depicted as an elderly peasant, is drawing water at the well, while in the front left-hand corner Mary bends over the infant Jesus. Much less prominently portrayed (looking through a rear doorway in fact) is a praying shepherd accompanied by ox and ass, and in the very distant sky there is a single angel to be seen. The difference in scale of these traditional nativity figures relative to the house and farm buildings is striking. But it is also a little misleading; the picture is not any the less a nativity scene than those in which shepherds and angels are more prominent. What Dürer has done, by a magnificently detailed representation of a common North European farmhouse, is to convey very immediately the compelling atmosphere of Holy Night with the purpose, we may suppose, of inducing a deeper sense of the mystery of the Incarnation in the sort of people for whom the picture was intended.

Compare Dürer's engraving with Jackson Pollock's *No. 14*. This painting is a result of Pollock's celebrated technique, later known as 'action painting', in which the canvas is placed on the floor and paint is dripped or thrown on it to make interesting and unusual patterns. At first sight, these two paintings could hardly be more different. Pollock's was intentionally the product of spontaneity and made with some speed, Dürer's the result of hours of painstaking work. Dürer's is representational to an unusually high degree, Pollock's wholly non-representational. Yet despite these striking differences, both works may be said to have something of the same purpose. Much of what is known as 'Abstract Expressionism', of which Pollock's painting is an example, was influenced by Eastern mysticism, and both the spontaneity of production and the resulting random patterns have been thought valuable because they shake ordered preconceptions. We are forced to see visual chaos rather than visual pattern and thus to see the uncertain, even unreal, nature of the world of appearance. Using the visual to create impressions of unreality is similar to the the way in which some versions of Buddhism try to shake our preconceptions as a means of spiritual enlightenment. The paintings of Abstract Expressionism might be thought of as visual equivalents of Zen *koans*, the questions which the novice is made to contemplate, such as 'What is the sound of one hand clapping?'. (Of course the creation and contemplation of *zenga*, or Zen pictures, for the most part abstract works of calligraphy, are an important part of Zen Buddhist practice also.)

Interpreted in this way, both Dürer's and Pollock's paintings, despite their striking differences, share the same purpose – to make people aware of spiritual realities behind everyday experience. It is not crucially important here whether the spiritual purpose so described fits either case. These two pictures illustrate the point that, in intention at any rate, the same artistic purpose may use representational and non-representational means, and this shows that we should not think of representation as the sole or even chief *end* of visual art, but rather as a prominent *means*. To see this is to reject representationalism because a means is only as valuable as the end it serves. Of course it remains the case that representation is the stock in trade of visual artists, and nothing in the foregoing argument involves denying this. Even the Surrealists, a school of which Salvador Dali is perhaps the best known member, who rejected the idea of 'rendering of the appearance of things' still made extensive use of, admittedly weird, representations. What we should infer from this is not that most painting is visual representation, but that representation is highly valuable in the range of methods available to the visual artist. But it is not the only one, and to understand the value that is to be found in the visual arts, we must explore other techniques as well. The conclusion to be drawn is that we need to ask what sorts of purpose both representation and these other techniques can be used to serve. This brings us back to the central concern of this book, 'What is the best end art can serve?' The answer aesthetic cognitivism gives is, 'Enriching human understanding'. Can painting do this, and if so how?

Art and the visual

Constable, commenting upon a new attraction on view in London, denied that it was art since it involved visual deception, and 'art pleases by reminding, not by deceiving' (quoted in E.H. Gombrich *Art and Illusion*). What this remark reveals is the assumption that the purpose of art is to please; the only question in Constable's mind is in the manner in which it does this, by reminding or by deceiving the eye. This assumption is probably widely shared. Yet, as we saw in Chapter 1, it sits ill with everyday social practice; works of imagination are not ranked according to the pleasure they give. The clearest possible examples of drawings, paintings, photographs, and films that are intended to give pleasure, and frequently do, are pornographic ones. It is hardly these, however, that will be held up to be the principal products of the art world. Of course it will be said, correctly, that there are pleasures other than sexual titillation. But this is not to the point. The arguments in Chapter 1 showed that there is no way of distinguishing between pleasures that will allow us to hold both that the value of art lies in the pleasure we get from it, and that there is a evaluative difference between serious and light art. We need not rehearse those arguments to see that they apply with equal force to a particular branch of art, in this case painting.

Someone persuaded by the arguments made in Chapter 1 might nevertheless be reluctant to abandon the idea that the value of visual art (or part of it) is the pleasure it gives, and may maintain that, at least in one respect – the skill displayed by the artist – the greater the art, the greater the pleasure. The history of Western art from around 1400 to 1900 is a history of the discovery of a wide range of techniques in the use of perspective, composition, and colour, and of the achievements these made possible. Both the skills of the great painters and the effects they achieved in their paintings are truly astonishing. They are, we might say, a delight to behold, and whether or not we call our delight in them 'pleasure', the fact remains that it is partly for the pleasure that we value them.

Still even if this is true it tells only half the story. Human beings have mastered many astonishing techniques, but the question of the value we should attach to those techniques remains unsettled until we know what they can be used to achieve. The *Guinness Book of Records* lists many achievements made possible only through the mastery of highly unlikely and unusual skills which accomplish largely trivial ends. When we consider, the remarkable ability of some painters to bestow tactile values on visual images – to convey visually a sense of how objects feel – we must also ask whether this serves any valuable end. Representation is part of the answer; representative power is greatly increased thereby. But in the preceding section we found reason to conclude that, if we are to understand the value of painting properly, representation must itself be viewed as a means to some further end. We assume that most representative painting has a serious purpose, so we unquestioningly admire the great skill that it displays. It is the task of a normative theory of art to justify this assumption.

The question then is why great skill in painting is to be valued. In the history of art the importance of this question has come to be recognized only relatively recently. Throughout most of its development, painting has so clearly had a social function – the decoration of churches, stately homes, and civic buildings, the painting of portraits, and so on – that the question of any further *raison d'être* of the visual arts has hardly arisen. As Gombrich says, in the 'good old days'

> no artist need ask himself why he had come into the world at all. In some ways his work had been as well defined as that of any other calling. There were always altar-paintings to be done, portraits to be painted; people wanted to buy pictures for their best parlours, or commissioned murals for their villas. In all these jobs he could work on more or less pre-established lines. He delivered the goods which the patron expected. True, he could produce indifferent work, or do it so superlatively well that the job in hand was no more than an occasion for a transcendent masterpiece. But his position in life was more or less secure. It was just this feeling of security that artists lost in the nineteenth century.
>
> (Gombrich 1977: 397)

Gombrich identifies several historical causes, including the invention of photography, for the rift between the artist and the public which brought into question the justification of painting as an occupation. An appreciation of these historical developments is important for understanding the relation between the value of art and the forms of art prevalent at any one time, but the question we are concerned with here is not itself an historical one. It could be asked at any historical period whether and to what extent skill at painting is to be valued. Charting historically the changing perceptions of the role of art may illuminate the answers we give, but of itself it cannot supply them because there may have been periods when this ability was overestimated or underestimated.

What is required is an examination of the issues with which earlier chapters were concerned. In Chapter 3 the discussion concluded with the claim that the social value attributed to art is warranted to the degree that art enhances the understanding of human experience. We may ask here, therefore, whether the visual arts do this.

One obvious way in which this can be so is through heightened experience of the visual itself. This suggestion may seem trivial: a reduction of painting to the level of mere coloured patterns. In fact something of this charge lies in much of the criticism and rejection of 'modern' art, especially so-called 'abstract art' – that it has laid aside centuries of achievement in the art of representation for the construction of mere pattern, and sometimes not even this. Many of the highly regarded paintings of Marc Rothko, for example, are just large patches of colour. Yet presentation and exploration of the strictly visual has long been a quest in the history of art. If this quest has only come to full self-consciousness of late, this does not imply that it was ever wholly absent.

Besides, whatever we may say of modern art, there is good reason to regard the exploration of the strictly visual as an achievement. In the preceding chapter it was argued that absolute music may be understood as a foregrounding of the aural, and so too one special accomplishment of painting is the foregrounding of the visual. We saw in the first part of this chapter that it is a mistake to think of representation as mere copying. Painters cannot merely imitate. They cannot be thought of as presenting the 'raw' visual data which the spectator then 'observes'. Painters have to choose from all the things that can be seen. Often what they present are hints and suggestions of what is seen. The mind of the spectator then supplies what is missing to form an image. In this way prior knowledge enters our perception of a painting. But this prior knowledge can also be a distorting of the visual, especially if it is the painter's knowledge as well as the spectator's. This is what is happening in the Egyptian figures referred to at the begining of this chapter. The painter knows what arms and legs and profiles look like and combines all these elements in the representation. But the result is not what the thing normally looks like at all. To suspend all our visual preconceptions is not an easy business, but once the move in this direction is made we may also find true representational likeness receding. The Impressionists were keenly aware of the fact that we do not give most of the things we see close attention and only receive a fleeting impression of their appearance. They knew that bright light and deep shadow eliminate visual features so they tried to capture something of this phenomenon in their paintings, one consequence of which was a loss of 'realism' as detailed features were suppressed. A particularly good example of this is Monet's *Gare St-Lazare*, in which the objects we would expect to find in a picture of a railway station are dominated and almost eliminated by the visual impact of sunlight, smoke, and steam.

Foregrounding the visual is not incompatible with representational art however. Whistler's famous painting entitled *Arrangement in Grey and Black* is a highly representational portrait of the artist's mother. The title reveals that we are invited to see the seated woman from a purely visual standpoint. This is why the work lacks a certain three-dimensional depth. So it is true that if the prime purpose of a work of art is to foreground the visual and make abstract all preconception of how things are to be seen, then representational faithfulness is of secondary importance. A desire to heighten awareness of colour, or draw attention to incipient patterns, as in many of the paintings of Van Gogh and Gauguin, may call for representational freedom. Only if without reason we insist upon the primacy of representation in art, can these be called distortions.

More than this, once we see that a painter can be concerned with experience and yet not primarily interested in representation, we admit the possibility of paintings supplying us with wholly novel visual experience. This is what happens to some degree in Cubism and Surrealism. Picasso's well known picture *Violin and Grapes* provides us with something we could not see without the artist's intervention, namely, the different aspects of a violin from several different angles and all at once. Many of Dali's paintings (whatever the theory behind them) exaggerate and hence draw attention to visual 'ambiguities': the shadow of a swan or the outline of an elephant, for instance, in *Swans into Elephants*.

The Dali example introduces again some of the themes of Chapter 3. There it was argued that we ought not to think of the relationship between art and reality as one of correspondence, meaning that art exactly reflects reality. Rather, art enhances our understanding by providing us with images and perspectives through which everyday experience may be seen afresh. The general theme is then to see that representation in the visual arts is not to be thought of as copying and that even the attempt to capture the purely visual is not a matter of passively recording what is seen. Rather the painter gets us to attend to our visual experience in certain ways. Monet's painting of the Gare St-Lazare is in one sense a picture of what is actually seen, but in another it is not, because normally our minds would supply details that are cloaked by the steam and the sunlight. Monet's achievement is to get us to attend to one usually neglected aspect of our experience. Dali's Surrealist paintings, on the other hand, can hardly be said to depict real experiences, yet we must admit that the visual ambiguities in his pictures are merely exaggerations of real features of our visual experience. Dali creates an alternative experience rather than capturing the visual in our normal experience, and at the same time his creations can be seen to be explorations of that experience. The same can be said for the engravings of M.C. Escher, many of which are now famous for just this reason. These explore perspective. The eye is drawn around, for instance, a waterfall. Each level seems lower than the one before, yet somehow as the eye moves round we reach the top of the waterfall again. These engravings are not merely technical puzzles;

they show how the mind and thus experience may be manipulated in the perception of the visual.

To construe visual art as a medium for the enhancement and exploration of visual experience does not trivialize it. It also allows us to make sense of certain important developments in the history of contemporary painting. But if this were all that could be said for visual art as a form of understanding human experience, we would lack any explanation of the importance of representation in our search for an adequate theory of art. On the face of it, there is no special role for representation in 'the foregrounding of the visual'. This means that as an explanation of the value of the visual arts, such a theory of painting is skewed in the direction of modern developments, and gives little or no account of many of the great achievements of the past. Additionally, though painting might in these ways reveal interesting aspects of our strictly visual experience, the strictly visual is a small item in our experience as a whole. If painting cannot move beyond the visual, it is of limited value and interest.

Visual art and the non-visual

Can the non-visual be portrayed by visual means? There is an abstract painting by Mondrian entitled *Broadway Boogie-Woogie*. As the title suggests, the picture aims in some sense to present in a purely visual medium a dimension of the same thing that is found in boogie-woogie sound. This move across the senses is sometimes called 'synesthesia' and Gombrich has argued that, once we have understood it properly, Mondrian's picture is a good, if limited example of it (Gombrich 1987: 367–9). Now while it would be difficult to deny that, as a matter of brute experience, seeing a colour, say, can cause someone to feel tingling in the spine, it is debatable that synesthesia in the pure sense of the word is ever realized. It is certainly remarkable how successfully painters have managed to portray visually the sensual richness of fabrics and so on, such that we might almost speak of their having pictured how these things feel to the touch. Nevertheless, there are strong arguments that these and similar ways of talking about the senses must be regarded as less than literal. Some of the same points arise here as arose in the discussion of music in the previous chapter. Language that appears to bridge gaps between the different senses may be a matter of analogical extension. Let us suppose, then, that the strictly visual is limited in just the way that absolute music is. Even so there is an important difference between the two, and it is just here that representation becomes of consequence. Painting unmistakably has a power to represent that music lacks, and this power to represent is in fact a means of going beyond the strictly visual.

Consider a simple case. Thoughts are not visual; we can hear and understand them but not see them. Yet a cartoon character can be represented as thinking by a simple and well understood graphic device. It might be said that this is not a good case of the visual representation of the non-visual, since the thought within the bubble is usually conveyed by linguistic, not artistic, means. But in fact the thought can often be just as easily represented by a picture. Even small children can readily understand a cartoon without words as meaning 'He's thinking of his cat'. Clearly then, the visual can portray the non-visual. Moreover it can portray states of emotion. The child will as easily say of a cartoon character, 'He's missing his cat' even though there are no verbal clues. Now this identification is made possible by a process of highly selective representation on the part of the cartoonist. It is a remarkable fact that a few simple lines can portray a disconsolate face, and the same fact makes it possible for the cartoonist to ensure that what strikes us about the face is its disconsolateness.

The cartoon is a simple example. In the history of art there are many more sophisticated ones, often portraits which speak volumes about mind and temperament – Holbein's *Sir Richard Southwell* or Goya's *King Ferdinand VII of Spain* for example. At the same time it is important to see that these representations are not significant for what they tell us about what their sitters looked like – who knows whether Ferdinand really looked as stupid, arrogant, and smug as Goya's portrait? This is a point that Collingwood was anxious to stress in *The Principles of Art*. The aesthetic value and significance of great portraits does not lie in their faithfulness to the sitter, though no doubt most of them are faithful in this respect. Rather, such paintings present us, who are unfamiliar with the appearance of the original subject, with visual images of a state of mind and character which in a similar way to a poetic image can alter our everyday experience, including our emotional experience, by making us more aware of what that experience contains. The representative power of the visual arts, in other words, can enhance our understanding in precisely the general way described in Chapter 3.

Representation may not be the only means by which visual art enhances our understanding of life. The idea behind the Expressionist school of painting was that emotional states could also be portrayed by the more strictly visual. Thus Van Gogh wanted his picture of *The Artist's Room in Arles* to portray restfulness, and expected to accomplish this largely through the use of colour. There are difficulties about sustaining Van Gogh's view of emotion in painting, but it would be something of a digression to examine them properly here. Fortunately we need not consider them because it is sufficient for the general argument about the value of visual art to see that it has the power to portray mental and emotional states, whether this is accomplished solely through representation or by other means as well.

How far can this representational power go? Might it have something to offer in the way of intellectual apprehension of experience as well? Such a claim is made implicitly in a lecture to the British Academy on a cycle of frescoes by Ambrogio Lorenzetti of Sienna. Quentin Skinner claims that it was Lorenzetti, and not the most eminent philosophers of the thirteenth and fourteenth centuries, who 'made the most memorable contribution to the debate' about the ideals and methods of republican self-government. This suggests that Lorenzetti's frescoes can be thought of as structured forms of argument, a suggestion confirmed by the subtitle of the lecture 'The Artist as Political Philosopher'. In fact, upon examination, Skinner means to claim only that an 'ideal of social and political life is being held up for our admiration' in a 'dramatic way', and in his detailed analysis of the frescoes, he refers to such features as the placing of the various figures as an 'apt illustration' of a political theory. Almost nothing is said about how the frescoes might bear out the theory or sustain it as the truth.

Perhaps it is fanciful to suppose that they could. The artist *qua* artist cannot be a political philosopher. Nevertheless, if visual art is to be more than the dramatic or memorable illustration of truths arrived at elsewhere, if it is to be itself a source of human understanding, there must be some fashion in which it *directs* the mind to the apprehension of truth and reality.

We have in fact already encountered two ways in which visual art can do this. First, by forcing our attention to pure visual experience, it may lead us to explore that experience. Second, by providing us with visual images of emotion and character, painting and sculpture may heighten our awareness (not merely our consciousness) of those states in ourselves and in others. But third, if it cannot supply us with any 'philosophy', it may nevertheless broaden the horizons of our understanding by imagining possibilities and giving form to things whose substance is in doubt.

Consider this case. St Teresa of Avila is one of the most famous Christian mystics. It is clear from her own account that she underwent a very intense experience. What is less clear is just how this experience is to be understood. In the descriptions she herself gives, the language used is so closely associated with sexual experience that it raises a doubt about whether her mysticism may have had its origins more in sexual fantasy than in an encounter with the divine. But it is only a doubt because if her experience was a mystical one of peculiar intensity, perhaps the language of sexual excitement is the best available substitute, though a poor one. If we are to rely on her record alone, then, there must be some uncertainty about the nature and reality of her experience.

We might try to settle the question in another way, by denying that there is any such thing as mystical experience, for instance. If so, St Theresa can only have been engaged in sexual fantasy. But this implication and hence the claim upon which it rests is acceptable only if there is no distinguishable difference between the two. It is here that we might make appeal to imagination in the visual arts. Bernini's celebrated sculpture of St Theresa, in Santa Maria della Vittoria in Rome portrays her in a state of ecstasy, and about to be pierced by the angel with his golden arrow. Now there are many interesting things about this work of art, especially given its place in the historical development of art. But a further question is, 'Has Bernini succeeded in imagining a specifically religious state of mind? Is this a convincing representative image of a state of ecstasy other than sexual excitement?' We do not have to be in a position to answer these questions to see their relevance in the present context. If he has succeeded, then nothing has been proved about St Theresa, but what has been shown is that those who want to collapse religious ecstasy into sexual fantasy have overlooked important phenomenological differences of which, in this case, the work of art has made us aware.

Bernini's sculpture may or may not be a well chosen example, but at the very least it points us towards a real possibility: that visual art should contribute to the consideration of wider questions about the possibilities of human experience than those which arise within the confines of our own immediate experience.

If this is true, we have now seen three interesting ways in which visual art may be said to enlarge and enhance our understanding. It is important to record and underline these because only then can we give a satisfactory explanation of relative value in the visual arts. Nothing that has been said is intended to deny that one valuable feature of art is the development of skilful ways of creating beautiful objects. But the same may be said of the art of the jeweller. Many great works in the visual arts are indeed very beautiful and are to be valued as such. Not all are, however, and even among those that are, their beauty does not always exhaust their value. What we now need to ask is whether this other, and I should say deeper, capacity – the ability of the visual arts to enhance our understanding – also has its limits.

One obvious limit is this. The images with which we are presented in painting and in sculpture are essentially static. This is not to say that movement cannot be represented in painting – many of Turner's paintings show just how successfully this can be done (*Steamer in a Snowstorm* is an especially good example). But painting cannot present us with a developing point of view. Although as countless paintings of the Nativity demonstrate, a painting can show more of the significance of a particular event within a known story, it cannot itself tell the story. Of course an artist can paint a series of pictures, like the cycle of frescoes by Lorenzetti already referred to. But he must take a chance as to the order in which the spectator chooses to look at the frescoes, and indeed as to whether those who look at his work continue to see the paintings as importantly related in sequence. If sequential viewing is *not* to be left to chance, but determined by the artist, we must turn from painting and sculpture to another visual art, namely, film, which can transcend the limitations of the static image.

Film as art

The dynamic character of film has been regarded as one of its most important attributes, by both film theorists and the makers of film. The French film
critic and theorist André Bazin says

> photography is a feeble technique in the sense its instanteity compels it
> to capture time only piecemeal. The cinema [by contrast] makes a
> molding of the object as it exists in time and, furthermore, makes an
> imprint of the duration of the object.
>
> (Bazin 1967: 97, brackets added)

In a similar spirit, the great Russian director Sergei Eisenstein identifies
the peculiar strength of montage in the succession of filmic images.

> The spectator is compelled to travel along the selfsame creative road
> that the artist travelled in creating the image. The spectator not only
> sees the represented elements of the finished work, but also experiences
> the dynamic process of the emergence and assembly of the image just
> as it was experienced by the author. . . . [E]very spectator . . . creates an
> image in accordance with the representational guidance suggested by
> the author, leading him to understanding and experience of the authors
> theme.
>
> (Eisenstein 1943: 34)

Eisenstein's view is common, though not universal, among those who
have written about film. In order to understand his view in its proper context, we need to begin by looking at a more sceptical question. The claim
that film may be a more powerful visual art form than painting makes the
assumption that film is indeed an art form. This has been doubted and
continues to be doubted in some quarters. The basis for this doubt usually
arises from the fact that photography is a mechanical art and the corresponding belief that it employs a purely causal process into which artistry
cannot enter.

This doubt about photography has already been addressed in the course
of the discussion, and we need not now rehearse the arguments. It seems to
me evident that choice and deliberation enter into photography in ways that
clearly correspond to all the other arts, and that causality in art is not
restricted to photography. As Noël Carroll remarks,

> When I write a novelistic description of a room and my fingers touch
> the keyboard of my IBM typewriter, the process of printing the words
> is automatic. Is the mechanical process between me and the final text
> any less automatic with the typewriter than with the camera?
>
> (Carroll 1988: 155)

It is worth adding that arguments against photography as an art form could not in any case be applied without amendment to cinema, for although it is true that most contemporary cinema is photography based, its origins lie in the development of moving pictures and projection, not photography, and to this day some animation continues to exploit the development of cinema without recourse to photography.

Despite this rather obvious fact, from time to time, the charge continues to be levelled at film that there is nothing more to it than *mimesis*, in the sense of plain copying. This recurrent doubt is partly explained by the attitudes of those who first used photographic film as a medium. At its inception, film plainly had striking advantages as a method of recording real people and historical events, and was indeed largely valued as such. Second, early use of film for artistic purposes took the form of recording artistic performances. The camera was placed in a fixed position before a stage on which a drama was performed, and the aim of the filmmaker was largely to provide an opportunity for those who were unable to attend the live performance nevertheless to see the drama. In addition to its historical genesis, the view that photography and hence film is mere copying gathered further support from the undeniable facts that the objects in a photograph must 'be there', and the photograph does indeed reproduce them, whereas the objects in a painting or a drawing need not 'be there', and may on occasions be wholly the products of artistic imagination.

Montage versus long shot

The responses of film theorists to this sceptical view can be divided broadly into two groups. First there are those, of whom Eisenstein and Rudolph Arnheim are among the best known, who claim that film has the ability to escape the limitation of what might be called 'inevitable attachment to reality'. Thus, commenting upon the idea that the audience is merely the 'fourth wall' of a stage (the other three being the backdrop and wings), Leon Moussinac says, on the contrary, 'in film the fourth wall of the room in which the action takes place is not simply left out, but ... the camera is brought into the actual room and takes part in the story' (quoted in Arnheim 1958: 54).

Arnheim elaborates upon the idea by remarking that film becomes an art form when the mere urge to record certain actual events is abandoned for 'the aim to represent objects by special means exclusive to film'.

> These means obtrude themselves, show themselves able to do more than simply reproduce the required object; they sharpen it, impose a style upon it, point out special features, make it vivid and decorative. Art begins where mechanical reproduction leaves off.
>
> (*ibid.*: 55)

Arnheim's answer to the sceptic then is to insist that film can leave 'mechanical production' behind, and in this way film becomes an art form. A contrary view is to be found in the voluminous writings of André Bazin. Bazin thinks that it is precisely its capacity to copy what is 'there' that gives film its special role as an art form.

> The aesthetic qualities of photography are to be sought in its power to lay bare the realities. . . . Only the impassive lens, stripping its object of all those ways of seeing it, those piled up preconceptions, that spiritual dust and grime with which my eyes have covered it, is able to present it in all its virginal purity to my attention.
>
> (Bazin 1967: 15)

These two lines of thought are in large part reflections of different styles of filmmaking. But they are normative as well as descriptive theories and may thus be seen to recommend different techniques of direction. Thus Arnheim's view is both a description and a commendation of films such as Eisenstein's. In these the device of montage, a rapid series of short shots, is used extensively to focus the spectators' attention sharply and drive it through a selection of specific images. Montage departs from how things 'really are', since we do not see the world as a series of discrete visual episodes, and since in Arnheim's view the art in film depends upon such departures from reality, montage is to be commended in the construction of film. Bazin's theory, on the other hand, reflects the style of filmmaking dominant in America in the 1950s, in which much use was made of medium and long shots, which present a wide and continuous visual field, and this is just the sort of 'realistic' filmmaking Bazin commends.

To appreciate the contrast at work in these two views, consider the following simple episode. A family is having a picnic by a river. Unnoticed by her parents, the little girl is stumbling perilously near the water. The family dog barks and runs to the child. The parents are alerted and bring her out of danger. In a long shot of this episode, the camera and the scene would be so arranged that all the actors would be visible all the time. The camera might focus more clearly on one or the other from time to time, but at no point would anything be out of view. To treat the same episode in montage, there would be separate shots of the family, the child, the parents, the dog, the rescue.

One obvious difference between the two techniques is that montage focuses the spectator's attention in a way that long shots do not. Those like Eisenstein and Arnheim who favour montage, do so because it enables the filmmaker to select and emphasize what they want the spectator to see. 'It is essential', Arnheim says, 'that the spectator's attention should be guided' (Arnheim 1958: 44). In the episode just imagined, montage makes clear the role of the dog's barking. By contrast, Bazin and others favour long shot over montage chiefly because (they allege) this is how we actually see things.

We do not see events in separate snapshots. While in montage selected shots are artificially collated, in a long shot the camera follows the actors just as our eyes would, and this is why it is more 'realistic'. More importantly perhaps, they reject deliberate selection on the part of the filmmaker, believing it desirable to preserve a measure of uncertainty in order to preserve the spectator's freedom of interpretation. In the passage omitted from the quotation above, Bazin says, 'It is not for me to separate off, in the complex fabric of the objective world, here a reflection on a damp sidewalk, there a gesture of a child'. Spectators must be left to make such selections for themselves.

There is, however, something of a tension in Bazin's view. On the one hand he commends 'realistic' film because it 'lays bare realities', while at the same time wanting to preserve 'ambiguity'. But if viewers are to have reality forced upon their attention, this necessarily eliminates at least some of the ambiguity. It is not hard to see that at the level which matters, the dispute between montage and long shot is based upon a false dichotomy. Many of the differences between montage and long shot are matters of degree rather than kind, and the exclusive merits of each need not be in competition. The length of a shot is to be understood as merely the time given to the spectator, and this can obviously be longer or shorter. In montage it is less, in long shot more, but there is no radical difference between the two. If the collation of short shots serves some purposes and the presentation of long shot others, a director is free to employ both at different points in the film.

Bazin thinks that the ability of film to 'copy' gives it the means to direct our attention to reality. He would of course be wrong to draw the implication that the director is in any sense passive. The plot, direction, angle, and focus of every long shot still has to be worked out. The point to stress is, whatever else they may disagree on, the 'realists' as represented by Bazin share the view of the 'creationists' as represented by Arnheim: the value and interest in film are in its revelatory properties and these properties derive in large part from artistic use of the camera. In other words, both schools of thought in classical film theory aim to demonstrate that film is an art, one by showing how far the use of the camera enables us to depart from mere reproduction, the other how the peculiar power of photographic reproduction gives film an artistic advantage that other art forms cannot enjoy.

The interesting question for our purposes, then, is not whether film can be an art, but whether these theorists have succeeded in isolating features of film that will give it distinctive value. On this of course they differ, and not only between a preference for montage as opposed to long shot. They differ in fact over whether film is strengthened or weakened as an art by the introduction of sound. And this brings us back to the issue with which this section began. Is film a more powerful visual art than painting, or does it gain this additional power precisely in so far as it ceases to be a purely visual art?

'Talkies'

Arnheim believed that with the introduction of sound, the art of film had effectively been destroyed just when its truly artistic purposes had begun to be realized. His reasons for thinking this were partly that black and white film, without the stereoscopic vision of long shot, can provide unique visual experiences, and partly that film offers us a way of exploring the visual dimension of experiences that are not purely visual in reality. He gives the following example of the first.

> [I]n Jacques Feyder's *Les Nouveaux Messieurs* . . . [t]wo lovers . . . are seen in conversation, with their heads close together. Then a close up is shown in which half the picture is covered by the dark silhouette of the back of the man's head (the camera being placed behind him) and this head partially conceals the woman's full face, of which the remainder is seen in bright light. [. . .]
>
> The reduction of depth serves . . . to emphasize the perspective superposition of objects. In a strongly stereoscopic picture the manner in which these various objects are placed relative to one another does not impose itself any more than it does in real life. The concealing of certain parts of the various objects by others that come in front seems chance and unimportant. Indeed, the position of the camera in a stereoscopic picture seems itself to be a matter of indifference inasmuch as it is obvious that there is a three dimensional space which may just as easily, and at the next moment probably will, be looked at from another point of view. If however, the effect of depth is almost negligible, the perspective is conspicuous and compelling. . . . There is no leeway between the objects: they are like flat surfaces stuck over one another, and seem almost to lie on the same plane.
>
> Thus the lack of depth brings a very welcome element of unreality into the film picture. Formal qualities, such as the compositional and evocative significance of particular superimpositions, acquire the power to force themselves on the attention of the spectator. A shot like that described above where half of the girl's face is cut off by the dark silhouette of the man's head, would possess only a fraction of its effectiveness if there were a strong feeling of space.
>
> (Arnheim 1958: 54–7)

One of the examples Arnheim gives of the second special effect of film, namely, to draw attention to non-visual phenomena in visual terms, is now well known.

> [A] revolver shot might occur as the central point of a silent film; a clever director could afford to dispense with the actual noise of the shot. . . . In Josef von Sternberg's *The Docks of New York* a shot

104

is very cleverly made visible by the sudden rising of a flock of scared birds.

(*ibid.*: 37)

What Arnheim is chiefly concerned with and spends a long time detailing is the peculiar power of film as a *visual* art. Technical advances in filmmaking, especially colour and sound, precisely because they allowed greater naturalism, threatened this status, in his view, while to the 'realists' they brought greater representative power. But in fact, with the benefit of hindsight we can see that there is no need for exclusiveness on either side. Those features that impressed Arnheim are still available to the modern filmmaker; a revolver shot can still be 'made visible' in the way he describes, and perhaps to even greater effect just because sound as a normal accompaniment is the order of the day. So too with colour. Steven Spielberg's film *Schindler's List* is shot in sepia, which allows him to use red in just one scene to give special prominence and significance to a young Jewish girl. A similar point can be made about the technical preferences of Bazin and others. A film that uses montage or close-up extensively can also use long shots in which the camera follows the action continuously. Nor need we share Bazin's anxieties over montage's curtailing the interpretative freedom of the spectator; interpretative freedom (if it is indeed properly thought of in this way) merely enters at a higher level in understanding the significance, rather than the content, of the images in montage.

Nevertheless, there is a point of some consequence here. Film has advanced beyond the silent screen. Arnheim regarded the arrival of sound as a misfortune because it removed film from the sphere of the purely visual, and this he thought to be an impoverishment. Others have regarded the same development as an enrichment, since it supplies us with a medium of greater power for aesthetic purposes. But both views coincide with the fact that modern film cannot be regarded as a purely visual art.

Does this matter? In one sense, contrary to Arnheim, it does not. He thinks that artistry in filmmaking requires that we 'consciously stress the peculiarities' of the medium. But he gives no reason for this, and his examples and explanation of artistry in filmmaking aim to show only that films can go beyond mere recording to accomplish artistic purposes. He appears to conflate the idea that film has distinctive ways of achieving such purposes with the idea that it is only through these distinctive methods that film can achieve them. But this is obviously wrong. We can agree that montage is a method unique to film and at the same time hold that an accompanying sound track can make a film sequence still more arresting. To appreciate film as an art we certainly need to stress its distinctive powers, but this does not warrant the sort of purism Arnheim seems to think it does.

On the other hand, it is true that modern film has gone beyond the purely visual. While the techniques of close up, montage, special lighting, and so on are important, acting, dialogue, soundtrack, are no longer mere additions, but integral parts of filmmaking. It is odd that Arnheim should have regretted the introduction of sound, since the soundtrack of a film is no more 'mere recording' than is the photography, and can be used in many of the ways that Arnheim thinks important. Aural 'montage' is a familiar and useful technique. Loud noises can be used to much the same effect as the looming shapes he discusses.

Arguably such additions are not to be regretted but welcomed as ways in which we can both exploit visual experience and transcend its limitations. It has sometimes been claimed that in film almost all artistic limitations are overcome. It represents in such a way as to explore formal visual properties; it contains dramatic action as in a play while nevertheless retaining the greater control over spectator attention that directed photography allows; it provides the fullest possible context in which dialogue is made significant; it employs sound effects and, most notably, it supplies music with the visual clues necessary for the realization of its evocative powers. In short film is the supermedium, the sort of thing that Wagnerian opera aimed (but arguably failed) to be. In such a view nothing could be sillier than Arnheim's anxieties about departing from an original purity. Every technical advance is gain.

The 'auteur' in film

Yet, if the conclusions of the preceding discussion are correct, film should have come then to outclass other art forms, and the major works of modern art should be films. Neither of these things is so. What explains this gap between potential and actuality? Some of the explanation is sociohistorical. The power of film is equally great as a means of entertainment, and the money for moviemaking has come largely from the entertainment industry. Much of the effort in filmmaking therefore has been devoted to this end, and to its commercial success. It is as if the primary efforts of painters had been devoted to wallpaper design. The contingent associations that this fact has given rise to have further circumscribed film's actual use as an artistic medium, with the result that among the countless films that have been made, relatively little of lasting significance has emerged.

No doubt this is true, but it is not the whole story. There is something in the nature of film itself which must be woven into a complete explanation of film as art. We should observe first of all that the move to a supermedium is not *all* gain. There can also be loss. Where, for instance, music accompanies film it is possible for one to vie with the other for our attention, with the result that the impact of each, far from being heightened, is diminished. It is sometimes the case that the score for a film, or part of it, becomes a recognized piece of music in its own right, something that is worth listening to and better listened to on its own. (Some of Shostakovich's music is a good example.) Given modern conditions for the commissioning of music this may be an important way in which new compositions emerge, but taken by itself it is a mark of failure. The desirability of 'liberating' the music from the film demonstrates the existence of fragmentation where there ought to have been organic unity.

The potential scope for such fragmentation in filmmaking is immense. A film comprises the following elements: plot, dialogue, action, direction, screenplay, camera work, editing, score, and special effects. When academy awards are made, frequently a film scores highly in only a few, sometimes only one, of these respects. Superb camera work can record a poor plot, brilliant special effects may follow ham acting, memorable music may accompany a trivial story, and so on. Of course, paintings, novels, and musical composition can also be analysed by distinct elements which may differ in quality or even conflict with one another – colour versus subject, characters versus dialogue, harmony versus melody, for example. But there is still an important difference; in all these cases it is just such tensions that ought to be resolved by the creative imagination of a single mind, the painter, the author, the composer, whose greatness is measured in part by the degree of imaginative unity achieved. A film on the other hand has no single author.

Or so it can be argued. Another important point of discussion in the philosophy of film has been *auteur* theory, that is, discussion over different accounts of who might be regarded as the *auteur*, or author, of a film. The fact that this is a matter of dispute is a point of difference between film and the other arts to which sufficient attention is not always paid. In all art forms of course more than one party is involved. Books have to be read and music played and listened to, pictures looked at. But the assigning of books to their authors ('Tolstoy's *War and Peace*'), pieces of music to their composers ('Beethoven's *Fifth*'), and pictures to painters is unproblematic. In the case of films this is not so. The most natural candidate for the role of *auteur* is the director. *Citizen Kane* is regularly and repeatedly listed as one of the greatest films ever made and is universally regarded as the work of Orson Welles. But though there are some instances such as this one where there is no practical uncertainty about authorship, this is not generally true. Perhaps in many, even most, films the director is the principal influence on the final form of the film. Even so the role of the director is properly thought of as one of choosing rather than creating; directors do not construct the plot, write the screenplay, work the cameras, build the sets, or compose the score, and only occasionally do they take an acting part. What this means is that his or her relation to collaborators cannot be compared to that of the author of a play and those who perform it. This is demonstrated by the fact that whereas a good play can be performed badly, bad performance in a film makes it to that extent a poor film. Directors of films do not stand in the same relation to the outcome of their efforts as playwrights do to theirs.

It is not a necessary truth about film that it has no single mind at work to control it. One can imagine some one person superhumanly performing all these roles, and it is true that in some of the best films one person has a multiple role. It is perhaps no accident that Orson Welles not only directed *Citizen Kane* but also took the lead role. But it is an important fact about the medium nonetheless that it is a combined effort. Modern film is a multimedia art form and makes a single *auteur* practically impossible. Accordingly its power to transcend the limits of any one medium, the purely visual for example, and to work with dynamic and not merely static images, is offset by its liability to fragmentation. The greater the power, we might say, the harder it is to control. If the greatest works of art are those that direct the attention of the audience to and through an imagined experience which in turn illuminates real experience, this is somewhat paradoxically less likely in film than in other arts despite the powers at its disposal.

Thus Arnheim's purism and his anxiety about the introduction of elements other than the visual, though unwarranted on the basis of the reasons he gives, is not without some foundation. Interestingly Eisenstein, several of whose films are among those most fitted to Arnheim's analysis, went to extraordinary lengths to retain control over every aspect of the finished result. Eisenstein was famous for the large number of immensely detailed drawings, diagrams, and instructions he produced for the guidance of actors, cameramen, and setbuilders. And where he used music he required it to be 'composed to a completely finished editing of the pictorial element' (Eisenstein 1943: 136).

The account of the inherent weakness in film as an art form rests in part on the principle that 'the greater the power, the harder it is to control'. As a general principle in art, however, this is not quite correct. While it is true that the multimedia character of film gives it power, but also gives it potential for fragmentation, it is a mistake to think that such power is possible only through multimedia. In fact, there is a medium that can transcend the limits of the visual, the aural, the static, and so on, namely, language. Language allows us to import the visual, the aural, the narrative, the emotional, and so on in an intellectual rather than a sensual grasp of imagery. It has the power of film, we might say, without the disadvantages. Some of the powers and the problems of the literary arts are among the topics to be considered in the next chapter. But so far as visual art is concerned, the arguments of this chapter give us good reason to conclude that the capacity of film to transcend some of the limitations of the static visual image is not without its drawbacks.

Summary

'Art' is often used to refer to visual art, and painting in particular. This tends to give prominence to the idea that representation is especially important in

art. While it is true that much visual art is representational, representationalism, or the belief that representational accuracy is of greater importance or
value, is mistaken even in painting. Representation is a means and not
an end in art. The ends which it serves may be served in other ways, may
be satisfied in fact by abstract painting. What matters is the value or
importance of these ends. One of these is just to bring to prominence visual
experience itself, but painting can pass beyond the purely visual. Somewhat
suprisingly, it can supply us with images which capture and illuminate the
non-visual – states of emotion and character for instance. What painting
cannot do is depict the dynamic of a narrative sequence. It is here that film,
while also a visual art, succeeds where painting fails. Film has the resources
to construct and display dynamic visual images and may thus transcend the
limitations of the static visual image. Its own weakness arises from the fact
that it is a multi-media art, and this means that it is almost impossible for a
film to be the result of a single directing mind. Films thus tend toward
fragmentation. The sort of transcendence that film makes possible, but
which remains in the control of a single author, seems to be available in
literature which is thus the next art form to be considered in our discussion.

Suggestions for further reading

Philip Alperson (ed.), *The Philosophy of the Visual Arts.*
E.H. Gombrich, *Art and Illusion.*
Richard Wollheim, *Painting as an Art* chap. 1.
V.F. Perkins, *Film as Film.*
Gregory Currie, *Image and Mind: Film, Philosophy and Cognitive Science.*
Noël Carroll, *Philosophical Problems of Classical Film Theory.*

6

---•◎•---

Poetry and paraphrase

We have seen reason to think that art at its best significantly enriches human understanding. This is why, despite all the evident differences, it can justifiably be ranked alongside science in the achievements of the intellect. In the preceding two chapters we have been exploring the problems that arise for this understanding of art when we try to apply it to music and to the visual arts. Both it turns out are importantly limited from this point of view. Once we turn to the literary arts however all such limitations appear to vanish. Since language is the normal instrument for learning and understanding and at the same time the medium of the literary arts, it would seem to follow that literature is perfectly suited to the task of contributing to human understanding.

Unfortunately, the fact that language is a medium common to the literary arts and to other forms of human understanding such as history, philosophy, and the sciences introduces a different, but no less important difficulty. If language in its ordinary everyday form can be used to promote understanding, why should we need, value, or indeed even have literary *artistry*? To put the matter simply, though a little misleadingly, why would we need poetry as well as prose?

Poetry and prose

The eighteenth-century English poet Alexander Pope was the author of a couplet which has become very familiar.

> True wit is nature to advantage dressed,
> What oft was thought, but ne'er so well expressed.

Suppose that this is a proper description of poetic utterance. If it is true that the 'thought' in a poem may be indentified independently of the way it is 'expressed' as Pope seems to suggest, then what the poem has to 'say' can be said in other ways. Where, then, is the advantage in poetical presentation? Why from the point of view of what it has to say about our experience, should we value the poetic form?

Pope's view of poetry was common in the eighteenth century. The great literary critic and conversationalist Dr Samuel Johnson, for instance, believed that the purpose of poetry was to delight and instruct. The instruction lay in the content, the delight in the form. But he differed from Pope in that he further held that the delight which we get from poetry is of limited significance and value. This is why in matters of real import poetry is to be abandoned. To employ poetic devices in the service of religion for instance, so Johnson thought, is to set the serious around with frippery. 'Repentence trembling in the presence the Judge', he says,

> is not at leisure for cadences and epithets. . . . Poetry loses its lustre and its power because it is applied to the decoration of something more excellent than itself. All that pious verse can do is to help the memory, and delight the ear, and for these purposes it may be very useful; but it supplies nothing to the mind.
>
> (Johnson 1906: Vol. 1, 212)

His remarks here are directly concerned with religious verse, but the same view can be extended to any serious poetry, as it generally was in Johnson's time.

This does not necessarily mean that poetry is in every sense redundant. There are several explanations that we could give of its value – one example is that the manner of expression in a good poem is amusing, beautiful, moving, or more easily remembered – all of which usually do apply to poetry. But any such explanation of the value of poetry, because it employs a distinction between the form and the content of a poem, cannot say that poetry *as* poetry enhances the *understanding*; anything that a poem has to say, its 'content', can as satisfactorily, if not as strikingly or as memorably, be said in a prose paraphrase. If this is true , however, from the point of view of any increase in understanding we might hope to gain, the existence of a paraphrase renders the poetry itself superfluous, essentially a matter of decoration. And this would imply that the one art form which appears to have the means of transcending the limitations of all others with respect to understanding – literature – cannot after all be accorded the kind of power and importance that cognitivism in art theory requires.

Consider by way of illustrating this contention some more of Pope's poetry.

> A little learning is a dang'rous thing;
> Drink deep, or taste not the Pierian spring:
> There shallow draughts intoxicate the brain,
> And drinking largely sobers us again.

The first of these lines is so convenient a summary of one fact about human experience that it has taken on the status of a proverb. Probably most people nowadays think it *is* an authorless proverb in fact. The line provides a striking and memorable way of saying something people often have reason to say. But it is a simple matter to say the same thing in other words – people who know only a little about a subject are often strongly inclined to believe themselves to be expert. Pope's comparison between learning and drinking in the last two lines is (or was) novel, but once more the thought behind it is easily expressed without the poetry. The more we know about a subject the more sober a view we are likely to take of it. As far as the *content* of these lines goes, then, paraphrase will do just as well. The value of the poetic version has to lie elsewhere.

There are many examples of poetry in which the meaning of the poem and the manner of its expression can be independently identified. There is plenty of poetry, in other words, which does permit paraphrase without loss of significant content. It is a consequence of this that poetry cannot be said to *require* a unity of form and content. It follows from this that the value of poetry *as such* could not lie in its contribution to our understanding. This is not because poetry cannot have meaning or a 'message', but because, so long as the meaning can be conveyed independently in a paraphrase, the 'message' is not shown or revealed by the poetry; it is merely asserted in a poetic manner of expression. Poetic form in itself then as Johnson claims, 'supplies nothing to the mind'.

If this is true of all poetry, we have to say that the reason to write and read a poem must lie not in its intrinsic character but in its contingent usefulness, as an *aide memoire*, say, or because of the pleasure we derive from it. Such a view, however, has odd implications. It would mean, for example, that the importance of what Shakespeare's plays have to teach and tell us is not intrinsic to them. Even if no one happens to have said the same things, or if Shakespeare said them first, what is insightful and profound in them could as well be stated in other ways, in which case the plays themselves only provide us with a source of entertainment and a storehouse of memorable lines, expressing the sort of thoughts and sentiments people commonly have.

Now there is no doubt that poetry can be a pleasure to read and listen to, and that poetic devices can be employed and exploited for the purposes of amusement. But the clearest examples of this – the poems of Lewis Carroll in *Alice in Wonderland*, or Edward Lear, for instance – though they are good fun, are also clearly examples of less than serious poetry. Lear's poem 'The Owl and the Pussycat' does not aim to 'say' anything.

> The owl and the pussycat went to sea
> In a beautiful pea-green boat
> They took some honey, and plenty of money
> Wrapped up in a five-pound note.

Indeed at the extreme, such poems do not even *mean* anything. Take the first verse of Lewis Carroll's *Jabberwocky*:

> 'Twas brillig, and the slithy toves
>   Did gyre and gimble in the wabe:
> All mimsy were the borogoves,
>   And the mome raths outgrabe.

Both poems are fun to read and listen to, but they are clearly to be distinguished from serious poetry. Serious and substantial poetry may give pleasure as well, of course, but it also aims to be and is generally regarded as being deeply concerned with some aspect of human experience. But what then is the crucial difference between the two?

The unity of form and content

Some writers have thought that the attempt to paraphrase a poem is always a mistake. Cleanth Brooks, in a chapter of *The Well Wrought Urn* entitled 'The Heresy of Paraphrase', writes as follows:

> We can very properly use paraphrases as pointers and as shorthand references provided that we know what we are doing. But it is highly important that we know what we are doing and that we see plainly that the paraphrase is not the real core of meaning which constitutes the essence of the poem.
>
> (Brooks 1947: 180)

Yet it seems true that there are good poems in which the content and the form are easy to separate. The truth in Brooks's claim is that this is not true of all poetry. There are many poems in which the interconnectedness of image and utterance is so marked that it is difficult to differentiate the two. A verse in which the Metaphysical poet John Donne offers us a summation of Christian doctrine, begins like this:

> We hold that Paradise and Calvary,
> Christ's Cross and Adam's tree, stood in one place;
>   (*Hymn to God my God, in my Sicknesse,* fifth stanza)

The verse comes in the middle of an extended geographical metaphor and it is difficult to see how Donne's conception of the theological relation between pre-Fallen Man and the Crucifixion could be otherwise expressed. Any attempt at paraphrase which departed from the geographical idiom would lose not just the form but the essential idea at work in the poem. The thought and the manner of expression are in this way inseparable. Nor is this close association between thought and image a peculiarity of the Metaphysical poets or even of poetry with metaphysical or theological aspirations. In *Portrait of a Lady*, T.S. Eliot has this marvellous description:

113

We have been, let us say, to hear the latest Pole
Transmit the Preludes, through his hair and finger-tips.

These two lines capture not only a certain style of musicianship but an attitude to it *and* a further view of that attitude. This complexity can be pointed out, but it would be impossible to say the same thing to the same effect in a paraphrase. This is because the lines do not merely record a scene or episode; they get us to apprehend it in a certain way. It may be incorrect to say that the same idea cannot be conveyed in any other way, but it is clear that paraphrase would require extended explanation and equally clear that this process of spelling everything out would destroy the inner complexity of the lines which makes the poetic expression arresting.

There are countless other examples which might be given, but even these two are sufficient to show that there is poetry in which content and expression are for practical purposes inseparable. With respect to such poetry, paraphrase in the ordinary sense is possible; we can always give a short summary of the general import of a poem. But where content and expression are closely allied in this way, a prose paraphrase however useful for other purposes will always bring with it significant loss of meaning. Given examples of this second sort, as well as those from Pope and others, the possibility opens up of a comparative evaluation between the two. While admitting that poetic form is sometimes largely decorative, it can be argued that not all poetry is of equal value and further that the degree to which poetry cannot be paraphrased is an indication of its worth; inseparability of form and content in a poem is a mark of its quality. We might summarize this normative doctrine in the slogan 'the harder to paraphrase, the greater the poetry'. What reasons are there for believing this?

The idea we are trying to substantiate, in line with earlier arguments, is that if the poetic is to be serious and substantial it must, contrary to Johnson, 'supply the mind' and not merely 'delight the ear'. As we have seen, if the thought in a poem can be restated in prose without significant loss, it cannot be the poem, strictly speaking, which is directing the mind but only what the poem says. What needs to be shown then is that mental direction is sometimes accomplished by the devices of poetry itself – rhythm, rhyme, alliteration, assonance and such, and above all imagery. To show this is to demonstrate that poetic form can be an essential part of what a poem says and not merely an agreeable addition to it.

Figures of speech

Showing that the devices of poetry can themselves contribute to increased understanding encounters an important obstacle. There is a longstanding belief among philosophers not only that poetic devices are at best merely ornamental but that their use actually *diminishes* the prospect of arriving at a proper understanding of reality. One of the best known and most uncompromising expressions of this view is to be found in the seventeenth-century English philosopher John Locke's *Essay Concerning Human Understanding*, a highly influential work in the history of philosophy. According to Locke,

> in discourses where we seek rather pleasure than information and improvement, such ornaments [metaphors, similes and the like] . . . can scarce pass for faults. But yet if we would speak of things as they are, we must allow that all the art of rhetoric, besides order and clearness; all the artificial and figurative application of words eloquence hath invented, are for nothing else but to insinuate wrong ideas, move the passions, and thereby mislead the judgment; and so indeed are perfect cheats: and therefore, however laudable or allowable oratory may render them in harangues and popular addresses, they are certainly, in all discourses that that pretend to inform or instruct, wholly to be avoided.
>
> (Locke 1896: Vol. 2, 146)

What lies at the back of Locke's view as expounded in this passage is the idea that language can be plain and fact stating, or it can be embroidered and embellished by the figures of speech which oratory and poetry usually employ. It is the former which we must use if we are to grasp clearly and plainly truths about the world and human experience. Figures of speech which in flowery and poetical language 'can scarce pass for faults' cloud and distort things. So by this account since plain speech is what understanding requires, the devices of poetry, whatever other values and pleasures they may give rise to, must be abandoned if what we are concerned with is understanding.

This is a familiar view in the history of philosophy, but it is mistaken because it is impossible to purge *any* use of language of literary devices. There is no such thing as the plain speech which Locke imagines. This is evident from a consideration of even mundane levels of language use. Metaphor, simile, analogy, synecdoche, and so on are common in the simplest attempts to understand and explain and are not restricted to poetry or even 'harangues and popular addresses'. Take the common expressions 'I *see* what you mean', 'I *follow* your argument', or 'I *get* your point'. These are all metaphors, but if we were to try purge them from argument and explanation, what could we put in their place? It does not take much imagination to manufacture endless examples of the same sort – *catching* the bus, letting wine *breathe*, *spinning* a tale, and so forth. Even Locke, contrary to the doctrine he is defending, happily (and effectively) employs metaphor himself when he describes literary devices as 'perfect cheats'.

What is true for ordinary language is also true for more specialized uses. It is just as impossible to engage in science, history, sociology, or philosophy without figures of speech. We say that electricity *flows* in a *current*, magnetic *forces* arrange themselves in *fields*, electoral *campaigns* are *fought*, and that social *pressures mount*. Were we systematically to expunge all such literary devices from the natural and human sciences of every type of literary device, we should not find ourselves enabled to apprehend reality in an undistorted form, but rather rendered silent. The question whether 'poetic' utterance, where this means the use of metaphor, simile, and so on, can direct the mind has to be answered in the affirmative. The important question is not whether it does this, which it obviously does, but to what end it may be done and what counts as doing it well.

There is no one answer to the first of these questions. Figures of speech are common to many different uses of language. As well as having an important role in scientific and historical investigation, they are to be found in advertising, speech making, and religious practice as well as the literary arts. It follows from this that although figurative language is an important feature of poetry and works of literature, this is not their distinguishing feature. We will not have understood the nature and value of imaginative literature until we have isolated the special use to which the poet and the novelist puts such devices in literature.

Expressive language

Imaginative and clever use of language can entertain and delight us. Everyday puns are straightforward instances of this, and more sophisticated 'literary' examples are easy to find, in the writings of Oscar Wilde, for instance, whose wit has a very marked linguistic component. In short, the use of language can in itself be amusing. But a highly literary use of language can go beyond the amusing. It can, for instance, supply us with heightened and more effective means of expression. The commonest cases of this are to be found in proverbs, such as the one cited and originating with Pope, where a specific image or a memorable phrase expresses our own attitude better than we could ourselves. One of the commonest occasions for this use of poetic language is in the expression of religious feeling and sentiment. In fact, there is much to be learnt about poetry and literature by thinking about hymns, psalms, and set forms of prayer.

The Anglican *Book of Common Prayer*, written for the most part by Thomas Cranmer, and the Christian hymns of Isaac Watts and Charles Wesley are very good examples of literary writing that is useful from an expressive point of view. All of them have provided generations of English-speaking Christians with the means of giving expression to religious feeling. But hymns and prayers are also good instances of the importance of the distinction between 'being an expression of' and 'being expressive of' discussed in Chapter 2, a distinction which needs to be borne in mind if the value of literature is to be understood properly.

In hymns and set prayers beautiful and affective language can obviously serve as the means of expressing the religious emotions the people who use them are actually feeling. However, it is doubtful if this is often their real function, because ordinary people only rarely feel the elevated and refined emotion that religious poetry typically expresses. Most hymn singers are not themselves mystics. Consequently it is only rarely that the hymns they sing express what they are actually feeling. More usually, religious poetry is 'expressive of' religious emotion rather than an 'expression of' it. The literary critic Helen Gardner makes this point.

> A complaint is often made that . . . it is absurd for a congregation of ordinary wayfaring Christians to be expected to sing sentiments that even saints can hardly be expected to feel habitually. There is a well-known joke about the Duchess singing in a warm tremulo 'Were the whole realm of nature mine, That were an offering far too small' while she hunted in her purse for a sixpence to put on the plate. But the joke is misconceived. A hymn is not intended to express the personal warmth of feeling of an individual singer, but a common ideal of Christian feeling and sentiment which the Christian congregation acknowledges as an ideal.
>
> (Gardner 1983: 156)

Gardner's point is that the sublime expression of feeling may serve purposes other than actually expressing feelings. A hymn that is truly 'expressive of' feeling enables ordinary worshipers to apprehend and understand something of the nature of Christian devotion, whether or not they actually experience feelings of devotion within themselves on any particular occasion that the hymn is sung. An expressive hymn may at some point allow worshipers to come to have such feelings, but whether it does or not it can still provide a measure of insight and understanding in regard to those feelings. In other words the imaginative expression of religious feeling and sentiment *can* 'supply something to the mind'.

This is not a peculiarity of hymns or of religion. The same point may be made about other forms of expressive poetry. A lot of John Donne's love poetry has an intensity which cannot be the standard for the much more mundane romances that most of us have known. Yet even if we never feel such intense sentiments towards anyone, we can nonetheless acknowledge them as comprising *a* state of the human mind and from there be led to a better understanding of that state. Similarly, First World War poetry, which includes both Rupert Brooke's patriotic fervour and Wilfred Owen's hatred of war, arose from an historical episode of great intensity which none of the poetry's contemporary readers have experienced. It is a mistake to think of this poetry as an expression of that experience, because not having been through the war ourselves we could not tell whether it was an adequate expression or not. Indeed even if we had been in the war, it would be impossible to tell if the poetry was an adequate description of *their* experience. But if instead we think of it as *expressive* of attitudes and emotions, these problems disappear; its value can be seen to lie in and be assessed according to its power to reveal and make intelligible the experience of war. In short, we learn from expressive poetry.

Poetic devices

The questions now arise: 'How do poetic devices perform this act of revelation? How do they direct the mind?' In formulating an answer to these questions it is useful to recall the parallel between art and logic that was drawn in Chapter 3. Arguments, which are governed by logic, direct the mind by steering our thoughts through patterns of validity, and the task of logicians is to devise generalized accounts of these patterns. It is, however, a mistake to think of the principles of logic as providing us with an *a priori* checklist of valid and invalid moves. In reality, arguments, even in philosophy where factual evidence plays a very small part, are complex. They do not follow simple forms and need to be considered in detail as free standing pieces of thought. The devising and application of logically valid formulae may sometimes assist in producing greater clarity of argumentative structure, but they do not provide us with a general and semi-automatic method of testing for validity, and have little to say about the loose inductive reasoning we most usually employ. In other words, the discipline of logic is not specially useful when it comes to deciding upon the cogency of actual arguments. Similarly, the ways in which poetic devices – rhythm and rhyme, metaphor, assonance, alliteration, onomatopeia, and so on – direct our attention and work together to weave a composite image upon which a poem focuses our minds can only be formulated and generalized about to a degree. As in the case of philosophical arguments, each poem must be examined in its own right, and this is the business of literary criticism, not of art theory.

Still, if we are to conclude that poetry does indeed direct the mind, some indication needs to be given of the ways in which literary devices can serve this end, and so the next task is to indicate and illustrate a few poetic devices and how they work.

The first and most obvious of these is the use of sound and stress. Indeed in the absence of any better definition, poetry can best be characterized as the deliberate use of sound and stress in language, although of course it is not only this. Where the sense or meaning of a sentence lies is a very large philosophical topic. Using a distinction of the German philosopher Gottlob

Frege, we may say that the meaning of an utterance combines sense and force, and it is not hard to see that the force of an utterance (and possibly the sense as well) depends in part upon stress and inflexion. The simple sentence 'He was there' is an assertion or a query depending upon whether I raise or lower my intonation on the last word. Poetry works upon facts like these and uses patterns of sound and stress to oblige us to read and to hear a line in one particular way. A simple example of this is to be found in Keats's sonnet *On First Looking into Chapman's Homer.*

> Oft of one wide expanse had I been told
> That deep brow'd Homer ruled as his demesne
> Yet did I never breathe its pure serene
> Till I heard Chapman speak out loud and bold:
> Then felt I like some watcher of the skies
> When a new planet swims into his ken.
>
> (lines 5–10)

The first four lines here prepare us for the momentous discovery of Homer through the good offices of Chapman, and the placing of 'Then' at the beginning of the fifth line forces us to focus upon the culmination. To see this, compare 'I felt then ...' The effect is quite different. There are in fact two devices at work here, stress and word order, but the sound of words themselves can also be used to create special effects, the reinforcement of an image, for instance. The fourth stanza of Hopkins's *Wreck of the Deutshland* reads:

> I am soft sift
> In an hourglass – at the wall
> Fast, but mined with a motion, a drift.

It is impossible to say 'soft sift' without an audible reminder of the image employed. Hopkins combines the use of sound and stress in fact. The emphasis appropriately falls on 'Fast' only to be eroded by the alliteration of 'mined' and 'motion' which audibly emphasizes the idea of slow but inevitable movement.

A second poetic method is what we might call 'wordplay', the distortion of language and syntactic structure. There are poems where this is done for fun – Lewis Carroll's *The Jabberwocky* which was quoted earlier for instance – but it is not hard to find examples of the same thing serving more serious purposes, manipulating a reader's previous knowledge in new directions. The opening line of *The Calls,* an unfinished poem by Wilfred Owen, runs:

> A dismal fog-hoarse siren howls at dawn.

This line is so constructed that to the very last moment we expect (and are expected to expect) the familiar word 'foghorn'. We only register in retrospect the occurrence of something different and unfamiliar. The principal effect of this is to draw out the element of 'fog' in the word 'foghorn' even though this word is unused and thus to emphasize an element which both ordinary and metaphorical uses of this common word have largely suppressed. 'Fog-hoarse' is an invented portmanteau word which captures elements of two familiar words. This juxtaposition of the familiar and the unfamiliar forces us to hear and to consider afresh things to which we would otherwise pay little attention. 'Playing' with words in this fashion is chiefly effective as a device for disturbing expectation. It is given extensive use in the poetry of Gerard Manley Hopkins. Hopkins does not merely combine existing elements in unusual ways. He makes one part of speech into another, constructs sentences and phrases whose grammar sounds nearly correct, and largely by the use of sound and stress patterns which the ear has to follow shakes up the expected order. For example:

> As kingfishers catch fire, dragonflies draw flame;
> As tumbled over rim in roundy wells
> Stones ring; each tucked string tells, each hung bell's
> Bow swung finds tongue to fling out broad its name;
> Each mortal thing does one thing and the same:
> Deals out that being indoors each one dwells;
> Selves – goes itself; *myself* it speaks and spells,
> Crying Whát I dó is me: for that I came.

These lines are quite hard to say. (Even harder is Hopkins's poem *Harry Ploughman*.) It is almost impossible to stress them in ways other than those intended, and the distorted grammatical constructions force our attention on what is being said. Both sound and structure lead to the invented verb 'selves', which is of course a summation of the thought of the poem.

Grammatical distortion may also be used to enliven an image or mental picture. Here is Donne in *The Progresse of the Soule*, describing the movements of the mandrake as it stirs from its 'darke and foggie plot'.

> And as a slumberer stretching on his bed
> This way he this, and that way scattered
> His other legge.

>   (Stanza XV)

'This way he this' is not grammatically correct but for that very reason highly effective in creating before our minds a striking picture of the first stirrings of the mandrake.

Donne also provides us with an example of a third poetic device, which may work to similar ends, namely the accumulation of imagery. A poem can work to draw out or suppress the normal associations we make not by word play or grammatical distortion but by the systematic assemblage of unusual figures of speech. Consider *The Sunne Rising*. In common thinking the sun has, so to speak, a good reputation. It is easily associated with positive ideas – light, life, warmth, and so on. To draw attention to a quite different attitude generated by contexts and occasions when the sun is unwelcome requires a special effort, and Donne uses a sustained sequence of unlikely images to accomplish this.

> Busie old foole, unruly Sunne
> Why dost thou thus,
> Through windowes, and through curtaines call on us?
> Must to thy motions lovers' seasons run?
> Sawcy pedantique wretch, go chide
> Late schoole boyes, and sowre prentices,
> Go tell Court-huntsmen, that the King will ride,
> Call country ants to harvest offices;
> Love, all alike, no season knowes, nor clyme,
> Nor houres, dayes, months, which are the rags of time.

The opening words of the stanza set the tone. Donne piles contemptible references one upon the other (including the reference to King James VI and I's addiction to hunting), and the rhythm contributes to this effect by driving us through all these references to 'rags' in the last line as their culmination. The effect of this is that he is able to retain the generally favourable associations of the sun, which a few images will hardly destroy, while at the same time comparing it unfavourably with the relative value of his lover. So he continues:

> Thy beames, so reverend, and so strong
> Why shouldst thou thinke?
> I could eclipse and cloud them with a winke,
> But that I would not lose her sight so long.

One final example of poetic method is often referred to as dramatic irony, but it is more instructive to call it multilayered representation. A multilayered poem trades on another familiar feature of language: ambiguity and the possibility of multiple interpretation. By the systematic exploitation of differing shades of meaning, a set of utterances and images may be made to present us simultaneously with more than one perspective. Something of this sort was found in the lines of Eliot's *Portrait of a Lady*, but a more sustained example is Robert Browning's *My Last Duchess*. This poem takes the form of a monologue by the duke as he shows an unnamed visitor a portrait of his wife now dead. What he reveals unintentionally, as the monologue proceeds, is an attitude and a history which he would be at great pains to deny. In fact, he has had her murdered out of peculiar sort of jealousy and finds the inanimate portrait more suited to his purposes than the living woman whose portrait it is.

>   She had
> A heart . . . how shall I say? . . . too soon made glad,
> Too easily impressed; she liked whate'er
> She looked on, and her looks went everywhere.
>   [. . .] She thanked men – good; but thanked
> Somehow . . . I know not how . . . as if she ranked
> My gift of a nine-hundred-years-old name
> With anybody's gift.
>   [. . .] she smiled, no doubt,
> Whene'er I passed her; but who passed without
> Much the same smile? This grew; I gave commands;
> Then all smiles stopped together. There she stands
> As if alive.

In the course of the poem Browning manages to represent the duke's thought in language which reveals an external perspective on the duke's attitude and conduct from which his motivation seems mad, and at the same time the duke gives us access to the internal mindset from which his own mad jealousy seems eminently reasonable. The deliberate employment of multilayered language is doubly revealing of the duke's mentality and so provides us with a more rounded understanding of a certain sort of mentality; we see both how it is and how it feels.

The use of sound and stress, word order, the distortion of grammar, accumulation of imagery, and construction of multilayered language are all devices by which poetry may be said to reveal or show things, analogous to forms of reasoning by which an argument might show or an experiment uncover something. There are of course important differences, but it does not seem misleading to describe the devices identified here as means by which the mind is directed. To speak of poetry in this way is not to suppose that what is revealed or shown is incontestable, any more than a belief in the power of dialectic to lead us to the truth implies that every argument must supply a conclusive demonstration of the thesis it means to support. We can be led in many different and competing directions by arguments and experiments which all claim validity, and so too we may expect poetic revelation to throw up a variety of images for our consideration. But enough has been said to establish the claim that poetic form is not just an agreeably ornamental way of saying things whose truth or substance is to be established in some other way. The relation between what is said in poetry and how it is said can be more intimate than that.

However, even if it is accepted that poetry as a form of understanding does not yield to paraphrase without significant loss there is a further question for this chapter to address – can the same be said of the other literary arts? The poetic forms described and discussed are closely connected with poetry narrowly understood. Other literary arts have other forms, and it needs to be shown that these are also ways of directing the mind to a better apprehension of some aspect of human experience. Can storytelling, whose form is narrative, be used in this way?

Narrative and fiction

The device of multilayered representation is to be found in novels as well as in poetry. A striking counterpart in this respect to Browning's *My Last Duchess* is Kazuo Ishiguro's novel *The Remains of the Day*, subsequently made into a highly successful film. Ishiguro's story is set in the England of the 1950s. The principal character is a butler, Stevens, who takes a few days' holiday motoring across the countryside with the ultimate purpose of seeking out a former colleague. The journey provides the occasion and the context for extended reminiscences of previous, rather more glorious periods of service. The story is told in the first person from the butler's point of view, and to a degree Stevens reminisces in order to construct an *apologia*, a self-justification of his past actions and attitudes. Nevertheless, in the telling the reader is led to see the butler's life from several different points of view. As in Browning's poem, Ishiguro uses his story to draw our attention to the contrast and complementarity of 'how it is' with 'how it feels'. One of the most notable instances of this is the butler's recollection of the night his father died, also the night of a major social event in the household. What emerges is both a strong sense of absurdity arising from Stevens's belief that the trivial requirements of social grandees generate duties strong enough to call him away from the deathbed of a parent, and at the same time we get a sense of the perspective from which his doing so has a certain moral substance to it.

Some of the other devices which typify poetry can be found at work in novels. But here the devices take on a special role in contributing to the business of storytelling. There is something comparable to Donne's accumulation of imagery in the opening pages of Dickens's *Bleak House*. The plot of *Bleak House* revolves around a law case of great complexity that seems to have been lost permanently in the labyrinthine structures of the English legal system of the nineteenth century. The result is that none of the parties or their lawyers understand any longer what the legal point at issue is. The novel's second paragraph begins:

> Fog everywhere. Fog up the river, where it flows among green aits and meadows; fog down the river, where it rolls defiled among the tiers of shipping and the waterside pollutions of a great (and dirty) city. Fog on the Essex marshes, fog on the Kentish heights. Fog creeping into the cabooses of collier-brigs; fog lying out on the yards and hovering in the rigging of great ships; fog drooping on the gunwales of the barges and

small boats. Fog in the eyes and throats of ancient Greenwich pensioners, wheezing by the firesides of their wards; fog in the stem and bowl of the afternoon pipe of the wrathful skipper down in his close cabin; fog cruelly pinching the toes and fingers of his shivering little 'prentice boy on deck. Chance people on the bridges peeping over the parapets into a nether sky of fog, with fog all around them.

Dickens pursues this compelling description of the physical condition of the river into the surrounding streets to Lincoln's Inn Hall and finally into the courtroom. As he does so he converts, almost imperceptibly, the literal fog of the river into the metaphorical fog of the court case. 'Never can there come fog too thick, never can there come mud and mire too deep, to assort with the groping and floundering condition [of] this High Court of Chancery.'

The fog, both literal and metaphorical, occupies several pages during which a single master image of enveloping obscurity is created before we reach the first spoken words in the story, from the Lord High Chancellor who sits 'in the midst of the mud and the heart of the fog'; thus Dickens obliges us to take a certain view of the venerable legal persons and procedures with which he is concerned.

The example from *Bleak House* shows that imagery in narrative can be used in a fashion similar to ways in which poetically constructed lines can. This is not surprising. One of narrative's distinguishing features is that it presents material in an order – beginning, middle, and end. Accordingly, just as a poet may use sound and stress to get us to hear and understand words in a certain way, so an author can construct a story that obliges us to attribute a certain significance to the events related. Moreover, this can be done in ways peculiar to narrative that have no obvious poetic counterpart (ignoring the complications introduced by the hybrid, epic or narrative poetry). An author can choose to keep the reader in ignorance for a time and thus let the relative importance of events emerge in a striking manner. The dénouement of a story can cause us to reinterpret earlier episodes, to see in them a significance we did not see on first encounter. In this way our understanding is positively directed by the structure of the story. All sorts of devices of this nature are available to the storyteller. For example, an author might systematically suggest, without explicitly stating, as Katherine Mansfield does in her short story, *The Woman at the Store*, that the first person narrator of the story is male. When it is revealed that she is female, the ambiguity of previous actions and attitudes cannot but be stressed in the mind of the reader.

Devices of this sort can be used to various ends. Storytelling is perhaps the oldest and most persistent form of entertainment, and the special features of narrative construction can be used to entertain. The method of revealing the significance of earlier events in the dénouement is a notable feature of mystery stories, most marked in the most hackneyed kind. In stories of no other evident literary value, Agatha Christie uses this device again and again to entertain the reader by having Hércule Poirot or Miss Marple reveal all. This is not to deny that there can be good stories whose sole purpose is entertainment. A more subtle form of narrative construction, in which earlier events are only properly understood later is to be found in the spy stories of John Le Carré (especially in *The Honourable Schoolboy*), where a large number of fragmentary episodes are related and whose significance is revealed through slow accumulation, a method of construction which has now been copied rather tediously by a large number of less good writers.

Stories can be moving and deeply captivating as well as entertaining – Tolkien's *Lord of the Rings* is a well known example – and the peculiar devices of narrative may be used to these ends also. But narrative can do more than this. Because it has the structure of beginning, middle, and end and is a work of imagination, it can create a unity out of actions and events that the flow of real historical events never has. When did the French Revolution begin and end? This is a foolish question from an historical point of view, even though there will be some wrong answers, because a historian may find significant historical connections before and after any dates we arbitrarily designate. But a novel has a beginning and an end (though not always an ending; some stories are open-ended); there is no 'earlier' or 'later' into which it might be extended. Similarly, there are no 'facts' about the characters or events other than those the author chooses to invent. The world of the novel, unlike that of the history book, does not go beyond that which it contains.

Occasionally, people have thought that the contrast between history and fiction tells against fiction, but this betrays a gross misunderstanding of the possible significance of imaginative literature. Compare hindsight and dénouement. When we apprehend the significance of events in retrospect they are, so to speak, brought fully into the story. They are no longer merely interesting fragments, but integral parts of the whole. The difference between history and fiction is this. While the historian, with the benefit of hindsight *discovers* events to be significantly related and assembles evidence to persuade us of this conclusion, the novelist with imagination *makes* the events relevant, and uses dénouement to direct the mind of the reader into seeing a significant relation between them.

In a parallel fashion, the historian selects out of pre-existing material to make a coherent narrative. It is always possible for the narrative to be amended or corrected by a demonstration of the relevance of some of the material omitted. But nothing of this sort can happen with a novel. However flawed it might be, we cannot correct a novel because there are no events and characters external to it out of which its story is made. Of course a novel can be badly written, its plot inconsistent, and its characters unconvincing. But these are not faults of misrepresentation or omission but of construction – it does not 'hang together' and does not therefore impress upon our minds a single image or set of interrelated images.

If this way of thinking about novels is correct, it may prompt yet another doubt about whether works of fiction can enhance our understanding of human life. If, unlike an historical narrative, a novel is not a selection from a multiplicity of facts, but a free-floating creation of the imagination, how can it have the necessary reference to human experience? The answer to this question has already been surveyed in an earlier chapter. We must think of works of art as being *brought to* experience rather than being *drawn from* it. This is not meant to imply that the author works in a vacuum. It is obvious that in realistic as opposed to fantastical stories, constraints operate that reflect the way life is. Nevertheless, a novel is not to be thought of as providing us with a faithful reflection of experience or a skillful summary of it, but as obliging us to view some aspect of experience through an image which allows us to attain an illuminating perspective upon it.

A simple illustration of this point is to be found in Malcolm Bradbury's novel *The History Man*. One of the best known episodes in this novel is a departmental staff meeting. Commentators have said both that Bradbury has described academic staff meetings with deadly accuracy and that it is a gross distortion. Neither remark is pertinent, however, to the novel as imaginative literature. We should not think of the novelist's purpose as that of recording reality, as a newspaper report might, and thus liable for praise or blame according to the accuracy or inaccuracy of the report. Rather the novelist is engaged in imagining things, and what an episode of this sort offers is an image of a staff meeting; it bears upon real staff meetings just in so far as we can view them afresh in its light, see both how close they come to farce, and how far short they fall of it as well. In brief, a good literary image does not distill experience; it lends perspective to it.

The History Man arguably is essentially a lightweight work. But something similar can be said of much greater works of literature. Take for instance Anthony Trollope's *Lady Anna*, which Trollope himself thought the best of his novels. Lady Anna is the daughter of the Countess Lovell, the course of whose unhappy life has been determined by doubts about the legality of her marriage to the Earl of Lovell. She has spent countless years in trying to secure her rights and title, assisted only by the constant friendship of a Keswick tailor and his son. When the novel opens a law case is underway over the proper beneficiary of the Earl's will, but it soon becomes clear that the Countess's claims are to be vindicated and that her only daughter will accede to a title and great wealth. It then emerges that Lady Anna, in the days of their penury, has engaged herself to the tailor's son.

The larger part of the novel is concerned with both the pressures that operate upon her to break her engagement and with the moral rights and wrongs of her doing so. However, the story is not simply an occasion for airing views about the individual in a class structured society, though there is plainly an element of social comment, if only in the fact that Trollope represents Anna's disregard of social sentiment and convention sympathetically (a fact which partly explains the poor reception of *Lady Anna* on publication). Rather the novel presents us with contrasting images of fidelity – the faithfulness of the old Countess to the cause for which she has given so much, and the faithfulness of Anna to her childhood lover. The first dehumanizes the Countess; the second attests to the true humanity of Anna. Almost everything that happens or is said in the novel contributes to the fashioning of these images, for unlike many Trollope novels, it has virtually nothing in the way of subplot. Through these images we can come to see something of the close connection between on the one hand faithfulness and fanaticism and on the other faithfulness and moral self-indulgence.

But there is more at work than this, and there is a still deeper theme. Throughout the larger part of the novel, Anna has a choice to make. Yet at the same time the final result is never in doubt. What determines this second fact is the conception of womanhood operating in this as in many other of Trollope's novels. At one level Anna can be said to stand out against the norms of her society, can even be said to reject them (though that society, in true English fashion, accommodates itself to her and the tailor in the end), while at another level her behaviour is determined as she herself may be formed, by social norms.

There is not the space here to expand upon or defend a claim about this particular novel, nor is it necessary. The example is intended only as an illustration of the way in which imaginative literature can create images through which the realities of our own experience are illuminated. The episode from *The History Man* may not only amuse but throw interesting light on the experience of those few people who have attended academic staff meetings. *Lady Anna*, on the other hand, enables us as human beings to look again at steadfastness and to see expressed in moral character a conception of half the human race, namely women.

Literature and understanding

The arguments and examples of the last two sections have been intended to show that the literary devices of poetry and the novel can be used to create images which oblige us to view our experience in certain ways and thus illuminate aspects of it. It is this possibility, perhaps relatively rarely realized, that allows us to describe imaginative literature as a source of understanding and which entitles us to attribute considerable importance to it. This claim can be misinterpreted, so it needs to be emphasized that what we have been discussing are possibilities. Normative theory of art is not concerned with the essential nature of 'art' but with explaining the different ways in which it can be of value and the relative importance that we should attach to each. Nothing that has been said in reference to literature (or the other arts), about art and understanding, therefore, implies that imaginative literature uniformly takes the form of a stimulus to human understanding or that it is commonly valued on these grounds. Probably the majority of poems and stories are to be valued because they are amusing, delightful, absorbing, or interesting, in short, a good way of passing the time. But it is also true that there is more than this to the works of Shakespeare, Donne, Racine, Goethe, Tolstoy, and so on. This both explains and justifies us in regarding them as we do. For in great imaginative literature, the devices of poetry, story, and drama can be harnessed, not just to please and entertain, but to create images through which the reader is given an enhanced apprehension of human experience. It is the fact that literature can play this role that gives us reason to value it highly. But in fact, along with other arts, it can go further. Some works do not merely enable us to reflect upon our social and moral experience but actually create the world of that experience for us.

This possibility is most easily illustrated by a non-literary example. The Russian Revolution is an event which played an important part in the conduct of Soviet life and in its relations with the rest of the world for almost seventy years. Yet the 'Russian Revolution' that played this role is not the event historians investigate. What influenced subsequent history through the minds of its participants was an *image* of the Russian Revolution and a sense of its significance only loosely based on historical realities. A powerful version of that image is to be found in Eisenstein's film *Oktober*. There is a famous scene in the film where the proletarian crowd storms the Winter Palace. Enormous, ornate doors, the symbols of power and wealth, are finally forced back by a crowd whose only, but invincible, strength is their solidarity. As far as history goes, no such event ever took place. What explains the power of this scene is not that this is how things actually were, but that this is how things would have had to have been, if the Russian Revolution were truly the event it was widely believed to be. In creating this fine film, however, Eisenstein was not engaged in servile propaganda. No doubt he created his image in ignorance of the real history of events (an ignorance no greater than that of most people at the time, it should be said), but he knew the mentality of the times. More than this, he in turn supplied the times with a clearer image, and henceforth 'The October Revolution' in which the Soviet Union was born and to the defence of which future policy was supposed to be directed, was not the history of 1917 (about which the leaders and people of the former Soviet Union knew and know relatively little), but an image supplied by *Oktober* and other artistic sources.

This is an example of an artistic image not merely reflecting upon, but also structuring, the world of political experience. Art can have the same sort of relation to moral and social experience. One way of putting this point is to say that we should think of artistic creations not as *stereotypes* but as *archetypes.* The images of the greatest artists do not provide us with distillations or summations of the variety in experience (stereotypes) but imaginary models against which we measure that variety (archetypes). And in certain contexts these archetypes may be said to constitute the only reality that there is. Things such as 'a lover', or 'a gentleman', or 'the perfect marriage', or 'a consuming passion', or 'innocence', do not await our discovery in the way that black swans or seams of gold do. They are patterns which structure our approach to the social and moral world in which our lives have to be lived and determine our attitudes to the behaviour of ourselves and others. Works of art that come to have a common currency contribute to the formation of these patterns, and in the case of the greatest works – some of Shakespeare's plays for instance – they have been definitive. Art thus contributes to social and moral experience, and for this reason may be said to provide us with the possibility not only of understanding but also of self-understanding.

Take for example the relationship between two people who might be or become lovers. How are they to think of the relationship it would be good to form and the sort of human pitfalls that lie in their way? Every relationship has an external and an internal aspect and the internal is rarely on view. In the works of imaginative artists this division is surmountable. Fiction and poetry put both mind and action equally on view; characters and events can be seen entire. Novels and poems supply patterns of human relationship, its fulfillment, destruction, or corruption, and these can enter directly into the moral experience of those who are reflecting upon how best to live, because the devices of art reveal to us the internal 'how it feels' as well as the external 'how it is'.

In fulfilling this function literature can be specially important. Music, as we have seen, can structure aural experience. Visual art can do the same for visual experience and, as I argued in the previous chapter, can to some extent go beyond the purely visual. A painting or a sculpture can certainly reveal something of the personality as well as the appearance of a figure represented – see for instance the mentalities revealed by faces in Caravaggio's *Beheading of John the Baptist.* But literature can create and explore inner lives to a far greater extent. It is in literature – poems, novels, plays – that our self-images are fashioned with the greatest complexity and where exploration of the constitutive images of moral and social life is most obvious. This is one of literature's peculiar powers and gives it, in this respect, pre-eminence among the arts.

Summary

This chapter has addressed the difficulties in the way of sustaining the contention that imaginative literature is an important source of human understanding. These difficulties arise chiefly because it is natural to think that any understanding which poetry or novels offers us lies in what they say and not in the way they say it. Yet if the form in which poets and novelists write is not central to the content of their writings, it seems that literary forms are merely decorative and that paraphrase can replace poetry without significant loss of meaning. But closer examination has shown that form and content in literature are often impossible to disentangle and that a variety of poetic and literary devices can be integrally employed in the creation of imaginative literature which prompts us to see and think about our experience of life differently. It is this power which gives literature its cognitive value.

It is not obviously true that such a power is possessed by all art forms. In addition to those already examined there is another for which the case seems specially hard to make, namely architecture, the topic of the next chapter and our last look at a given art form.

Suggestions for further reading

Monroe C. Beardsley, *Aesthetics: Problems in the Philosophy of Criticism* chaps 3 and 5.

Cleanth Brooks, 'The heresy of paraphrase' in *The Well Wrought Urn*.

Stanley Cavell, 'Aesthetic problems of modern philosophy' in *Must We Mean What We Say?*

Robin Mayhead, *Understanding Literature*.

Peter Lamarque and Stein Haugon Olsen, *Truth, Fiction and Literature*.

Martha Nussbaum, *Love's Knowledge: Essays on Philosophy and Literature*.

Yvor Winters, 'The experimental school in American philosophy' in *In Defense of Reason*.

7

——·◎·——

Architecture as an art

The question on which this introduction to philosophy of art has focussed is the *value* of art. We have seen reason to think that art can be given greatest significance in so far as we can attribute to it the status of a special source of understanding. However difficulties arise once we set about applying this thesis to particular forms of art, and the preceding three chapters have been concerned with the special problems of music, the visual arts, and literature. But there is at least one art form – architecture – where it seems we need not even try to apply the general thesis. Architecture, by which is meant the building of houses, hospitals, churches, theatres and so on, is valued in large part because it serves the functions for which these buildings are intended. It might therefore be argued that in architecture we have an art form for which the question 'What is its value?' is easily settled; it is valuable because it is useful.

The undisputed usefulness of architecture raises another question. If architecture is valuable because it is functional, might we on this same ground raise doubts about its artistic credentials and ask whether it is properly called an art at all. It is widely accepted that there is something essentially correct in the slogan 'art for art's sake'. In the course of the argument we have found that the full implications of this familiar slogan are difficult to support. Nevertheless, the artistic is indeed to be contrasted with the strictly utilitarian, and if so, there is reason to wonder whether architecture, which is *not* engaged in for its own sake but for its usefulness, can claim the status of art.

The peculiarities of architecture

On the face of it, 'Is architecture an art?' is an odd question. Surely there cannot be any doubt. Ordinary ways of thinking and speaking place architecture among the arts no less than music or drama. And does not the practice of doing so receive ready confirmation in even the briefest visit to the extraordinarily beautiful buildings of the Italian Baroque, for instance, or the striking classical orderliness of Regency London? Unfortunately, the question of the status of architecture as an art is not so easily settled because architecture has features that appear to set it apart from the other arts.

The first of these, though not the only one, is indeed its usefulness or utility. This is a feature worth thinking about further. Architecture is useful in a way that all the other arts are not; the architect's products are *essentially* functional, whereas those of the painter and musician are not. It is important to be clear about this difference. Music and painting can obviously serve practical purposes. It is not hard to imagine examples. The sound of an orchestra, for instance, can be used to drown out a baby crying. A painting can be used to cover an ugly crack in the wall. Of course such uses are quite accidental; they are not *intrinsically* related to the character of music or painting as art. For this reason we might dismiss them as philosophically unimportant. Yet even if this is true, music and painting can also serve aesthetically functional purposes. For example, incidental music performs an important function in the theatre and cinema, and the designer and painter of stage sets may contribute a great deal to the overall artistic effect of a drama or an opera. Unlike the earlier examples of purely fortuitous use, this deployment of painting and music serves an artistic function, and so cannot be viewed as contingent in quite the same way, and consequently cannot be dismissed so easily.

Even so, in neither of these second examples – music and painting – can the aesthetic purpose be regarded as essential. This is because, removed from the context of their artistic use, music and the painting can survive in their own right. It is possible to listen to incidental music for its intrinsic merits and disregard the contribution it makes to the play for which it was written. Mendelssohn's music for *A Midsummer Night's Dream* is a good example. Indeed nowadays most people probably know it best as a piece of music in its own right rather than as an accompaniment to Shakespeare. Similarly, stage sets and backdrops, though not often exhibited as works of art in their own right, clearly could be. Even more important than the possibility of independent worth is the fact that we can intelligibly *prefer* to listen or look to such things in isolation from their original context, in the belief that they have greater artistic merit on their own. Arguably this is the case with Schubert's music *Entr'act from Rosamund*, which is rarely heard in the setting for which it was written.

The possibility of independent existence and independent merit is important because it shows that music and painting can fail to satisfy the artistic use for which they were originally intended and yet continue to have aesthetic value. Music that does little or nothing to intensify the drama for which it was written, for instance, may nevertheless succeed as music. The spectacular backdrop of a play that fails may be the only aesthetically interesting thing to emerge from it. A poor film may have an excellent score. Something of the same can be said for sculpture, drama, poetry, and so on. But the same *cannot* be said for architecture. Whatever else architects may be said to do, they build things, and this means that they necessarily operate under certain functional constraints. A building which fails in the purpose for which it is intended is an architectural failure, regardless of whatever other more decorative merits it might have. The simplest mark of such failure is that the building falls down, but there are others of greater interest. The architect who designs a house in which comfortable and convenient living is virtually impossible has failed, however attractive his building may appear in other respects. Something of this sort can be said about some of Frank Lloyd Wright's highly praised houses, despite his express intention to the contrary. The same is true of those who build office blocks, hospitals, universities, factories, and so on, which, however attractive the appearance, prove expensive or unpleasant as a place of work. In each of these cases, the building must satisfy a user, and the purpose of the user is always something other than merely admiring the building. As someone has said, it is important in buying a house to remember that we do not live in the garden.

What this means is that, unlike other art forms, the outcome of the architect's work must have a use and hence a value other than an aesthetic one. More importantly it cannot fail to satisfy this requirement without losing its merit as architecture.

Still this last remark might be disputed. Could not a building which was erected for one purpose serve another? Yes, is the answer, but contrary to first impressions this fact confirms rather than counters the point about the essential usefulness of architecture; it is still a building with a use even if it is not necessarily the use originally envisaged. The possibility of changing use does nothing to refute the suggestion that any work of architecture must have some purpose or other. It implies, at most, that no architectural function is fixed.

But why *must* a building have purpose? Surely there are buildings – the miniature temples and other follies which decorate eighteenth-century gardens for instance – with no purpose at all? With this sort of example in mind, it is tempting to think that the purpose of at least some architecture is mere ornamentation. Though this might be described as a purpose of sorts, any building whose purpose is pure ornamentation has been constructed solely with the aim of being admired and enjoyed and is therefore more nearly sculpture. Admiration and enjoyment are not utilitarian purposes and hence not purposes of the sort the 'art for art's sake' principle means to exclude. Does this not imply that architecture can be engaged in, just as the other arts are, entirely for its own sake? It may be relatively rare for buildings to be erected solely for this reason, but this is just a matter of empirical fact, not of any special philosophical interest. To see this, suppose that almost all the music we have was composed with a view to performing a certain function – accompanying ceremonial occasions perhaps. If so we would no doubt be inclined, but wrongly, to make utilitarian purposefulness an essential feature of music, as we are equally wrongly inclined to do for architecture.

Or so someone might argue. But the case for functionless architecture cannot be made out so easily. The ornaments of the eighteenth century are clearly parasitic; they are rather delightful copies of buildings whose original purpose was *not* merely to delight. Many are imitations of the temples of ancient Greece and Rome, which did have a purpose. Moreover, even in these cases we are admiring buildings, and what is it for a building to be 'admired and enjoyed' if this does not include admiration for the economy of its structure, the cleverness of its design, and so on? When we admire a building, we cannot merely be admiring how it looks. If we were, a model of the building would suffice. It is not enough, therefore, for a building to be elegant or delightful to the eye. Appreciation of the means of construction the architect has chosen is always an essential part. This is confirmed by the fact that although many ruins are impressive pieces of architecture from a distance, it would not have been acceptable for the architect to have built any of them that way. The abbey ruins at Rievaulx are wonderful to look at, but they are still architectural *ruins*.

Where occasionally the appearance of a building seems to be wholly divorced from its useful function and to aim at a purely aesthetic aspect, we have good reason to wonder how it differs from a large-scale piece of sculpture. Roger Scruton, in his important and influential book *The Aesthetics of Architecture*, supplies us with a convincing example. Gaudí's Chapel of the Colonia Güell takes the form of a tree-like growth which seeks to disguise its character as a piece of engineering. What are in fact supporting pillars look like the trunks of palm trees and the laths of the ceiling are disguised by being in the form of leaves. But, as Scruton remarks, so extraordinary is it that 'what purports to be architecture can no longer be seen as such, but only as a piece of elaborate expressionist sculpture seen from within' (Scruton 1979: 8).

It seems we must agree that architecture is essentially useful. This is to say, architecture *must* be useful while other arts only have the *possibility* of usefulness. Utility, however, is not the only peculiarity of architecture, not the only thing which sets it apart from the other arts. A second such feature is the importance of place. A building which in other respects is attractive and effective enough, may be marred by failing to fit its location. It can be so out of keeping with its situation for instance, that it is too grand, or too small, or in some other way wholly at odds with its surroundings. This is an important demerit in a building. Irrespective of its other merits, incongruity of place can make a building look ridiculous or ugly. We have only to think of some of the modern buildings set in otherwise coherent streets or squares of Victorian houses to see that this is so.

The same thing cannot be said of paintings, poems, or pieces of music. These can at least be placed and appreciated in a large number of different settings. Change of location does not alter their aesthetic merits. There are limits certainly. As Scruton points out, it may not be possible to appreciate medieval church music properly in a modern concert hall. But for the most part, such works of art are not tied to location in the way that architecture is.

A third differentiating feature is this. Architecture has what is called 'a vernacular'. That is to say, architecture is never made up of wholly novel elements. The architect composes buildings out of standard features, things such as doorways, windows, and roofs. Even the less functional aspects of a building, such as cornices, corbels, and turrets, as well as more specialized features like Doric and Ionic columns provide a standard 'vocabulary' which architects use. And at least some of these can also be used in other contexts, furniture and ornaments for example. There are no parallels to these in the other arts, no accumulated features which the poet or composer simply puts together. Thus even when it is true that most poetry before the twentieth century employed standard verse forms, which are not in any case strict parallels to the architectural vernacular, it is still possible as in this century for wholly free verse to appear.

One way of viewing architecture then is to see it as a utilitarian deployment of given techniques to fulfill given functions within a given location. But if architecture is strictly useful and constrained in this sense, wherein lies its art? To regard architecture as essentially useful is surely to concede, in accordance with one of Collingwood's well known distinctions, that it is a craft and not an art at all. If so, architecture is not an exercise in art properly so called, but in design, and, as much architectural thinking of the last hundred years has supposed, buildings are 'machines' for living and working in.

Does this signify? If a building conforms to a given function and executes it well, what can it matter whether it also possesses the sort of attributes that would normally be associated with a work of art?

Form and function

We can put the issue most plainly by employing the familiar distinction between form and function. Music and painting though they may have functions are also interesting for their form, and usually for their form alone. Buildings on the other hand must have a function. If, however, that function is satisfied by a variety of forms, from what point of view are we to adjudicate between the different forms a building might take? From a utilitarian or functionalist point of view it seems to make no difference. If two different forms serve the same function equally well and function is what counts, must we not regard them as equally good pieces of architecture?

What counts against this strictly utilitarian point of view is that the form of buildings does seem to matter. Indeed there is a measure of absurdity in even attempting to deny this. While there is no escaping the fact that how well a building serves its function is important, the finest buildings are commended and admired at least as much for their appearance. In other words, people care not just about how efficiently functions are satisfied, but how buildings look.

Can we not just say that both form and function matter independently, and that the architectural point of view is best thought of as a combination of different interests and considerations? This is the opinion expressed by a seventeenth-century Provost of Eton, Sir Henry Wooton, who wrote that 'Well-building has three conditions: firmness, commodity and delight', which is his translation of the views of Vitruvius, the ancient theorist of building. That is to say, structural soundness, functionality, and an aesthetically attractive appearance are all equally important in architecture.

Now there is obviously something right about this. The question however is just how the first two (structure and purpose) and the third (artistry) might be related. Is there a mere combination of interest here? Or can we speak of a fusion of interests which would give architecture the integrity of an art?

It will simplify matters to combine structure and purpose and express these two possibilities in the traditional terms of form and function. Either form and function in architecture are quite independent and are held together contingently by the fact that some of those who build functional buildings also care about their form artistically or form and function in architecture are more intimately related in some way. This way of expressing it also has the advantage of connecting this philosophical question with the central issue in architectural thinking over the last hundred years.

Consider the first possibility. Can we build in such a way that form and function are divorced but given equally close consideration? Sometimes it seems that we can. For example Orchestra Hall in the city of Minneapolis is a building which aspires to this sort of separation. The inside was designed independently of the outside and in designing it the dominant consideration was the functional one of acoustics. Consequently behind the stage there are large blocks projecting at odd angles from the wall and though these may be regarded by concert-goers as an unusual or extravagant decorative feature, their purpose is not decorative at all but the absorption and reflection of sound. Around this acoustically designed hall an outer shell has been erected. In its construction the sole consideration has been aesthetic form or how it looks to the non-concertgoing observer who cares nothing for its function, nor for its interior.

One can imagine objections to building in this way. A building ought to have a unity, it might be said. But what is the force of this 'ought'? By what authority is this principle laid down? Purists of a certain kind may balk at such a ruthless division of technical competence and artistic imagination, but if those who want to go to concerts and those who want their city embellished by impressive buildings are both satisfied, the architect can claim to have done all that can be done.

Façade, deception, and the *'Zeitgeist'*

A more modest claim would be that buildings in which form and function are unified are better than those in which they are divorced because the kind of building we have been considering constitutes a sort of fraud or deception. This is the thought which often lies behind objections to façades and similar forms of ornamentation. In the days when bankers sought greater respectability than was usually associated with the borrowing and lending of money, banks were erected for this purpose only to be clad with an imposing façade copied from buildings, often classical, that had been erected for some other purpose. The same phenomenon is to be found in a great deal of post-revolutionary architecture in the USA, where classical styles were used to lend the new republic the appearance of a political solidity it did not really enjoy. In this the architectural styles of the temples and public buidlings of the ancient world were 'robbed' of their outward appearance by those who had neither use nor sympathy for the religious or civic purposes which had generated them.

David Watkin, in a book entitled *Morality and Architecture*, vigorously repudiates this way of thinking, connecting it with moralistic ideas, introduced into architecture by the author of the nineteenth-century Gothic revival, Augustus Pugin. Pugin thought, 'Every building that is treated naturally, without disguise or concealment, cannot fail to look well' (quoted in Watkin 1984: 103). There is of course an important difference between a principled rejection of ornamentation and façade and the rather bolder idea that naturalness and 'honesty' in building guarantees aesthetic success. But both suggestions arise from one line of thought – that good architecture must meet standards that are not merely those of a pleasing appearance. Watkin finds the same kind of thinking in the writings of Nikolas Pevsner, author of a monumental guide to the architecture of Britain. Pevsner's concern with 'honesty', Watkin thinks, 'undoubtedly owes something to the Bolshevik language current in certain artistic and political circles in Europe in the early 1920s' (Watkin 1984: 104). Pevsner regarded any modern aspiration to classical forms as a failure to acknowledge the spirit of the times and for this reason as an architectural failure. In *The Buildings of England* he comments as follows on the architecture of London in the mid-1950s. '[I]t ought to be recorded first that the neo-classical, neo-Georgian spectre is even now not yet laid. In no other capital known to me would it be possible to see major buildings still going up which are so hopelessly out of touch with the C20' (Pevsner 1972: 111).

Pevsner thinks that architecture can be either 'true' and 'honest' in the appearance it presents to the world, or that it can be false and deceptive. Façade and ornamental copying are defects in architecture because they get in the way of honesty. They present an appearance at odds with the reality. Watkin, by contrast, is contemptuous of any such attempt to make architectural worth subject to independent non-aesthetic standards. Who is right about this?

To answer this question we need to ask where the standard of 'truth' in architecture is supposed to come from. The quotation from Pevsner suggests an answer: architecture is false or deceptive if it does not reflect the *Zeitgeist*, or spirit of the times, in which it is constructed. Pevsner is not alone in this view. In fact it is a thought shared by a school known as '*Kunstgeschichte*' or the historical school of art. The idea takes more and less ambitious forms. One of its most ambitious statements is to be found in the writings of the German theorist Wölfflin.

> Architecture is an expression of its time in so far as it reflects the corporeal essence of man and his particular habits of deportment and movement, it does not matter whether they are light and playful, or solemn and grave, or whether his attitude to life is agitated or calm; in a word, architecture expresses the '*Lebensgefühl*' [feeling for life] of an epoch.
>
> (quoted in Scruton 1979: 53, material in brackets added)

Others have said the same with respect to other art forms. The painter Kandinsky held that:

> Every work of art is the child of its time. . . . It follows that each period of culture produces an art of its own, which cannot be repeated. Efforts to revive the art principles of the past at best produce works of art that resemble a stillborn child. For example, it is impossible for us to live and feel as did the ancient Greeks. For this reason those who follow Greek principles in sculpture reach only a similarity of form, while the work remains for all time without a soul. Such imitation resembles the antics of apes: externally a monkey resembles a human being; he will sit holding a book in front of his nose, turning over the pages with a thoughtful air, but his actions have no real significance.
>
> (Kandinsky 1947: 129)

It is not hard to see how this stinging condemnation is to be applied to architecture. Those who seek to copy the building styles and ornaments of the past can only succeed in producing slavish and hence lifeless imitations. Each era must speak for itself, find its own voice, and in so far as architects and other artists fail to meet this challenge, their work is 'false'.

The view espoused by Wölfflin and Kandinsky, and in a milder form by Pevsner, is generally known as 'historicism', the belief that history determines both possibilities and necessities for the art and culture (including the religion and morality) of each 'epoch'. It is a view that derives in large part from the philosophy of the nineteenth-century German thinker G.W.F. Hegel, who is discussed briefly in Chapter 8. Fortunately we do not need to consider here the full range of topics Hegel's philosophy raises, because there is a simpler account of the falseness of façade in architecture which can be used to advance the discussion.

It is not necessary to take so stern a view as Pevsner or Kandinsky of those architects who, in what is a rather innocent way, ignore the fashions of the day, 'plunder' the ancient world of shapes and forms, or look back to the building styles of previous eras, even with nostalgia. Nor need we invoke ambitious theories of the *Zeitgeist* or spirit of the age in order to think that the copying of styles and the extensive use of façades can properly be called 'deceptive'. The point of building in this way, after all, has often been to make things seem other than they are, to disguise the humble function of a building by a grand exterior, for instance. Consequently, we need not engage in historicist moralizing to think that, other things being equal, it is better to avoid such deception if we can. That is to say, a building which declares its function openly, and yet succeeds in conveying all those attributes which the use of a façade was intended to do, would be preferable because it would have a certain unity or integrity. The qualification 'if we can' is important here. It is easy to imagine circumstances in which, as architects say, there is no appropriate vocabulary, and grandeur can only be accomplished by copying other styles and simply affixing them to the outside of the building. But this does not prevent us from agreeing that in an ideal world the architect would have no need to disguise. To castigate 'non-modern' styles of architecture for 'dishonesty' in the way Pevsner does may require the support of a highly contentious philosophy of history, and it may even be ridiculous, as Watkin argues. But it is not ridiculous to hold out as an ideal for architecture a style of building in which nothing can be dismissed as copying, façade, or mere decoration.

To accept this ideal does not necessarily advance our understanding of the relation between form and function in architecture. We could agree that façades are better avoided and yet at the same time deny that architecture should not pursue the concerns of function and form separately. After all, not all ornamentation is façade. The more modest argument against façades, however, is easily extended. If a building can show its structure in an aesthetically satisfying way, then, other things being equal, this is better than if its structure has to be hidden or elaborately adorned to attain the same effect. Some such principle of artistic integrity has commended itself to generations of architects.

We may conclude on the strength of the argument so far, then, that an architecture in which form and function are treated separately may be said to be deficient just in this sense; since it is widely agreed that unity in any work of art is to be commended, there is reason to regard a more unified architecture as preferable. This brings us then to a direct consideration of the alternative – that form and function in architecture may be more intimately related. On the face of it, there appear to be two possibilities here also. Either form follows function, or form determines function.

Functionalism

The first of these possibilities, form follows function, is recognisable as an architectural slogan, one coined by the American architect Louis Sullivan, although it expresses a sentiment that has influenced architecture on both sides of the Atlantic for the larger part of this century. 'Functionalism' is a normative view, a view of how architects ought to build, and this explains the campaigning zeal with which both functionalism and opposing theories were promoted among architects themselves, a zeal most clearly displayed in the architect Adolf Loos's somewhat extreme remark that 'ornamentation is crime'.

Form follows function – the function should determine the form. Such a view is usually associated with Modernism rather than neo-classicism in architecture. Yet this is the view, though not the slogan, of Augustus Pugin, the reviver of Gothic building styles, whose architectural views and whose extraordinary productivity in the space of a short life did much to create and sustain the dominant style of nineteenth-century Britain, where neo-Gothic churches in particular were commissioned and built by the hundreds. It was Pugin's view that there should be no features about a building which are not necessary for convenience or construction and that ornament should be limited to the essential structure of the building. Architecture served the business of living well. This is what made him a functionalist. But Pugin was also an enthusiastic Christian, and believed that since the best form of life was Christian, the best form of architecture was to be found in that period when life was most extensively Christianized, namely medieval Europe. Functional building consequently is best realized in 'pointed' or Gothic architecture, to which, accordingly, Pugin advocated a return.

To say that form must follow function is another way of saying that how a building is constructed must depend on its use. There is some obvious truth in this. A school which was so organized that it made teaching virtually impossible – voices did not carry, the blackboard could not be seen and so on – would be an architectural failure. But though close attention to function will determine many features of the building, it cannot determine them all. For example, a school serves its function just as well whether yellow or red brick is used for its walls. And even more ambitious features of a building may remain indeterminate even when the demands of function have been apparently satisfied.

The inability of function to fully determine form is illustrated by many of the buildings which were constructed under the influence of this focus on function. Take, for instance, the Houses of Parliament in London. The competition to replace the buildings destroyed by fire in 1834 was won by Charles Barry. His basic design was for a structure similar to those he had erected in other parts of London (the Reform Club for example), but the British government decided that the Parliament building should express the sort of 'Englishness' associated with Elizabethan and Jacobean styles, about which Barry was somewhat ignorant. So he called upon Pugin to design a great deal of the detail, and it is this detail that gives the building its distinctive and memorable character. But none of this detail is in any sense required by the fact that this was to be a legislative assembly. No doubt the number of seats, and offices, and supplementary service rooms was determined by the original brief, and perhaps the natural demands which the voice makes upon a debating chamber were also important. There is latitude in the satisfaction of these demands, however, and the point is that Pugin's contribution, far from being functional, is an embellishment of a structure which might have been decorated in other ways and yet serve its function, including its expressive function, equally well.

Form then *cannot* simply follow function, for even in buildings of considerable functional complexity, a grasp of function leaves too many issues concerning its construction undecided. Sometimes people have been inclined to deny this, on the grounds that function can supply a complete account of form, if only we are prepared to accept simple buildings – the sort of stark and unadorned building associated with Modernism. However, there are two errors here. The failure of function to determine form is a logical failure, not the practical one of ignoring simplicity – even a wholly determinate description of function cannot be made to imply a determinate description of form. Secondly, the sort of simplicity characteristic of Modernist buildings is not the logical consequence of a belief in functionalism, but its opposite, the belief that function should *follow* form.

Formalism and 'space'

The principal influence on Modernist architecture was the Swiss Charles-Edouard Jeanneret, better known by his pseudonym Le Corbusier, one of the founders of CIAM (the *Congrés Internationaux des Architects Moderne*). Le Corbusier was himself a painter and his conception of architecture, which he contrasted with mere 'building', is of a pure art which explores space and shape through the medium of construction. The relation to function is essentially creative and revisionary. In their designs, architects ought not to take the function of a building as preconceived and given, but as something which is itself moulded by the form of the building. It was this aspect of Le

Corbusier's idea of architecture which appealed to so many architects of the post-First World War generation, who saw in it the possibility of their contributing to fashioning a new world, building a new society. In this light, the architect becomes not merely the observer and servant of socially ordained functions but the creator of new ones, a role which gives architecture and architects a far greater significance than that of simple builders, designers, or engineers.

The influence of this line of thought was most marked in the design of housing. Here architects set out not to satisfy preconceived ideas of domestic accommodation but to show what domestic accommodation could be. The examples are legion, but in his famous *Unité d'Habitation* in Marseilles, Le Corbusier himself supplies as good an example as any: 337 apartments on top of massive *pilotis* or pillars of concrete marked with the lines of the timber shuttering into which it was poured. It was a model of public housing which was to be followed thousands of times in many countries.

The aim at the heart of this school of thought was not to accept but to create a conception of living. The relative simplicity of the style and lack of ornamentation arose not from a desire to let function determine form but from a realization, and confinement, of function within geometrically simple forms, namely, the artistic exploration of space itself.

The impact of this conception of architecture was immense. It even reversed the roles of architect and client in accordance with its theories, for whereas formerly clients had decided what sort of building they wanted and had found someone to build it, increasingly they turned to architects to tell them what sort of building they ought to want, the theme of Tom Wolfe's polemical book, *From Bauhaus to Our House*. But the result, as almost everyone concedes, was widespread failure to satisfy need. Houses and apartment blocks were built in which no one wanted to, or could, live, and gigantic offices were created in which working conditions were often intolerable. This functional failure was illustrated most dramatically in 1972 when the Pruitt-Igoe flats in St Louis, Missouri, which had won an award from the American Institute of Architects only seventeen years before, were blown up at the unanimous request of the residents, because they had proved impossible for daily living. Similar steps have been taken elsewhere. In October 1990 the largest ever controlled destruction of buildings took place, when eight huge blocks of council flats in Britain were destroyed in under three minutes. Not only was life in these buildings intolerable but their construction was so poor that it would have been prohibitively expensive to repair them.

'Modern' architecture is now almost universally deplored and generally regarded as having failed. It is easier to record this failure than explain it adequately. One of its causes was undoubtedly the disregard for history which the Modernist school displayed (despite some affinity with the 'historicism' Watkin condemns). An early declaration of the CIAM expressed the intention that 'It is only from the present that our architectural work should be derived' and this meant ignoring the experience of the ages in satisfying the real needs of the people who were to make use of that work. Not surprisingly, what resulted was regarded as unsatisfactory by those for whom it was planned.

Some of the leaders amongst the modernists were happy to accept this rejection because they believed that people would have to be educated in the new architecture, would have to learn to shed their preconceptions of what the experience of living in a building should be. Le Corbusier himself took this view of objections to his designs, believing that his work constituted a crusade against unthinking convention.

It is probably true that there is a tendency among ordinary people to cling to the tried and familiar and to resist anything new. Nevertheless, the opposition to Modernism in architecture can be seen to be based on something deeper than mere conventionality. The deep source of the opposition is evidenced by the fact that eventually it led to the defeat of the Modernist school. It was grounded in the real needs and purposes which many modern housing schemes, schools, and office blocks have failed to meet. This failure arises at least in part from a philosophical flaw in the central idea behind Modernism. Whatever form we give a building must in part be determined by its function, whether consciously or not. A multi-storey car park, for example, could have a design which explores volume and space in manner so striking that it thoroughly alters our idea of what a car park could be. Even so in the end it must satisfy the purpose of housing cars safely and conveniently. Moreover no artistic conception, however brilliant, can make a multi-storey car park into a dwelling place, because people being the sorts of creatures they are want and need a different sort of shelter. It is not because of artistic integrity but because of differing needs and practical requirements that car parks and houses have to differ. In short people are not cars, and aesthetic form can no more determine function exhaustively than function can determine form.

We have now considered three possibilities: first, that form and function in architecture may be treated quite separately; second, that form must follow function; and third, that architectural form can itself establish functions. Interpreted as normative principles of architecture, none of these has proved wholly satisfactory. Each however has something to be said for it. Clearly it is possible to deck a strictly functional building with ornamentation, and this has often been done. The most we can say in criticism is that a style of architecture which satisfies both functional and formal considerations and thus has a greater unity, is intelligible as an ideal, in fact one to which almost all generations of architects have aspired. Just why it might be considered an ideal is hard to explain. The best we can say perhaps is that it brings to prominence requirements of coherence and integrity, which play an important part in almost all human endeavour.

In considering more closely this ideal of architecture satisfying both form and function it is not easy to see just how form and function might indeed be unified. Form must in part be determined by predetermined function but never wholly so, and while architectural forms can enlarge our ideas of how given functions may be satisfied, they cannot create them from scratch. What we want, then, is architecture in which form and function are not wholly independent concerns, but in which neither can be subsumed under the other. Ideally form and function in architecture must *complement* each other, and one way in which this might be accomplished is through a style of building which not only *serves* but also *expresses* the function, thereby establishing a relationship between 'firmness, commodity, and delight'.

Architectural expression

How might the form of a building – its design and appearance – express the function it is intended to serve? It is easy enough to say in the abstract how this is to be done: the most striking architectural features must not only make its use convenient, but also convey to the observer the idea of its function. The problem is to see just how it is possible. How can architectural features convey ideas? At least part of this problem arises from the fact that in many cases the ideas of function involved just seem the wrong sort of thing to be expressed in building style. We can easily imagine a telephone kiosk for instance which both serves its purpose well and is attractively designed, but it seems absurd to suppose that its lines or colour might in any sense convey the idea 'making a telephone call'. The same sort of absurdity attaches to similar interpretations of much grander projects. How could St Pancras railway station in London, though undoubtedly impressive, be thought to express the idea of travelling by train? Besides, there is a further question about what exactly the idea to be conveyed is. Should St Pancras say 'travelling by train' to the spectator or just 'travelling', or even more abstractly 'movement'? It is not so much that we find it difficult to answer these questions but that they seem inappropriate questions to raise.

It is easy to raise such difficulties and make them out to be absurdities. We can, however, overlook real possibilities. It is not absurd to think that a building might express *some* ideas – grandeur or elegance, for instance – and not too difficult to connect these with the function a building might have. For instance the Marble Hall in Holkham Hall, Norfolk, is rightly described as both elegant and grand, a fine blend of classical and Baroque styles in fact, and its purpose was to allow both guests and hosts to display their elegance and grandeur. The Marble Hall may thus be said both to show and to serve elegance. In this way its form expresses its function.

But yet more plausible as examples of buildings which express ideas closely associated with the function they are intended to serve are the medieval churches of Western Europe. It has been pointed out many times that everything about a Gothic cathedral, but especially the spire, draws our attention upward, just as the minds and souls of those who worship in it should also be drawn upward. The gigantic nave of the cathedral at Rheims must fill those who stand in it with a sense of how small and fragile they themselves are. The important point is that this is an attitude singularly appropriate for those entering the presence of God. Similar remarks can be made about church architecture of other periods. It has been observed, for instance, that the colonnades which Bernini built around the piazza at St Peter's in Rome

> providing welcome shade in the midday sun . . . suggest the embracing, protective arms of Mother Church, wrapped around the faithful in the piazza . . . [and] . . . draw the eye to the steps or to the window and balcony in the Vatican palace from which the Pope gives his blessing.
>
> (Nuttgens 1983: 200)

Such an interpretation of this building can be disputed, but this is not crucial here. What matters is that remarks of this sort are *intelligible*, and this is enough to show that, at its finest, architecture *can* unify form and function in just this way: form can express as well as serve function.

Architecture and understanding

There is then at least one way of thinking of architecture as a unity of form and function and thus as a form of art and not merely craft or design. But given the general conclusions of Chapter 3, this question remains: 'If art at its best is a source of human *understanding*, can architecture be art at its best?' In other words, is there any sense in which architecture can contribute to understanding? What the argument of this chapter has shown is that, against the functionalists and the formalists, we cannot only conceive of, but also have good reason to aspire to an architecture in which neither form nor function are divorced, and where neither is subservient to the other. Moreover, it is easy to find examples of existing buildings which realize something of this ideal.

This is architecture in which the form of the building expresses its function. Describing it in this way gives rise to three possible misunderstandings. First, this is not a descriptive definition of the term 'architecture' intended to capture each and every instance in which the word is used. It is rather the outline of an ideal which it makes sense for architects to aspire to in their work. Second, the reference to expression does not signal a return to expressivism. It is not the feelings or emotions of the builder which are said to be expressed by architectural form but the function of the building. Third, to

145

say that the function is expressed by the form does not imply that the architectural ideas of the builder in some sense pre-exist their realization in the building.

To appreciate these points and to see how they might lead to a conception of architecture as a contribution to the understanding of human experience, consider again some of the most striking buildings ever constructed: the Gothic cathedrals of Northern Europe constitute a good test because any ideal conception of architecture must accommodate them. But there are several facts about them that are of importance. To begin with, these were not the work of any one designer or architect. They were often in fact constructed over long periods of time by a number of builders, masons, and craftsmen and with the oversight of clerics and benefactors. It makes no sense, therefore, to say that they express any one person's ideas or feelings, or that they embody someone's conception of a church's function. It is more accurate to say that in the course of their construction people *discovered* how to build adequately to this end. We can think of the history of a cathedral as involving countless problems of design, material, engineering, finish, space, and so on, to which a great deal of deliberation was devoted, and out of which these magnificent buildings finally emerged. What their founders and builders set out with was a commitment to a religious ideal, not a given set of feelings or ideas, and during the course of its being realized they learned how to build an appropriate place of Christian worship. And we, as the users and spectators of these building, consequently learn from them in something of the same way.

Scruton uses one such building, the cathedral at Amiens, to make this point. Looking at its West Front, he says,

> We are compelled to believe that what we see is a mass of masonry, and therefore to see that it is so. But we are not compelled to attend to the building in such a way that the thought of the celestial city seems an apt or appropriate expression of our experience. It is an activity of ours to attend to the cathedral in this way.
>
> (Scruton 1979: 85)

Scruton's point in stressing the freedom we have here is to show that attention to great architecture is a function not of the passive reception of emotion or sense perception but of active mind and imagination. Like any exercise of the mind it has to be free, but for this very reason it results in new experiences and enhanced understanding. In the example Scruton gives, the mind applying itself in the presence of this building passes beyond the facts of structural economy and beauty of form and glimpses something of the idea of paradise. It is in this way then that architecture can take on the sort of significance that we have found in the other arts.

How widely, and to what extent architecture illuminates human conceptions and ideals for us in this way is another question. Great cathedrals are no doubt among the most plausible examples to cite. But that other works of architecture, including those by a single architect can do so, cannot be seriously in doubt. Some famous industrial buildings can be said to have this sort of importance – Battersea Power Station, for example. Even so we may expect that the world of architecture, as of the other arts, has a great deal of variety, and this includes a variety of profundity and importance. In the case of many buildings, perhaps the vast majority, it would be absurd to attribute to them an ability to enhance our understanding of human purposes and the human condition. The conception of architecture we have been concerned with here is an ideal, and the fact that it is only occasionally and mostly imperfectly realized should not lead us to ignore the more obvious values of beauty and utility which many buildings possess. Just as in the other arts, there is a *scale* of values, both positive and negative. The expressive unity of form and function comes higher on this scale than commodiousness; draughtiness is less of a blemish than ugliness. But commodiousness is still desirable in a building and draughtiness to be avoided if it can be.

Summary

Unlike the other art forms architecture seems to have a special feature relevant to its value: it is useful. Its usefulness explains its value however only if we focus on the function of buildings to the exclusion of their form. Yet it is the form of the building in which the art of architecture is usually supposed to lie. Architecture plainly must encompass both form and function. The central problem in the philosophy of architecture is to explain the relation between them that allows us to classify architecture as an art.

Architectural theory in this century has seen a sustained rivalry between functionalism, which believes that form should be determined by function, and formalism, which believes that form should realize ideas of function. To a large extent this rivalry is based upon a false dichotomy. All buildings need both form and function and neither can wholly determine the other. An alternative idea is that unity of form and function in architecture can be achieved by the relation of expression: the form of a building can give public expression to its function. This account of the way in which architectural form and function can ideally be unified has the advantage of enabling us to explain the value and importance of many great architectural achievements.

Does this explanation of the value of architecture connect in any way with the cognitivist aesthetic theory? In answering this question we can see that it is plausible to interpret some of the very finest buildings as being vehicles for the exploration and elaboration of certain human ideals, religious devotion being an obvious example. The ability of a building to do this may be rare, but the fact that it is a possibility shows that even in architecture where there is plainly a scale of values – usefulness, durability, attractiveness, and so on – it makes sense to place cognitive value at the top of the scale.

The idea of a scale of values returns us to a major topic in aesthetics – normative theory of art. At the beginning of this book the assumption was made that the most promising way to explore art and its forms is by asking 'What is the value of art?' This is an assumption that must now be examined, and the merits of rival approaches considered. At this point we leave not only specific art forms behind but any immediate concern with the arts because we must concern ourselves with the much more abstract topic of the nature of art theory itself.

Suggestions for further reading

Nelson Goodman, 'How buildings mean', in Philip Alperson (ed.), *The Philosophy of the Visual Arts*.
Roger Scruton, *The Aesthetics of Architecture*.
David Watkin, *Morality and Architecture*.

8

———◦◎◦———

Theories of art

The approach taken over the last seven chapters has been a normative one. The question with which we began was 'What is valuable about art?' and this question has been used to guide us through, and adjudicate between, the competing claims of hedonism, expressivism, and cognitivism, and of the arguments of philosophers associated with these positions. But now we must return to the logically more fundamental question which was suspended in the introduction, namely whether this is the best approach to take in aesthetics.

This question arises for two reasons. First, the normative approach to art is not the commonest. Traditionally philosophical aesthetics has been concerned with the definition of art, of trying to say what art is, rather than why it is valuable, and consequently, some defence must be made of taking a different approach. Second, and more importantly, contemporary art theory, of which aesthetics more narrowly defined is a branch, is marked by the great variety of methodologies that different writers adopt. Moreover, these are not just alternatives; they are usually in express competition. The highly influential ideas about art and literature described as Marxism, structuralism, deconstruction, or postmodernism, purport to have revolutionized the subject in a way that makes philosophical aesthetics outmoded and renders it redundant. If this is true, almost all of the argument in preceding chapters is seriously undermined. So we need to ask whether it *is* true, and this means that we have to examine the basis of theories of art. Let us begin with those traditional theories which seek to define art.

Defining art

The aim of philosophical theories of art that try to define and analyse the concept of art was perhaps most uncompromisingly stated by Clive Bell, who though not himself primarily a philosopher, was an influential figure in twentieth-century aesthetics, and is best known for the elaboration of one such theory.

[I]f we can discover some quality common and peculiar to all the objects that provoke it, we shall have solved what I take to be the central problem of aesthetics. We shall have discovered the essential quality in a work of art, the quality that distinguishes works of art from all other classes of objects.

Bell then goes on to say:

[e]ither all works of visual art have some common quality, or when we speak of 'works of art' we gibber. Every one speaks of 'art', making a mental classification by which he distinguishes the class 'works of art' from all other classes. What is the justification of this classification? What is the quality common and peculiar to all members of this class? Whatever it be, no doubt it is often found in company with other qualities; but they are adventitious – it is essential. What is this quality? What quality is shared by all objects that provoke our aesthetic emotions? What quality is common to Sta Sophia and the windows at Chartres, Mexican sculpture, a Persian bowl, Chinese carpets, Giotto's frescoes at Padua and the masterpieces of Poussin, Piero della Francesca, and Cezanne?

(Bell in *N&R* 1995: 100)

Bell's answer to his own question is that what is shared by all works of art is 'significant form', but what he takes to be 'the central problem of aesthetics' is of primary concern here. Bell is interested chiefly, perhaps exclusively, in the visual arts. Even so, he gives expression to a general aim found in many writers, namely, the hope of formulating a definition of art which will state the necessary and sufficient conditions for something's being properly classified as a work of art.

To state the necessary and sufficient conditions of art is to set out the properties something must have in order to be a work of art, and the properties it does have which will guarantee that it is. It is in the spirit of the same endeavour that the American philosopher Suzanne K. Langer, also a leading figure in twentieth-century aesthetics 'make[s] bold to offer a definition of art, which serves to distinguish a "work of art" from anything else in the world. . . . Art is the creation of forms symbolic of human feeling' (Langer 1953: 53). So too the Italian philosopher Benedetto Croce advances the simple, if somewhat obscure, theory that art is 'the expression of intuition', and clearly he offers this formula as an account of necessity and sufficiency.

A British philosopher, E.F. Carrit, who was impressed by Croce's view as getting 'nearer the root of the matter than any previous philosopher' concluded that '[i]f we find ourselves unable to accept it . . . we should have either to say that the explanation of beauty is still undiscovered or to accept the alternative . . . that beautiful things have no other common and peculiar quality which makes them beautiful' (Carrit 1932: 88). Carrit assumes that theory in aesthetics can take only the form of specifying a defining character-istic, and that if no such theory can be formulated satisfactorily, aesthetics has failed.

This assumption that a theory of art must be a definition of the concept 'art', characterizes a whole approach to philosophical aesthetics. Under the general label 'aesthetics' philosophers have been engaged in many different things, but it is the pursuit of a distinguishing definition that has dominated philosophical aesthetics in the period since the work of Immanuel Kant. Indeed, although philosophers since Plato have talked about art, and have frequently followed Plato in the search for philosophical definitions, it would not be an exaggeration to say that Kant was the founder of *aesthetics* as it has generally been understood.

Kant's major work on aesthetics is entitled *The Critique of Judgment* (discussed in some detail in my first chapter). It is not in fact a free-standing work on aesthetics, but part of a much broader 'Idealist' philosophy, which he elaborated in three lengthy *Critiques*, and Kantian Idealism can be found still at work in a good deal of aesthetics. Sometimes philosophical aesthetics, understood as the search for a necessary and sufficient definition of art, has been thought inextricably tied to Idealism, which is at heart the belief that philosophy is the understanding of the abstract ideas of the intellect rather than of objects experienced in the world around us. W.B. Gallie, for instance, argues that all definitional theories are

> vitiated through and through by the essentialist fallacy: they presume that whenever we are in a position to define a substance or activity, we must know its essence or ultimate nature – and know this by methods that are entirely different from those used in the experimental and mathematical sciences.
>
> (Gallie 1948: 302)

However, the stated task of philosophical aesthetics – to arrive at a definition, conception, or characterization of art that makes explicit the necessary and sufficient conditions for something's being a work of art – does not need to be and as a matter of fact is not always accompanied by Idealist metaphysics. Contrary to Gallie's claim, in other writers, the search for the defining characteristic of art is more readily construed as empirical or factual, a survey of the facts about art as we know it, one which *does* use something like the methods of the sciences. John Hospers, for instance, thinks the expression theory of art (which was examined in Chapter 2) is to be construed in this way. His famous essay which scrutinizes the claim that 'all art must be expressive of something or other, so much so that a non-expressive work of art is a contradiction in terms', criticizes it for failing to fit relevant facts.

> If the [expression] theory is presented not as an *a priori* pronouncement but as an actual account of the creative process in artists, it will have to stand the empirical test, namely: in all cases of admitted works of art, was the process of its creation such as the expression theory describes? And I do not see any evidence that it holds true in all cases.
>
> (Hospers 1955: 315)

That the generally opposing philosophical doctrines of Idealism and empiricism may *both* accommodate the traditional project of aesthetics is clear testimony to how dominant an approach this has been. Indeed, according to Morris Weitz (who does not take into account Marxist or other sociological theories), the aim of arriving at a definition of art is common to all the major aesthetic theories of the modern period.

> Each of the great theories of art – Formalism, Voluntarism, Emotionalism, Intellectualism, Intuitionism, Organicism – converges on the attempt to state the defining properties of art. Each claims that it is the true theory because it has formulated correctly into a real definition the nature of art; and that the others are false because they have left out some necessary or sufficient property.
>
> (Weitz in *N&R* pp. 183–4)

It is Weitz's belief that all such theories fail. He shares Gallie's view that this search for definition is essentialist and therefore impossible, although he thinks it may still serve a purpose. But essentialist or not, the marks of its failure are unmistakable: no theory of this sort has met with universal, or even very widespread, approval. Kant's definition of the aesthetic (not quite the same, admittedly, as a definition of art) as 'purposiveness without purpose', Croce's 'intuitionism', Bell's 'significant form', or Langer's 'symbolic feeling', have all had as many critics as advocates. Philosophical fashion has for a time seized upon some favoured theory, but almost at the same time problems inherent in this same theory have been detected.

Problems with a theory do not constitute a conclusive objection to the enterprise; much the same may be said about every branch of philosophy. More important here is the reason for each theory of this sort being rejected. It is very easy, too easy in fact, to counter any of these general claims about 'Art', as Hospers counters expressivism, by pointing out recognized art forms or works of art which the theory simply cannot accommodate. For instance many works of literature appear to have significant content as well as significant form. It seems plainly perverse to hold, in the spirit of Kant or Bell, that architecture has purposiveness but no purpose. Again while poetry and drama, and representational works in general, may easily be thought to be expressive – a love poem is an obvious example – it is difficult (and may be impossible) to say what, or even whether, absolute music could be said to express. Absolute music and abstract art can be made to fit the 'significant form' theory better, and so perhaps can ballet, but films cannot because they are usually made up of scenes and actions and tell a story. And opera, which is in many ways an amalgam of all the arts, can always be relied upon to produce counterexamples to any definitional theory. In short, philosophical definitions of 'art' invariably involve unwarranted generalization. This is the first major objection. There are, it is true, rejoinders that can be made on behalf of all these theories, but their uniform and manifest failure to fit the facts about art is a major difficulty for philosophical aesthetics as a whole.

In response to this difficulty, philosophers have sometimes made an important and interesting move. If a form or a work of art does not fit their preferred definition, they claim it is not 'art proper' or 'true art'. The validity of invoking this distinction needs to be considered closely. It has often been regarded as a bit of cheating, a way of bending the theory to fit the facts. But what it actually does is to convert a *descriptive* definition of art into a *prescriptive* or normative one, and there is no reason not to try expressly to formulate a normative conception of art. The difference is that the aim of a descriptive definition is to include all the things called art; the aim of a normative one is to sort out from among the things known as art those which truly deserve the label. Normative conceptions of art is a topic to which we will be returning at the end of this chapter. For the moment, however, let us remain with descriptive definitions and see what other difficulties they present.

Croce, who offers one such descriptive definition of art, sees that there will be cases it cannot cover, but he argues that since the different art forms simply cannot be everywhere distinguished one from another clearly – there is no sharp division between fine art and jewelry, for instance – we have no choice but to resort to generalization. It is not only legitimate but inevitable, and not peculiar to aesthetics. A clear distinction between 'light' and 'dark', for example, will not encompass the 'partially lighted'. But even if Croce is right in this, there is a further deeper difficulty: what is the generalization to be about?

This is the second major difficulty confronting philosophical aesthetics. In the history of the subject since Kant, there has been continual uncertainty as to whether the subject matter of art theory is subjective states of mind, that is, do we theorize about the attitudes of observer or audience, or is the subject matter objectively existing artefacts, that is, the works of art themselves? That is to say, is a theory of art a theory about the kind of human judgment and/or perception that arises when we are confronted with a work of art, or is it a theory about actual objects – paintings, poems, plays, pieces of music, and so on? The origin of this uncertainty is found in Kant himself. While Kant is primarily interested in the status of a state of mind which calls an object beautiful, he also has a theory of what it means for something to be a work of art, and the relation between the state of mind and the external object itself is very uncertain.

Arguably this uncertainty has plagued philosophical aesthetics ever since Kant. Despite the opening words of the passage from Clive Bell quoted above, the theory of 'significant form' has for obvious reasons focussed attention on created objects – it is the form of the objects which matters – while expressivism, and more specifically Romanticism, have tended to give pride of place to states of mind both of artist and spectator. The problem has been compounded by the emergence of a third possibility. Functionalist and institutional theories of art tend to focus on neither the aesthetic attitude nor on individual works, but on the general activity of art making and art viewing, and on their social role. The result of all this is that aesthetics has in part come to be a dispute about what it should dispute about, and what one theorist regards as central another will regard as irrelevant. In addition to the problem of unwarranted generalization then, philosophical definitions of art have a problem about subject matter. Are we seeking a definition or generalization about attitudes or artefacts or functions or activities?

Even if both these difficulties could be overcome, and many writers have thought they can be, there is a third. This is the objection that most alternative sociological theories have made their starting point. It arises from the observation that every language is a cultural product with a history, and that consequently concepts themselves have a history. When philosophers have spoken about 'Art', this objection runs, they have implicitly supposed that there is some object or category or activity or attitude which finds universal application and is indifferent to cultural context and historical development. But socio-historical investigation seems to show this to be false. One sociologist of art, Janet Wolff, puts it this way.

> The social history of art shows, first, that it is accidental that certain types of artefact are constituted as 'art'.... Secondly, it forces us to question distinctions traditionally made between art and non-art ... for it is clear that there is nothing in the nature of the work or of the activity which distinguishes it from other work and activities with which it may have a good deal in common.
>
> (Wolff 1988: 14)

Her point is that what is regarded as art at any one time is the outcome of social influences, not of the nature of the art objects themselves. This important fact, according to Wolff, will not be overcome by appeal to the accepted conclusions of art criticism:

> aesthetics can find no guarantee of any corpus of works or canon in art criticism or literary criticism. These discourses, too, are the historically specific product of social relations and practices, and hence as partial and contingent as art and literature themselves.
>
> (*ibid.*)

In other words, the mind of the art critic, or the reading public for that matter, is not itself immune to social interest and conditioning. Art critics do compile lists of 'classic' works, but this list is as subject to historical influence and change as the concept of art itself.

The precise force of the sociological objection to traditional aesthetics will be considered more closely a little later on. For the moment, it is enough to observe that something in this sociological line of thought is incontestable. What is to be called 'Art' is not even today universally agreed upon, and we do not have to look very far to see that the concept of 'Art with a capital A' does not have application in many other times and places. The distinction between art and craft, for example, brought to prominence in modern aesthetics by Collingwood, whose version of expressivism was examined in Chapter 2, cannot be translated into the language of Plato and Aristotle. Nor is it easy to relate this distinction to that which the eighteenth century made between fine and mechanical arts. This way of thinking about language and concepts reveals that philosophical aesthetics, even if it is not essentialist, is Platonist. Plato held that everything has an eternal unchanging 'Form' which the things we see around us mirror or imitate, and in a similar way, it can be argued, philosophical aesthetics supposes that there is a universal unchanging form called 'Art', which can be apprehended at any and every time. But the truth is, or so the sociologist of art holds, that the practice, the criticism, and the institutions of art are all social products, and have to be understood in terms of historical development. They are neither fixed nor final, and they differ both in time and place. If this is true, philosophical aesthetics is not merely using the wrong methods, but seeking to explain the nonexistent.

To summarize: philosophical aesthetics as inspired by Kant seems to suffer from three major difficulties. First, it proceeds on the basis of a certain generalizing which, whether or not it is informed by the essentialism of Idealist metaphysics, seeks the defining characteristic of art when there is no warrant to suppose that there is any one property or feature which all works of art must or do share. Inevitably, every definition fails to accommodate all the facts, because the facts are just too various. Second, philosophical aesthetics has a deep-seated uncertainty about what the possessor of this characteristic is, even if it could be found. Is it the work, the attitude we bring to it, or the whole complex of activity of which these are both part? Third, approaching art in the traditional manner of philosophical aesthetics ignores the incontrovertible fact that the concept of art is not an unchanging 'Form' laid up for all eternity, but a socially and historically determined conception whose application, if it has one, is correspondingly limited.

There are further rejoinders to all these objections, but it is not germane to consider them here, for the purpose of this chapter is merely to describe the thinking which has determined where the battle lines between modern art theories are drawn. Whether or not these rejoinders are sufficient to overcome the difficulties, the fact is that serious doubts have been raised about philosophical aesthetics, and this gives us good reason to consider more closely its rivals.

Art as an institution

There is one theory of art which has commanded attention and which can be thought of as occupying a middle position between the philosophical and the sociological. This is the institutional theory, whose best known exponent is the American philosopher George Dickie, though Jerrold Levinson is another prominent exponent of a similar idea. The institutional theory takes seriously the idea that motivates sociologists of art, namely, that what counts as a work of art can differ over time and place. But it is also an exercise in traditional aesthetics because the institutional theory aims to make this fact the basis of a philosophical definition of art.

Dickie originally formulated his definition as follows:

> A work of art in the classificatory sense is (1) an artefact (2) a set of the aspects of which has had conferred upon it the status of candidate for appreciation by some person or persons acting on behalf of a certain social institution (the artworld).

> (Dickie 1974: 34)

This is a convoluted definition, and it is one that Dickie himself later abandoned (see Dickie in *N&R* pp. 213–23). Nevertheless it captures a general idea which continues to have attractions and can be stated more simply as follows: an artifact becomes a work of art if relevant critics regard it as being a candidate for this status. Art is what the artworld decides it is. This social definition of a work of art has certain advantages over a purely conceptual or *a priori* definition. A definition arrived at independently of the real artworld, based perhaps like Kant's on a general philosophical system, can in principle be wholly at odds with what is commonly thought of as art. But if what philosophy tells us is art is not what the world of artists, critics, and audiences regards as art, what possible interest could the philosophical definition have? By defining art in the way he does, Dickie avoids any such disparity. A second connected advantage is this: the institutional theory of art can accommodate an occasional but important feature of the artworld, that is, the transformation of everyday objects into works of art. To take a famous example: in 1917 Marcel Duchamp, an established artist, responding to an open invitation to all comers, sent a manufactured enamel urinal, which he entitled *Fountain*, to an exhibition in New York. Understandably, the exhibition committee refused to show it, although later 'experts' came to hail it as a work of art after all. On the institutional theory an everyday object, selected rather than created, can indeed be a work of art, if the artworld so regards it, whereas on any other definition this, or some other object, will be ruled out in advance.

These advantages of the institutional theory arise because the theory takes seriously the social context of art, which is the feature the sociologists are keen to stress. Even so, the institutional theory has met with even more contention than other definitions. Three problems have emerged as being especially intractable. First, the definition appears to suffer from circularity. A work of art is defined in terms of the artworld. But how is the artworld to be defined if not as the world concerned with works of art? Not all circularity is vicious, and Dickie has defended his view on the grounds that his definition, though circular, is not viciously circular. Even if he is correct in thinking this, two other objections are not so easily met.

The idea of a social institution that has the power to confer status is neither unfamiliar nor peculiar to art. The law, for instance, is a much plainer example. An action's being a crime is a matter determined entirely by the institutions of law declaring it to be so. Crime is whatever the legal system says it is. Similarly, someone's being a priest is a result of a bishop's having bestowed this status. But both these examples refer to institutions with known and established authorities. In the case of the 'artworld' there are no such authorities. Who exactly is it that confers the status 'work of art' and by what authority do they do so? The 'artworld' is neither sufficiently corporate nor does it have recognized procedures for bestowing status. The crucial point is that people in anything plausibly called 'the artworld' often disagree about the value and status of a work. This possibility is illustrated by the Duchamp example. First, established critics rejected it as a work of art; later, for whatever reason, equally established critics came to regard it as such. Since the same object must either be or not be a work of art, this implies that one of the groups of critics was mistaken, and hence nothing about its status as art follows from either response.

The consequence of the artworld's being mistaken is different from that of the law's being mistaken, and this reveals a crucial difference between the two institutions. Although judges and legislators can make mistakes, their doing so does not eliminate the authority of their decisions. Until the law is changed or the judicial decision reversed, the status of crime and criminal remain, even though a mistake has been made. What this shows is that social authority derives not from opinion, however well informed, but from recognized social function. What Dickie's 'artworld' lacks is not so much the function he attributes to it, as the social recognition of some 'invested' authority it would need to have for his theory to work.

This leads to the third objection. We might agree with Dickie that the artworld has a function, but to assume that this function is that of bestowing status, is to accept the artworld on its own terms. It may be true that artists and critics think that they are the determiners of what is and is not art. Why should we accept their own estimation of themselves? To begin with, this would make for a deep conservatism in the arts – anything which the artworld does not accept becomes unacceptable. Furthermore, it takes too narrow a view of the social context of art. The artworld, if indeed it does make sense to speak of such a thing, is not a distinct and isolated entity, but a complex of institutions and activities bound up with society as a whole. To understand art in its social context properly requires us to take into account this wider context, and in doing so we may well discover that art has functions different from those the people engaged in it claim for it or are willing to admit. Dickie has taken a step in the right direction by focussing upon the social institution of art, but his focus is too narrow. It is this thought that leads us on to broader theories, which I have here labelled 'sociological'.

Marxism and the sociology of art

Sociological alternatives to philosophical aesthetics may be grouped under a variety of labels: Marxist aesthetics, structuralism, critical theory, deconstructionism, postmodernism. These are all familiar terms in contemporary art criticism, but the precision of these labels is slightly misleading because there is a good deal of overlap between the ideas they represent. However, Marxism, structuralism, deconstructionism, and so on, are convenient labels for some highly influential movements in recent thinking about the arts, and it is important that they be considered.

Let us begin with Marxism. There are recognizably Marxist theories of art, but since Marx himself had little to say about art, these theories consist of an extension of basic Marxist concepts. Indeed if Louis Althusser, a leading French Marxist theorist, is right, a proper understanding of art can only come about through understanding fundamental Marxist conceptions.

> [T]he only way we can hope to reach a real knowledge of art, to go deeper into the specificity of the work of art, to know the mechanisms which produce the 'aesthetic effect', is precisely to spend a long time and pay the greatest attention to the *'basic principles of Marxism'*.
>
> (Althusser 1971: 227, original emphasis)

On this view,

> in order to answer most of the questions posed for us by the existence and specific nature of art, we are forced to produce an adequate (scientific) knowledge of the processes which produce the 'aesthetic effect' of a work of art.
>
> (*ibid.* 225)

Althusser is here effectively generalizing the approach Lenin took in an essay on Tolstoy:

The contradictions in Tolstoy's views are not those of his strictly personal thinking; they are the reflection of the social conditions and influences, of the historic conditions ... that determined the psychology of the different classes and different strata of Russian society at the time.

(Lenin 1968: Vol. 14, 293)

Of course from the Marxist perspective, the purpose of intellectual activity is not merely to understand the world but to change it, and for this reason Marxists have also been interested in the practical effect of art, both conservative and revolutionary. The history of Marxist art theory as summarized by Tony Bennett, himself a Marxist critic, reflects these two aims. (Bennett is talking about literature, but his description can legitimately be extended to art in general.)

[W]ithin the context of the topography of 'base' and 'superstructure' mapped out by Marx, there has been a sustained attempt to explain the form and content of literary texts by referring them to the economic, political and ideological relationships within which they are set. In addition, Marxist critics have always sought to calculate what sort of political effects might be attributed to literary works and accordingly, to judge for or against different types of literary practice.

(Bennett 1979: 104)

Bennett detects a third concern in Marxist aesthetics, to which we will return. The two he identifies here – interest in the socio-economic context of art, and in its political effects – have led to a theory of art as falling between ideology on the one hand and science on the other. 'Science' and 'ideology' are terms from Marxist social theory according to which science is the true perception and understanding of reality while ideology is the false and distorting set of ideas in which reality is presented by those who have a vested interest in resisting radical change. To say that art is halfway between the two, therefore, is to say that it has a dual nature. On the one hand, we do find a reflection of the world in art, but not as it really is, so much as how people take it to be. Art expresses, in part, the historically limited perceptions of each particular society and period. To this extent art is ideological, for it disguises reality. On the other hand, art is recognized as art. That is to say, it is understood to be the outcome of imagination, not scientific inquiry, and because it is understood in this way it can also reveal the *unreality* of the ideological world, show it to be made up of ideas and images. In this way art inclines to science because it tells us something about the world of capitalism and thereby increases real understanding. Althusser expresses this Marxist conception of art as a mixture of the ideological and the scientific when he says, 'the peculiarity of art is to "make us see", "make us perceive", "make us feel" something which *alludes* to reality' (Althusser 1971: 222, emphasis original).

In revolutionary art the element of *alluding to* reality will be evident. Art as an instrument of radical social change shows something about reality by shaking the ideological false-consciousness of the spectator. It is for this reason that Althusser praises the painter Cremonini, because 'his painting denies the spectator the complicities of communion in the complacent breaking of the humanist bread, the complicity which confirms the spectator in his spontaneous ideology by depicting it'. This abstruse remark means that revolutionary art does not represent things in familiar and comfortable ways, which most art does, but in unfamiliar and hence disturbing guises. By implication, nonrevolutionary art, which in the view of most Marxists includes all forms of naturalist 'copying', leaves ideological images of the world undisturbed. It thus plays its part in sustaining the *status quo*. In bourgeois art, most Marxists would contend, the element of allusion escapes both artist and spectator, who are accordingly deceived. Similarly deceived are the critics, notably the so-called New Critics of the 1950s, who supposed their inquiries to be what the Marxist literary theorist Terry Eagleton calls 'innocent', that is, quite without social or political presupposition or interest. Such critics take art works at face value and imagine themselves to be commenting impartially upon what they 'find' in them. But mere 'finding' assumes an impossible neutrality; no one can stand completely free, above and outside their own social allegiances.

This understanding of art is typically Marxist. An example is the work of the Hungarian writer Georg Lukács who, although a dissident, has had considerable influence in Marxist aesthetics. Lukács draws an evaluative distinction between 'narration' and 'description'. 'The real epic poet', Lukács tells us, 'does not describe objects but expresses their function in the mesh of human destinies' whereas 'the decisive ideological weakness of the writers of the descriptive method is their passive capitulation' (Lukács 1970: 146). His point is that real poets play a part in social struggle; those who purport merely to 'describe', are in fact allying themselves with forces of oppression.

The Marxist theory of art ascribes to it both intellectual and practical importance. Compared with science, it is a defective form of understanding but one which can serve either to maintain the established political order, or to disturb it. The accuracy of this view of art is clearly bound up with, and in fact rests upon, the truth of the Marxist theory of history and society of which it is only a part. It might be thought therefore that we can only examine the Marxist theory of art if we examine Marxism in general, and since this would involve a large number of important issues in politics, history, and philosophy, the task of assessing the Marxist theory of art seems very extensive. Fortunately for present purposes we can ignore these larger questions. The truth of the Marxist theory of historical materialism is a *necessary* condition of the truth of Marxist theories of art, but it is not a *sufficient* condition. That is to say, if Marxist social theory is false, then the Marxist theory of art is false. But even if Marxist social theory is true, the application to art could still be erroneous. In other words, we can investigate the plausibility of the Marxist theory of art independently of Marxist theory as a whole.

When we do, even considered on its own terms, the Marxist approach to art encounters an important problem, a problem encapsulated in the question, 'What is the Marxist theory of art a theory *of*?' The Marxist alternative to philosophical aesthetics as traditionally pursued arises, it will be recalled, because of dissatisfaction with the ahistorical essentialism of Kantian aesthetics. Marxism finds here just the same fault that Marx found with Hegel's theory of the state. 'Art', like 'The State' is one of those 'abstract determinations which in no way really ripen to true social reality' (Marx 1970: 40). Yet in the elaboration of their views, the idea of something called 'art' (as well as several related abstract concepts), is employed by Althusser, Lukács, Bennett and many other Marxists nonetheless. Indeed, references to 'art' are no less frequent in the writings of Marxist theorists than in the writings of philosophical aestheticians. Nor is this surprising because it is hard to see how *any* such theory could be elaborated without relying on some abstract conception of 'art'. Furthermore, it is clear from the examples the Marxists use that they are drawing precisely the sort of distinction between art and non-art that Wolff claims social investigation has exploded.

According to Bennett, the continued use of this discredited abstract concept 'art' arises from the fact that in addition to the two aims he cites in the passage quoted above, Marxists have a third, incompatible one.

> with the possible exception of Brecht's work, every major phase in the development of Marxist criticism has been an enterprise in aesthetics. It has attempted to construct a theory of the specific nature of aesthetic objects. . . . Indeed, if there is a single dominant thread running through the history of Marxist criticism it is the attempt to reconcile . . . two sets of concerns: the one consistent with the historical and materialist premises of Marxism and with its political motivation, and the other inherited from bourgeois aesthetics.
>
> (Bennett 1979: 104)

Bennett holds, rightly in my view, that these two elements in Marxist criticism cannot be reconciled. 'The inheritance of the conceptual equipment which goes with the concerns of aesthetics constitutes the single most effective impediment to the development of a consistently historical and materialist approach' (*ibid.*) The remainder of Bennett's book is, consequently, an attempt to develop such an approach. The net effect of his impressive efforts in this direction is instructive. Bennett's more consistent Marxism results in what might be called the disappearance of art (or in Bennett's case, the literary text). Since the very idea of 'a work' is one of the categories of aesthetics, the Marxist cannot consistently maintain that 'works' either reflect, reveal, sustain, or subvert social reality.

> It is rather *Marxist criticism* which, through an active and critical intervention, so 'works' upon the texts concerned as to *make them* 'reveal' or 'distance' the dominant ideological forms to which they are *made to* 'allude'. The signification of ideology that they are thus said to have is not somehow 'natural' to them; it is not a pre-given signification which criticism passively mirrors but it is a signification they are *made to have* by the operations of Marxist criticism upon them.
>
> (Bennett 1979: 156, emphasis original)

This way of speaking is not easy to understand. What Bennett means to say is that if the importance and true meaning of works of art is their social function, this is brought out not by an examination of their internal content, but by a Marxist analysis of the place of art in a culture. Possibly he is correct in thinking that this is the inevitable conclusion of a consistent attempt to abandon the abstractions of philosophical aesthetics, but if so, a very high price is exacted. This is not so much because the concept of a work of art must be given up, but because if *all* the work is done on the part of Marxist criticism, the object of that criticism may be anything whatsoever. Marxist critics may as readily, and perhaps more satisfactorily, create their own material as rely on anything those commonly called artists may produce.

This drastic result is well illustrated towards the end of Bennett's book. There he refers approvingly to a work by Renée Balibar in which he says, 'the decisive theoretical break is finally located'. Balibar offers two contrasting texts of a passage from George Sand's *The Devil's Pool*. One is an edited (1914) version for use in schools, the other the text of a 1962 critical edition. The two differ widely, but because all that matters to the Marxist critic is how they differ in social function and effect, according to Bennett, 'neither one of these is the "original" or "true" text'. If this is correct, we are forced to the conclusion that *from the point of view of Marxist criticism*, what Sand wrote, or indeed whether she wrote anything at all, is a matter of indifference. The text not only means but *is* whatever Marxist criticism says it is.

Bennett is happy to accept this conclusion, and perhaps consistency requires this of him. The point to be made here, however, is that there is no special connection between his consistent version of Marxist criticism and any known phenomena commonly called art, no matter how broadly that label may be applied. As a result, we have no reason to regard Bennett's version of Marxist criticism as an exercise in the theory of art at all. Since 'art' is a false abstraction which should be abandoned, there cannot be any theory of it, Marxist or otherwise. Marxism, pushed to its logical conclusion, does not mean a different or better way of doing what philosophical aesthetics has done badly, but a total abandonment of any such enterprise. Bennett concludes that 'there are no such things as works or texts which exist independently of the functions which they serve' (p. 157). If so, the theory of art must be replaced by the analysis of society.

This is not an outcome that many Marxist theorists have expressly accepted, and it is important to note that so far this conclusion has been found to derive only from the views of Althusser and Lukács. Other Marxist theorists have had slightly different conceptions of art. The exploration of these might have different implications. For instance, Terry Eagleton, one of the best known Marxist literary theorists, holds that texts do not reflect or express ideological conceptions of social reality, but are rather themselves products of that reality. Consequently the task of criticism

> is to show the text as it cannot know itself, to manifest those conditions of its making (inscribed in its very letter) about which it is necessarily silent. . . . To achieve such a showing, criticism must break with its ideological prehistory, situating itself outside the space of the text on the alternative terrain of scientific knowledge.
>
> (Eagleton 1978: 43)

It is not altogether easy to understand what Eagleton means by this, but if the proper object of criticism is something about which the text or work is *necessarily* silent and if criticism must put itself 'outside the space of the text', there does seem a distinct possibility of the disappearance of art here too. One response to this lies in interpreting Eagleton's endeavour as a matter not of ignoring the text but, so to speak, reading past it in the same way perhaps that natural science goes beyond bare experimental data and constructs a theory to explain the data, or that anthropology offers interpretations of myths and rituals which go beyond the level of mere observation. Though neither analogy is perfect, this way of putting it draws attention to similarities between Eagleton's line of thought and some other more general structuralist conceptions. Accepting for the moment that consistent Marxism means not the revision, so much as the end of aesthetics, it is the associated structuralist approach which now needs to be explored.

Lévi-Strauss and structuralism

Structuralism made its first appearance in the field of linguistics, and it would be true to say that the role of language in human thought and understanding remains of central importance. Moreover, the extension of the role of language to art in general generates a conception of music, painting, architecture, and so on, that preserves several lingusitic concepts by viewing these as systems of signs and signifiers somewhat comparable to natural languages. In linguistics the pioneer of structuralism was the Swiss linguist

Ferdinand de Saussure. Saussure made the now famous distinction between *parole* – utterance – and *langue* – the unspoken and inaudible system of language which determines the structure and meaning of an utterance. The things we say are constructed out of, and depend for their meaning upon, a grammar and vocabulary that is not itself expressed, and generally is not explicitly known by language speakers. The task of linguistics as Saussure conceived it is to construct or deduce the *langue* from its realization in *parole*.

Two features of this way of thinking are especially worth noting. First the hidden *langue* behind a manifest *parole* is not to be thought of as something existing apart from language as it is used. Although the hidden *langue* may be distinguished from concrete utterances, nonetheless it can only manifest itself in these same utterances. The grammar of a natural language, for instance, is not identical with grammatical utterances themselves, yet it can be realized only in real spoken sentences. The distinction at the heart of structuralism thus holds out the promise of something which in a sense all intellectual endeavour strives for – the detection of reality behind appearance – while at the same time invoking no occult or strangely metaphysical entities. This explains much of structuralism's attraction in a wide variety of fields, social anthropology as well as the study of language, for instance. Second, structural linguistics opens up the possibility of theoretical explanation, that is to say, explanation of linguistic phenomena in terms of the internal nature of language and thought, and not merely their appearance or development as seen in varying time and place. Sometimes this is expressed by saying that structuralism allows for synchronic (simultaneous) and not merely diachronic (historical) explanation. In other words it provides a way of understanding appearances *via* an ever-present structuring system and not merely by means of a historical process of development. It was for this reason that structural linguistics seemed to provide a source of theoretical liberation from the mere recording of historical changes which had marked the study of language hitherto.

Given the intellectual attractiveness of structuralism it is not surprising to find the basic ideas of linguistic structuralism extending into wider spheres of inquiry. Most notable of these is anthropology as it was developed by Claude Lévi-Strauss. Lévi-Strauss himself seems to have thought of his employment of ideas from the field of linguistics merely as an extension and not a special adaptation of them, for he says, '[W]e conceive anthropology as the *bona fide* occupant of that domain of semiology which linguistics has not already claimed for its own' (Lévi-Strauss 1978: 9–10). The effect of this extension, however, was to give the concept of underlying structure a more abstract form, and hence one that allowed it to be applied to systems other than language. In his view, 'even the simplest techniques of any primitive society take on the character of a system that can be analyzed in terms of a more general system' (*ibid.* p.11).

164

Lévi-Strauss's definition of a suitable object for structuralist analysis is as follows.

> An arrangement is structured which meets but two conditions: that it be a system revealed by an internal cohesiveness, and that this cohesiveness, inaccessible to observation in an isolated system, be revealed in the study of transformations through which similar properties are recognized in apparently different systems.
>
> (Lévi-Strauss 1978: 18)

It is not difficult to see that such abstract conditions can be applied to art and art making. Indeed Lévi-Strauss himself was one of the first to make this connection in the field of anthropology, by drawing attention to work on fairy tales by the Russian Vladimir Propp. Propp thought that certain constant functions and spheres of action, delineated by character types such as 'the villain', 'the provider', 'the sought for person', and so on, can be detected in the various characters of particular tales. More abstract and ambitious still was the approach of Tzvetan Todorov, who employed a close parallel between grammatical and literary structures so that characters were seen as 'nouns', their attributes as 'adjectives' and their actions as 'verbs', with 'rules' again conceived on the model of grammar, which of course determine the combinations of the parts of speech.

The most important implication of the structuralist approaches to literature was the creation of a new view of literature itself, namely, that in it we find not merely the manifestation of an underlying structure, but a conscious or partly conscious reflection upon the structure itself. To use the terminology of the linguistics, the field in which this development began, contrary to other forms of writing, in literature we do not find a clear distinction between signifier (words) and signified (the objects the words refer to). Rather, in literary compositions the signified *is* the signifier itself, and the effect of this equation is to draw the attention of the reader not to an external reference, but to the very means of reference themselves. It is this function that the semi-technical term 'foregrounding' aims to capture.

> The function of poetic language consists in the maximum of foregrounding of the utterance ... it is not used in the services of communication, but in order to place in the foreground the act of expression, the act of speech itself.
>
> (Jan Mukarovsky, 'Standard language and poetic language' quoted in Hawkes 1977: 75)

The impact of structuralism in thinking about the arts has clearly been greatest in literary theory, no doubt because of its origins in the study of language. But there is no great difficulty in seeing how the extension to other arts can be made. Lévi-Strauss's two conditions for the existence of a structured system make no explicit reference to language, and it seems quite plausible to conceive of art forms other than literature as structured arrangements analysable in terms of constants and variables. Indeed it is natural and quite common for artists and art critics to speak in this way. Thus, painting can be understood as a way of foregrounding the visual, architects often speak of an architectural 'vocabulary', and it is difficult to talk about music at all without referring to the structure of a composition.

It is easy enough to see, then, how structuralist ways of thinking can be made to generate an understanding not merely of poetic function, but more widely of the arts in general. The resultant view is one which plainly has connections with Marxism, as many writers have acknowledged. There is a crucial difference between the two however. On structuralist theories properly so called, the systems of meaning and perceptions that are self-reflected in art are universal and for the most part fixed. That is to say, structures of the sort Lévi-Strauss describes, even if ultimately subject to change, are atemporal 'grammars' manifested in particular historical cultures. In Marxism, by contrast, everything is subject to historical change, and especially perhaps, social and cultural structures.

Derrida and deconstruction

Structuralism has its difficulties of course. In fact, it is probably correct to claim, as Edith Kurzweil does in *The Age of Structuralism* (1980) that the age of structuralism is over. The reasons for its decline may have as much to do with intellectual fashion as with its intellectual problems, but for present purposes it is instructive to explore some of these problems.

First, and in some ways least interestingly, no one has been successful in actually deriving a convincing structure of axioms and rules of transformation. Lévi-Strauss's universal system of binary opposites (light/dark, good/ bad, and so on), after a promising start, ran into innumerable difficulties which could only be resolved by retreat to a degree of complexity that removed most of its theoretical power. And Lévi-Strauss himself, despite an abiding admiration for the pioneering nature of Propp's work on fairy tales, revealed considerable weaknesses in his treatment of the same. In short, in none of the spheres over which structuralist theorists have ranged has anything like a 'grammar' emerged.

Second, it will have been clear, even from this brief exposition, that the move from structural linguistics through anthropology to a structuralist theory of literature and finally art, is questionable. To treat music, for instance, as comparable to a natural language is mistaken, as we saw in Chapter 4. But even if we accept the legitimacy of this extension, the resulting view seems to encounter precisely the same objection as we found in philosophical aesthetics. That is, we end up with something called *the* function of poetic language, *the* role of literature. These are ways of talking which seem just as subject to sociological objection as the pursuit of a Platonic definition of art or poetry or literature.

But third and most importantly, the theories that emerge from structuralism appear to contradict its originating thought. This is the line of objection developed by the French literary theorist Jacques Derrida who is perhaps the major influence on post-structuralist thought. Derrida's corpus of writing is very large, hard to understand, still harder to generalize about, and impossible to summarize. Here I shall elaborate his criticisms of structuralism as they appear in the essays 'Force and signification' and 'Structure, sign and play in the human sciences' both of which appear in the collection of essays entitled *Writing and Difference* (Derrida 1990).

Derrida thinks that structuralism arises from and reflects an important 'rupture' in the history of human thought, a final break with Platonism of the sort some people have detected in philosophical aesthetics. A Platonist view of language thinks of words and signs as substitutes for the things they signify, and further thinks that these transcendental objects are the fixed centre on which structures of thought and language are built. But the crucial rupture in the history of thought consisted in a recognition that:

> the substitute does not substitute for anything which has somehow existed before it. Henceforth, it was necessary to begin thinking that there was no centre ... that [the centre] was not a fixed locus but a function, a sort of nonlocus in which an infinite number of sign-substitutions come into play. This was ... the moment when in the absence of a centre or origin everything becomes discourse.
>
> (Derrida 1990: 280)

What Derrida is saying here is that whereas most theorists have thought of human language and the external world as two distinct entities which are related by correspondence, structuralism sees that the underlying reality is not some fixed world, but the reality is the structure of thought and language itself. It is in fact upon this recognition that the whole of structuralism rests. According to Derrida however, its proponents (in these two essays he refers chiefly to Lévi-Strauss and the literary critic Jean Rousset) do not pursue the basic insight of structuralism to its logical conclusion. 'Structuralism' he says 'lives within and on the difference between its promise and its practice' (*ibid.*, p. 27). Structuralism denies the independent existence of the structures upon which it rests. To this extent it treats *parole* (the utterance) as basic and has no place for reified or concretized Platonic forms. Yet instead of recognizing that if everything has become discourse, a series of utterances, 'structure' is itself a metaphor, structuralists continue to treat 'structure' as a sign in the Platonic fashion, as an existing entity upon which theories may be built. Thus despite pretensions and appearances of being a radical alternative to Western philosophy, 'modern structuralism [is] a tributary of the most purely traditional stream of Western philosophy, which, above and beyond its anti-Platonism, leads from Husserl back to Plato' (*ibid.*).

> For as long as the metaphorical sense of the notion of structure is not acknowledged as such, that is to say interrogated and even destroyed as concerns its figurative quality . . . one runs the risk through a kind of sliding as unnoticed as it is efficacious, of confusing meaning with . . . its model. One runs the risk of being interested in the figure itself to the detriment of the play going on within it.
>
> (*ibid.*: 16)

This notion of 'play' is important in Derrida, but before looking at it further we should note that Derrida acknowledges the extreme difficulty of recognizing fully the implications of the 'rupture'. To express, or even merely to signal, our abandonment of traditional ways of thinking requires us to use the language of tradition, and hence to run the risk of being recaptured by it. Derrida thinks this is what has happened to the structuralists as well as the literary and art critics who have pursued structuralist methods.

> [S]tructure, the framework of construction, morphological correlation becomes in fact and despite his theoretical intention the critic's sole preoccupation . . . no longer a method within the *ordo cognoscendi*, [the realm of knowing] no longer a relationship in the *ordo essendi*, [the realm of being] but the very being of the work.
>
> (*ibid.*: 15)

It is arguable that this difficulty is of Derrida's own making and that it cannot in fact be overcome, because what he is demanding is that structuralists, and philosophers quite generally, speak in a wholly new language, when of course there cannot be any such thing – we could only invent a new language by translating terms and concepts we already employ. A less flatly contradictory interpretation is that Derrida does not demand a completely new language, but only that we use language in a different way, 'knowingly', which is to say, conscious of its limitations. In other words, there is a way out of the linguistic 'trap' if we stop trying to devise replacements for old theories and instead understand them in a different way. '[W]hat I want to emphasize is simply that the passage beyond philosophy does not consist in turning the page of philosophy . . . but continuing to read philosophers *in a certain way*' (*ibid.*: 288, emphasis original).

This alternative way of reading is to be contrasted with the older way of thinking, back into which structuralism slides. It is here that the notion of 'play' becomes important.

> There are thus two interpretations of interpretation, of structure, of sign, of play. The one seeks to decipher, dreams of deciphering a truth

168

or an origin which escapes play . . . the other, which is no longer turned toward the origin, affirms play and tries to pass beyond man and humanism.

(*ibid*.: 292).

Faced with a work or a text or a myth or a story, then, we cannot hope to detect within it something which will determine for us *the* correct interpretation of it. We can only 'play' upon it, and a good deal of Derrida's later work consists precisely in 'play' of this sort, as does the work of critics inspired by similar thoughts. Such a prospect, he thinks, could be greeted negatively. Having lost all prospect of there existing a thought-determining centre or origin we may incline to the 'saddened, negative, nostalgic, guilty, Rousseauistic side of the thinking of play'. Or we might find instead a cause for 'the joyous affirmation of the play of the world and of the innocence of becoming, the affirmation of a world of signs without fault, without truth, and without origin which is offered to an active interpretation' (*ibid*.: 292).

Derrida's conception of free interpretation has been taken up with enthusiasm by some students of literature, notably the American critics Hillis Miller and Paul de Man, though the same free interpretation could as easily be applied to paintings, drama, or music. This sort of interpretation has come to be known as 'deconstruction', the systematic unravelling of 'imposed' structures. Literary criticism of this sort, as inspired by Derrida, seems to have capitalized on ideas arising from a number of different but contemporaneous sources. Derrida's distinction between two types of interpretation, for instance, bears a close similarity to Roland Barthes's distinction between *lisible* (readerly) and *scriptible* (writerly) texts. In the former, the reader is expected to be passive, to 'receive' a reading of the text and hence absorb an established view of the world. In the latter the writer and the text itself (for it is not just a matter of intention but of style) acknowledges its malleability and involves the reader's interpretation as part of the creation of the work. Barthes seems to think that the most we can hope for from 'readerly' texts is pleasure, whereas from 'writerly' texts, which invite our active participation, we can expect something much more exhilarating – *jouissance* – a term deployed by the Marxist/post-structuralist theorist Lacan – something similar to Derrida's 'joyous affirmation of play'.

The point to be stressed in the thought of both thinkers is that a proper understanding of structuralism leads to a liberation from the very idea of structure itself. It leads to a certain sort of freedom, the freedom of indefinitely many 'readings'. These are to be teased out from the work in a host of different ways, and much of Derrida's later writing consists precisely in doing this (as does Hillis Miller's). The idea that must be abandoned is that of natural, innate, or proper meaning, and interpretation must recognize that it moves in a world without fault, without truth, without origin.

But if this liberation from the idea of structure is so, no interpretation can be wrong. (This is one reason why the influential German philosopher Habermas thinks the thought of Derrida to be irrationalist.) Moreover, no distinction or discrimination can be *required* of us, and this includes the distinction between art and non-art and the discrimination between the aesthetically valuable and the aesthetically valueless. Derrida appears to recognize and to accept this implication when he anticipates an objection from Rousset.

> Does not one thus run the risk of identifying the work with original writing in general? Of dissolving the notion of art and the value of 'beauty' by which literature is currently distinguished from the letter in general? But perhaps by removing the specificity of beauty from aesthetic values, beauty is, on the contrary, liberated? Is there a specificity of beauty, and would beauty gain from this effort?
>
> (*ibid.*: 13)

It is fairly clear what Derrida takes the answer to these rhetorical questions to be – there is no one thing that is aesthetic beauty, and once we see this we are freed to discover beauty everywhere and anywhere, not just in those things conventionally accepted as 'works of art'. But we may reasonably raise questions about the cost of accepting this way of thinking. As with consistent Marxism, it seems to involve us in the abandonment of art theory altogether. Indeed worse than this; at least Marxism points us in the direction of an alternative type of inquiry, namely the sociohistorical, whereas for Derridian studies everything, and hence anything, goes. Thus, should literary critics choose to interpret the railway timetable, or art critics 'explore' the wrapping from a hamburger, there is nothing to be said about the fitness or unfitness of the objects of their attention. We can ask only whether joyful affirmation in a system of signs is possible, whether the result is *'jouissance'*.

As with Marxism, so Derrida, Barthes and those who think in this way can consistently accept this conclusion and regard it as an honest recognition of the wholly unconstrained or liberated condition in which critics find themselves. But there are at least two further points to be made. First, in the work of the deconstructionists there is a measure of the same tension between promise and practice which they allege is to be found in structuralism. Although it is impossible to classify Derrida as a philosopher, critic, or social theorist, because he refuses, on theoretical grounds, to work within these traditional distinctions, he does nevertheless discuss almost exclusively the work of philosophers, critics, and anthropologists. He does not discuss the scribbles of race track punters or the instructions on packages of medicine (though Barthes does examine 'literary' works such as these). In other words, distinctions *are* being made within the sphere of 'the letter in general', even if these distinctions are not the most familiar and are treated with a greater degree of flexibility than the study of literature traditionally has done.

Second, it is hard to see how this could conceivably be avoided. Indeed a certain measure of Platonic realism seems to lurk in Derrida's thought itself and to be for this reason inescapable. It seems tempting to express his view by saying, for instance, that those critics who persist in looking for a centre or an origin do not acknowledge the *fact* of their condition, that their criticism is *really* free, thus reintroducing the idea of an independent reality against which understanding and interpretation are to be tested.

What exactly is wrong with speaking in this way? Some version of the Marxist idea of 'false-consciousness' runs through nearly all of the critical attacks on philosophical aesthetics we have been considering. Essentialism, unwarranted generalization, Platonism, or the failure to recognize the mind-dependent structures upon which systems of meanings depend, the transformation of 'structure' itself into a centre or origin – the error in each of these philosophies is said to lie in the assumption that there is a 'given' which can determine our understanding for us, whereas, according to the deconstructionist, the interpretative mind is free to 'play'. However, there must be a serious doubt whether the thrust of this criticism can be sustained. As I have suggested, some kind of Platonic realism seems inescapable if we are to speak of this assumption as an error, for 'error' suggests that these philosophies misrepresent how things really are. But suppose traditional metaphysics is erroneous in this regard. Even so, if the motivation behind deconstruction and its forerunners is to free critical interpretation from the imaginary metaphysical constraints, another line of thought deploying a different conception of constraint can be seen to open up.

Normative theory of art

If there is to be such a thing as theory of art, we must be able to distinguish art from non-art. Let us agree, however, that Platonism about art is false. There is no such thing as an essential 'Form' or universal 'Idea' called 'Art' which those things properly called works of art realize. Consequently this distinction between art and non-art is not a reflection of a reality independent of our thinking about art, and the words 'art' and 'non-art' are not substitutes for, or signs of, something that pre-exists them. However, to accept this does not carry the implication that we have to cease making the distinction. It only means that we cannot interpret the distinction descriptively; there is nothing to prevent us interpreting it *normatively*. That is to say, applying the distinction between art and non-art does not signal a *discovery*, but a *recommendation*. Thinking of art theory in this way not only avoids the strictures imposed by Wolff, Eagleton, Todorov, Derrida, and others, but it also resolves an ambiguity, noted earlier, which runs through a great deal of aesthetics, an ambiguity in the term 'work of art'.

Is 'work of art' a descriptive or an evaluative label? The only plausible answer, given the way the term is used, is 'It is both'. When, for instance, experts testify in court, on behalf of artists or writers, that a painting or a novel is not pornography but a work of art, they mean not simply to say what it is, but to give it a certain evaluative or normative status. Be its content what it may, the force of their testimony is that there is a value in it other than the value pornography has. To call something a 'work of art' in these circumstances, is not merely to classify it but to exonerate it. Most of the definitions of 'art' which have been devised in philosophical aesthetics treat 'art' as a neutral classification, but sooner or later this leads to the sort of Platonic essentialism or empirical generalization which, as we have seen, contemporary critics find so objectionable. The solution, however, is not to abandon all attempts at distinguishing between art and non-art, as some of these critics have done, but only to set aside the idea of 'art' as a neutral classification. A theory of art which explicitly and self-consciously set out to recommend a distinction between art and non-art in terms of relative value would avoid most of the problems we have considered.

We can make the point in Derridian language. It is a mistake to think that we can discover, in the nature of things as it were, interpretative rules by which to 'play'. But this does not mean that we cannot devise rules of 'play' and proceed to recommend them for the purposes of discussing art. Such rules would, of course, be mere stipulations unless there were rational grounds for recommending these rather than some other set of rules. But there is nothing in any of the critiques we have been considering that excludes the possibility rationally recommended norms of criticism. All that has been ruled out is a certain kind of metaphysical realism.

Deconstruction could itself be rationally grounded in this way. We might, for instance, recommend Barthesian rules on the grounds that they lead to greater *'jouissance'*. A parallel with a more straightforward example of 'play' will make the point clearer. Consider the game of chess. There is indeed a sense in which we 'discover' what the rules of chess are, but anyone who supposed that this means the rules are, so to speak, 'laid up in heaven' would have made a metaphysical error. The force of the error (or so critics allege) is that it leads to the rules being regarded as unalterable. On the other hand, acknowledging their alterability (or 'contingency' as some writers call it) does not imply that we can play chess in any way we choose. It means rather that we can make rationally grounded alterations in the rules. The grounds for altering them will have to do with improving the game from the point of view of the value we derive from playing it. Rules establish norms – how games *ought* to be played – and these norms are to be assessed according to their effectiveness in realizing values – pleasure is one such value. A rule can increase or diminish the pleasure of a game, and its ability to do so is a reason for or against adopting it.

Similarly, to distinguish art from non-art, or kitsch from art proper, need not be thought of as an attempt to unveil a metaphysical difference. At the same time, this does not mean that the distinction can be applied arbitrarily in any way we choose. If there is too great a measure of latitude we will end by making no distinctions at all. What we need, once the deficiencies of essentialist and sociological theories of art have been uncovered, are grounds for identifying art proper in one way rather than another; in other words, we need normative recommendations.

This suggests an alternative approach to aesthetics and art theory. It is one which, instead of striving for philosophical or sociological neutrality, expressly aims to formulate a reasoned conception of 'art proper', a conception that can then be applied in judging the objects and activities which lay claim to the status of art. Instead of seeking a definition of art in terms of necessary and sufficient properties, or seeking to determine its social function, we see what values music, or painting, or poetry can embody, and how valuable this form of embodiment is.

Such an approach to art is not a novelty. It is true that for the most part philosophers in the modern period have treated aesthetics as a branch of ontology (the nature of being or existence) and the philosophy of mind, chiefly because of Kant's influence. But the much older Greek tradition established by Plato and Aristotle was evaluative rather than metaphysical in character. Monroe C. Beardsley, one of the best known American philosophers of art, makes this point:

> the dominant movement of Plato's thought about art, taking it all in all, is strongly moralistic in a broad sense . . . it insists that the final evaluation of any work of art . . . must take into account the all important ends and values of the whole society.
>
> (Beardsley 1975: 48–9)

The normative approach is not exclusive to the Greeks. It is to be found for instance in Alexander Baumgarten's *Reflections on Poetry* written in 1735, the work to which, as far as one can tell, we owe the very term 'aesthetics'. Baumgarten's treatment of poetry could hardly be called 'moralistic' in even the broadest sense. But it *is* evaluative, implicitly if not explicitly. Baumgarten's concern is not to discover the essence of poetry, but, like Aristotle long before him, to establish principles of good poetry. He seems to have in mind the model of logic. Logical formulae do not distil the metaphysical essence of thought but establish rules for what is valid thinking. In a similar fashion Baumgarten's reflections, made largely upon his reading of the Latin poet Horace, are intended to provide a concept of 'true' poetry, or poetry proper, in the light of which we may judge any poem presented for our consideration.

A normative philosophy of art is developed to a much more sophisticated level by G.W.F. Hegel. Hegel's theory of art is what he refers to, in the *Science of Logic*, as a 'determination'. The difference between a definition and a determination is explained by Stephen Bungay as follows.

A determination is not a definition because a definition excludes possible examples by delimiting the object at the outset. [which is what
Hospers complains of] A determination is a theory, a framework of
universal explanation, which then must demonstrate its own explanatory power through its differences and its instantiation.

(Bungay 1987: 25, material in brackets added)

Hegel's own theory of art follows this conception. Like all his philosophy,
however, it is obscure to the point of being unintelligible. Here it is possible
only to offer a highly compressed summary, which will not be easy to understand, but which may still give some indication of its general character.
Hegel's theory does not consist in generalization drawn from an examination of acknowledged works of art, nor does the theory seek to discover
what is essential in the aesthetic attitude. Rather, in the elaboration of an
encyclopedic account of knowledge and understanding, something called art
is allocated a place. Very roughly, art stands halfway between intellectual
understanding and experience of the senses, and its distinguishing character
is thus what Hegel calls 'sensual presentation of the Idea', or the presentation of the idea of a thing by means of the senses. 'Sensual presentation of
the Idea' is something art makes possible through its ability to identify the
form of a thing (Idea), which we grasp intellectually, and its content
(appearance), which we encounter through the senses.

This line of thought clearly owes a good deal to Kant's treatment of art in
his third *Critique*, but it does not describe our everyday experience. Hegel
does indeed *begin* with '*Vorstellungen*', that is, things as they are presented
to us in our consciousness, but the aim of the whole of his philosophy – and
not just his aesthetics – is to reconstruct these *Vorstellungen* critically in
thought. Hegel is engaged in formulating a philosophy of 'the Absolute',
which is to say a complete philosophical understanding of everything, and it
is this Absolute which determines finally what the conceptual character of
art is. Once we have grasped its place in the Absolute, the Idea of art can be
used to order and explain our experience of art. Strictly, this last step is not
philosophy, according to Hegel, since the application of the Ideal to the
actual products of those thought to be artists requires judgment and not
merely philosophical theorizing. However, the adequacy of the philosophical theory must in part be proved by the explanations and discriminations it allows us to make, and in the *Aesthetics*, Hegel does go on (not very
satisfactorily) to apply his philosophy in an examination of architecture,
music, and literature.

This critical way of thinking about art has much to commend it, but with
Hegel, as even this brief summary shows, the chief difficulty lies not in what
he has to say about art, but in his obscure and ambitious metaphysical
enterprise, of which his theory of art is just one part. Hegel's philosophy is
notoriously difficult to understand, and this applies to his philosophy of art

as well. A more accessible approach of the same kind, however, can be found in the works of Hegel's great contemporary rival, Arthur Schopenhauer.

For Schopenhauer there is no distinction between 'art' and 'art proper'. True works of art are to be understood as having a distinctive value within human consciousness, and for any work claiming this status, the only question is whether it realizes this value. A work of art aspires to achieve something, and the only task for philosophical reflection is to decide what the proper object of this aspiration should be. Schopenhauer's account of artistic value and how it is realized in different art forms, is largely cognitivist. That is to say, it is what art allows us to see and to understand about human experience that lends it significance and makes it valuable. The cognitivist theory of art was examined in some detail in Chapter 3, and Schopenhauer is perhaps the clearest instance of a major philosophical author who clearly offers a normative theory of art along cognitivist lines.

A plainer example yet is to be found in Collingwood's *Principles of Art*, where 'art proper' is systematically distinguished from, for instance, art as craft or entertainment, in terms of the peculiar value it embodies. As we saw in Chapter 2, Collingwood, in contrast to Schopenhauer, is an expressivist, not a cognitivist. He thinks that the value of art lies in its character as the expression of feeling, and not some special apprehension of reality. Exploration of his version of expressivism showed that it easily gives way to Schopenhauer's type of cognitivism, but whether this is correct or not, Collingwood and Schopenhauer both believe that the chief task of aesthetics is to explain the *value* and *importance* of art.

The same ambition is to be found in several modern day writers. Roger Scruton, a prominent contemporary philosopher of art, tells us that 'philosophy aims at the discovery of value. The only interesting philosophical account of aesthetic experience is the account which shows its importance' (Scruton 1979: 3) and Malcolm Budd, another British philosopher, opens his most recent book by saying that 'The central question in the philosophy of art is, What is the value of art?' (Budd 1995: 1). Normative philosophy of art, then, is neither a novelty nor an aberration, but a promising theoretical approach to the arts. It is an approach that the preceding chapters have taken, and what this chapter has shown is that at a deeper philosophical level it has advantages over its traditional and sociological rivals.

Summary

Philosophical aesthetics has traditionally tried to formulate a definition of art which will serve as a neutral classification. Such definitions easily become stipulative, and in an attempt to avoid stipulation appeal has usually been made to Platonic essentialism or empirical generalization. But neither view can properly accommodate the social context of art. The institutional theory formulated by George Dickie tries to define art in terms of the social 'artworld', but it fails because it leads on naturally to a more radical sociological approach. The danger in this approach, however, whether in Marxist, structuralist, or post-structuralist forms, is that the distinction between art and non-art disappears, so that there remains no subject to theorize about.

We can avoid both sets of difficulties if we take an expressly normative approach to art, of the sort we find in Hegel, Schopenhauer, and Collingwood. Normative theories of art concern themselves not with the definition of the nature of art but with its value. Sociological theories explain this value in terms of the historically specific functions that art has performed in different cultures. But the fact is that generation after generation and a wide variety of cultures all have attributed a special value to certain works and activities, and this suggests that some of the things we call art have an abiding value. Consequently, the sociohistorical approach to art is importantly limited. Marx himself observed this in a remark about the art of antiquity.

> [T]he difficulty lies not in understanding that Greek art and the epic are linked to certain forms of social development. The difficulty is that that they still afford us artistic pleasure and that in a certain respect they count as a norm and as an unattainable model.
>
> (Marx 1973: 110–11)

The last few words of this quotation are crucial. People in different periods have abiding ideas about the *norms* of art, just as they have abiding ideas about what is and what is not a valid logical inference. And, just as logic can investigate the extent to which these ideas are correct, not by revealing metaphysical truth but by devising systems of rules, so an interest in the ideal of art can investigate the evaluative basis upon which that ideal might be founded. In this way, objectionable essentialism is avoided, but so is anxiety about the Derridian 'rupture'. Furthermore, by being self-conscious about its evaluative character, philosophy of art can be made to escape Eagleton's charge of seeking an impossible 'innocence' (see *Criticism and Ideology*). Other writers have seen this. Janet Wolff, whose views on art and sociology were quoted earlier in this chapter, argues that sociology of art, no less than philosophical aesthetics, has sought a similarly impossible neutrality, and closes her book by saying this:

> The sociology of art involves critical judgments about art. The solution to this, however, is not to try even harder for a value-free sociology and a more refined notion of aesthetic neutrality; it is to engage directly with the question of aesthetic value. This means, first, taking as a topic of investigation that value already bestowed on works by their contemporaries and subsequent critics and audiences. Secondly, it means

176

bringing into the open those aesthetic categories and judgments which locate and inform the researcher's project. And lastly, it means recognising the autonomy of the question of the particular kind of pleasure involved in past and present appreciation of the works themselves.

(Wolff 1988: 106)

What Wolff means to say is that the sociological study of art can only proceed successfully if we identify what is to count as artistically significant. This requires us to make critical judgments, and in turn this implies precisely the sort of normative investigation which, as we have now seen reason to think, is a more promising approach to the theory of art than either of its two major rivals. Wolff, in fact, makes an implicit assumption of just the sort that the proposed inquiry ought to investigate. She supposes, in what she says, that the 'value already bestowed on works by their audiences' will find its validation in 'the particular kind of pleasure' works of art supply. But the idea that the value of art proper lies in the pleasure it provides is itself, in a simple way, a normative theory of art. We cannot *assume* its truth since it is a claim that has yet to be investigated.

Our subject has now come full circle. We have seen how an examination of the philosophical basis of rival theories of art leads to a question about the connection between art and pleasure, and this was the topic with which the first chapter of our study began.

Suggestions for further reading

Clive Bell, 'The aesthetic hypothesis', *N&R* p. 98.
Morris Weitz, 'The role of theory in aesthetics', *N&R* p. 183.
George Dickie, 'The new institutional theory of art', *N&R* p. 213.
Jerrold Levinson, 'Defining art historically', *N&R* p. 223.
Roland Barthes, ' The death of the author', *N&R* p. 385.
Monroe C. Beardsley, ' The arts in the life of man', *N&R* p. 538.
Terence Hawkes, *Structuralism and Semiotics*.
Eric Matthews, *Twentieth-Century French Philosophy*, chaps 7 and 8.

Examples

—◦◯◦—

It is important for anyone studying the philosophy of art to have a good knowledge of examples from a number of art forms. The following is a list of all the examples used in this book, and readers are recommended to take steps to familiarize themselves with a good number of these at the same time as studying the arguments. Where the text mentions an artist, period, or style, a representative work is included in this list.

Architecture

Pictures of almost all the buildings cited below will be found in Patrick Nuttgens, *The Story of Architecture*, Oxford, Oxford University Press, Oxford, 1983 and R. Furneaux, *Western Architecture*, London and New York, Thames and Hudson, 1985.

Amiens Cathedral
Bernini – *Piazza at St Peters, Rome*
Gaudí – *Chapel of the Colonia Guëll*
Gothic Cathedrals of Northern Europe
Houses of Parliament, London
Holkham Hall, Norfolk, England
Orchestra Hall, Minneapolis
Pruitt-Igoe flats, St Louis, Missouri
Reform Club, London
Regent Street, London
Rievaulx, the abbey ruins
St Pancras Railway Station, London
Unité d'Habitation, Marseilles
Wright, Frank Lloyd – *Kaufman House*, Bear Run

Film and television

Eisenstein, Sergei – *Battleship Potemkin*
Eisenstein, Sergei – *Oktober*
Feyder, Jacques – *Les Nouveaux Messieurs*
film noir – John Huston, *The Maltese Falcon*
Godard, Jean-Luc – *Breathless*
The Good, the Bad and the Ugly
Marx Brothers – *A Night at the Opera*
Melrose Place
Neighbours
Nightmare on Elm Street
Spielberg, Steven – *Schindler's List*
Von Sternberg, Joseph – *The Docks of New York*
Welles, Orson – *Citizen Kane*

Literature

Austen, Jane – *Emma*
Bennett, Arnold – *Lord Raingo*
Bradbury, Malcolm – *The History Man*
Brooke, Rupert – *1914*
Browning, Robert – *Fra Lippo Lippi, My Last Duchess*
Carroll, Lewis – *Alice in Wonderland, Jabberwocky*
Conrad, Joseph – *Nostromo, Lord Jim*
Cranmer, Thomas – *Book of Common Prayer*
Dickens, Charles – *Bleak House, Hard Times*
Donne, John – *The Progresse of the Soule, The Sunne Rising, Hymn to God
   my God, in my Sickness*
[*John Donne: The Complete English Poems*, ed. A.J. Smith, Harmonds-
   worth, Penguin, 1971]
Eliot, George – *Middlemarch*
Eliot, T.S. – *Portrait of a Lady, The Waste Land*
[*Collected Poems*, London, Faber and Faber, 1937]
Faulkner, William – *The Sound and the Fury*
Fielding, Henry – *A History of Tom Jones*
Ford, John – *'Tis Pity She's a Whore*
Hopkins, G.M. – *Harry Ploughman, Wreck of the Deutschland*
[*The Poetical Works of G.M. Hopkins*, ed. N.H. Mackenzie, Oxford,
   Clarendon, 1990]
Ishiguro, Kazuo – *The Remains of the Day*
Keats, John – *On First Looking into Chapman's Homer*
Kipling, Rudyard – *Kim*

Lawrence, D.H. – *Lady Chatterley's Lover*
Le Carré, John – *The Honourable Schoolboy*
Lear, Edward – *The Owl and the Pussycat*
Katherine Mansfield – *The Woman at the Store*
Owen, Wilfred – *The Calls*
Plunkett, Joseph – *I See His Blood Upon the Rose*
Sand, George – *The Devil's Pool*
Shakespeare – *A Winter's Tale, Henry V, King Lear, Macbeth, Othello*
Stout, Rex – *Some Buried Caesar*
Tolkien, J.R.R. – *The Lord of the Rings*
Tolstoy – *Anna Karenina, War and Peace*
Trollope, Anthony – *The Eustace Diamonds, Lady Anna*
Watts, Isaac – *When I Survey the Wondrous Cross*
Wesley, Charles – *Jesu, Lover of my Soul, O Thou who Camest from Above*
Wilde, Oscar – *The Artist as Critic*
Wodehouse, P.G. – *Mr Mulliner's Nights*

Music

Recordings of most of the works listed here can be found on compilations of popular classics or are available on major recording labels.

Bach, J.S. – *Double Violin Concerto*
Beethoven – *Symphony No 5 in C minor, Op. 67*
Beethoven – *Sonata for Violin and Piano No 9 in A, Op. 47 'Kreutzer'*
Beethoven – *Symphony No 6 in F, Op. 68 'Pastoral'*
Beethoven – *String Quartet, Op. 135 in F*
Boccerini – *'Minuet' from String Quartet Op.13 No 5*
Britten – *St Nicholas*
Brubeck, Dave – *Take Five*
Brahms – *Violin Concerto*
Bruch – *Violin Concerto in G minor*
Bruckner – *Mass in E minor*
Cage, John – *4' 33"*
Elgar – *Cello Concerto*
Handel – *Messiah*
Joplin, Scott – *The Entertainer*
Mahler – *Songs of a Wayfarer*
Mendelssohn – *A Midsummer Night's Dream*
Messiaen, Olivier – *O sacrum convivium*
Mozart – *'Rondo' from Violin Concerto in D*
Mussorgsky – *Pictures at an Exhibition*
Prokofiev – *Peter and the Wolf*

Saint-Saëns – *Carnival of the Animals*
Satoh, Somei – *Litania*
Schubert – *Entr'act from Rosamund*
Shostakovich – *Symphony No 3 Op. 29 'First of May'*
Stainer – *Crucifixion*
Strauss – *Blue Danube Waltz*

Paintings and sculpture

Reproductions of most of the examples cited here will be found in E.H. Gombrich, *The Story of Art* 16th edition London, Phaidon, 1995.

Bernini – *The Ecstasy of St Theresa*
Bruegel the Elder – *Peasant Wedding*
Caravaggio – *Beheading of John the Baptist*
Constable – *The Haywain, Salisbury Cathedral*
Dali, Salvador – *Swans into Elephants, Christ of St John of the Cross*
Duchamp, Marcel – *Fountain*
Dürer – *The Nativity*
Egyptian art – *Portrait of Hesire*
El Greco – *The Opening of the Fifth Seal of the Apocalypse*
Escher, M.C. – *Ascending and Decending, Waterfall*
Gainsborough – *Portrait of Mr and Mrs Andrewes*
Giotto – frescoes at Padua
Goya – *King Ferdinand VII of Spain*
Holbein – *Sir Richard Southwell*
Lorenzetti, Ambrogio – frescoes at Siena
Michaelangelo – *Sistine ceiling*
Mondrian – *Broadway Boogie-Woogie*
Monet – *Gare St-Lazare*
Picasso – *A Cockerel, A Hen with Chicks, Violin and Grapes*
Piero della Francesca – *Constantine's Dream*
Pollock, Jackson – *No. 14*
Rothko, Marc – *White, Yellow, Red on Yellow*
Rubens – *Allegory on the Blessings of Peace*
Sta Sophia, Istanbul
Stubbs – *Gimcrack*
Van Gogh – *The artist's room in Arles*
Velásquez – *Pope Innocent X*
Whistler, James – *Arrangement in Grey and Black*

Bibliography

——•◎•——

Alperson, P. (ed), *What is Music? An Introduction to the Philosophy of Music,* Philadelphia, Pennsylvania State University Press, 1994.

—— *The Philosophy of the Visual Arts,* New York, Oxford University Press, 1992.

Althusser, L., 'Letter on art' in *Lenin and Philosophy and Other Essays,* trans. Ben Brewster, London, New Left Books, 1971 [originally published in *La Nouvelle Critique,* 1966].

Arnheim, R., *Film as Art,* London, Faber, 1958.

Baumgarten, A.G., *Reflections on Poetry,* trans. K. Aschenbrenner and W.B. Hatthner, Berkeley, University of California Press, 1954 [1735].

Bazin, A., *What is Cinema?* Vol. 1, trans. H. Gray, Berkeley, University of California Press, 1967.

Beardsley, M.C., *Aesthetics: From Classical Greece to the Present,* New York, Macmillan, 1966.

—— *Aesthetics : Problems in the Philosophy of Criticism,* New York, Harcourt Brace, 1958.

Bell, C., *Art,* Oxford, Oxford University Press, 1987.

Bennett, T., *Formalism and Marxism,* New York, Methuen, 1979.

Brooks, C., *The Well Wrought Urn,* New York, Harcourt Brace, 1947.

Bryson, N., Holly, M. and Moxey, K. (eds). *Visual Theory,* Oxford, Polity Press, 1991.

Budd, M., *Music and the Emotions,* London, Routledge and Kegan Paul, 1985.

—— *Values of Art,* Harmondsworth, Penguin, 1995.

Bungay, S., *Beauty and Truth: A Study of Hegel's Aesthetics,* Oxford, Clarendon Press, 1987.

Carrit, E.F., *What is Beauty?,* Oxford, Clarendon Press, 1932.

Carroll, N., *Philosophical Problems of Classical Film Theory,* Princeton, NJ, Princeton University Press, 1988.

Cavell, S., *Must We Mean What We Say?,* Cambridge, Cambridge University Press, 1969.

Collingwood, R.G., *The Principles of Art,* Oxford, Clarendon Press, 1938.

Cooke, D., *The Language of Music,* Oxford, Clarendon Press, 1957.

Cothey, A.L., *The Nature of Art,* London, Routledge, 1990.

Croce, B., *Aesthetic,* trans. D. Ainslie, London, Peter Owen, 1953.

Currie, G., *Image and Mind: Film, Philosophy and Cognitive Science,* Cambridge, Cambridge University Press, 1995.

Derrida, J., *Writing and Difference,* trans. A. Bass, London, Routledge, 1990.

Dickie, G., *Art and the Aesthetic: An Institutional Analysis,* Ithaca, NY, Cornell University Press, 1974.

BIBLIOGRAPHY

Eagleton, T., *Criticism and Ideology*, London, Verson, 1978.

Eisenstein, S., *The Film Sense*, London, Faber, 1943.

Gadamer, H.-G., *The Relevance of the Beautiful and Other Essays*, trans. N. Walker, ed. R. Bernasconi, Cambridge, Cambridge University Press, 1986.

Gallie, W.B., 'The function of philosophical aesthetics', *Mind*, 57, 1948, pp. 302–21.

Gardner, H., *Religion and Literature* Oxford, Oxford University Press, 1983.

Goldwater, R. and M. Treves (eds), *Artists on Art*, London, John Murray, 1976.

Gombrich, E.H., *Art and Illusion*, 5th edition, London, Phaidon, 1977.

—— *The Story of Art*, 16th edition, London, Phaidon, 1995.

Goodman, N., *Ways of World Making*, Indianapolis, IN, Hackett, 1968.

Hawkes, T., *Structuralism and Semiotics*, London, Methuen, 1977.

Hegel, G.W.F., *Aesthetics*, trans. T.M. Knox, Oxford, Clarendon Press, 1975.

Hospers, J., 'The concept of artistic expression', *Proceedings of the Arisotelian Society*, 55, 1955, pp.313–44 [also in Hospers, *Introductory Readings*].

—— *Introductory Readings in Aesthetics*, New York, The Free Press, 1969.

Hume, D., 'Of the standard of taste' in *Essays, Moral, Political and Literary*, Oxford, Oxford University Press, 1975.

Ingarden, R., 'Artistic and aesthetic values' in H. Osborne (ed), *Aesthetics*, Oxford, Oxford University Press, 1972.

Inwood, M., *A Hegel Dictionary*, Oxford, Basil Blackwell, 1992.

Isenberg, A., *Aesthetics and the Theory of Criticism*, Chicago, IL, University of Chicago Press, 1973.

Johnson, S., *Lives of the Poets*, Vol. 1, Oxford, World's Classics, 1906.

Jones, E., *The Origins of Shakespeare*, Oxford, Oxford University Press, 1978.

Kandinsky, W., *Concerning the Spiritual in Art*, New York, George Wittenborn Inc., 1947.

Kant, I., *Critique of Judgement*, trans. W.S. Pluhar, Indianapolis, IN, Hackett, 1987.

Kivy, P., *The Corded Shell: Reflections on Musical Expression*, Princeton, NJ, Princeton University Press, 1980.

Kurzweil, E., *The Age of Structuralism : Lévi-Strauss to Foucault*, New York, Columbia University Press, 1980.

Lamarque, P.V., and Olsen, S.H., *Truth, Fiction and Literature*, Oxford, Clarendon Press, 1994.

Langer, S.K., *Feeling and Form*, London, Routledge and Kegan Paul, 1953.

Lenin, V.I., *Collected Works*, Vol. 14, London, Lawrence and Wishart, 1968.

Lévi-Strauss, C., *Structural Anthropology*, Vol. 2, Harmondsworth, Penguin, 1978.

Locke, J., *Essay Concerning Human Understanding*, Vol. 2, Oxford, Clarendon Press, 1896.

Lukács, G., *Writer and Critic and Other Essays*, trans. A. Kahn, London, Merlin Press, 1970.

Lynton, N., *The Story of Modern Art*, Oxford, Phaidon Press, 1980.

Marx, K., *Critique of Hegel's Philosophy of Right*, trans. A. Jolin and J. O'Malley, Cambridge, Cambridge University Press, 1970.

—— *Grundrisse* [Basic sketches], trans. M. Nicolaus, Harmondsworth, Penguin, 1973.

Matthews, E., *Twentieth-Century French Philosophy*, Oxford, Oxford University Press, 1996.

Mellers, W., *Man and His Music*, revised edition, London, Barrie and Rockliff, 1962.

Mill, J.S., *Utilitarianism*, London, Fontana, 1985.

Morgan, D., 'Must art tell the truth', *Journal of Aesthetics and Art Criticism*, 26, 1967, pp.17–27 [also in Hospers, *Introductory Readings*].

BIBLIOGRAPHY

Margolis, J., (ed.), *Philosophy Looks at the Arts,* 3rd edition, Philadelphia, PA, Temple University Press, 1987.

Mayhead, R., *Understanding Literature*, Cambridge, Cambridge University Press, 1965.

Neill, A. and Ridley, A. (eds), *The Philosophy of Art: Readings Ancient and Modern*, New York, McGraw-Hill, 1995.

Norris, C., *Deconstruction: Theory and Practice,* London, Methuen, 1982.

Nussbaum, M., *Love's Knowledge: Essays on Philosophy and Literature*, New York, Oxford University Press, 1990.

Nuttgens, P., *The Story of Architecture*, Oxford, Oxford University Press, 1983.

Otto, R., *The Idea of the Holy*, trans. J. W. Harvey, 2nd edition, Oxford, Oxford University Press, 1950.

Perkins, V.F., *Film as Film*, Harmonsworth, Penguin, 1972.

Pevsner, N., *The Buildings of England*, Vol. 1, *The Cities of London and Westminster*, 3rd edition, Harmondsworth, Penguin, 1972.

Scruton, R., *The Aesthetics of Architecture*, London, Methuen, 1979.

—— *The Aesthetic Understanding*, London, Methuen, 1983.

Soskice, J.M., *Metaphor and Religious Language*, Oxford, Clarendon Press, 1985.

Storr, A., *Music and the Mind*, London, HarperCollins, 1993.

Tolstoy, L., *What is Art?*, trans. A. Maude, Oxford, Oxford University Press, 1955.

Walton, K., *Mimesis as Make-Believe*, Cambridge, MA, Harvard University Press, 1990.

Watkin, D., *The Morality of Architecture,* Chicago, IL, University of Chicago Press, 1984.

Weitz, M., 'Truth in literature' in Hospers, *Introductory Readings.*

Winters, Y., *In Defense of Reason*, Denver, CO, Alan Swallow, 1947.

Wolff, J., *Aesthetics and Sociology of Art*, London, George Allen and Unwin, 1988.

Wollheim, R., *Painting as an Art*, London, Thames and Hudson, 1987.

Young, J., *Nietzsche's Philosophy of Art*, Cambridge, Cambridge University Press, 1992.

Index

Wesley, Charles 116–17
What is Art? 24–5
What is Music? 86
whimsy: *see* imagination
Whistler, James 95
Wilde, Oscar 14, 116
Winter's Tale, A 27
With Malice Toward None 48
Wittgenstein, Ludwig 81
Wittgenstein, Paul 81
Wodehouse, P.G. 9, 59–60
Wolfe, Tom 142
Wolff, Janet 154, 161, 171, 176–7
Wölfflin 138–9

Wollheim, Richard 109
Woman at the Store, The 124
Wooton, Sir Henry 136
'wordplay': *see* syntax, of poetry
Wordsworth, William 25
World War I 117–18, 141–2
Wreck of the Deutschland, The 119
Wren, Christopher 25
Wright, Frank Lloyd 133
Writing and Difference 167

Zeitgeist 137, 138–9
Zen Buddhism 91
zenga 91